Navy
WINGS OF GOLD

True Love, Ferocious Combat
and Miraculous Survival

Personal Accounts of Heroic U.S. Naval Aviators
in World War II

by
F. Willard Robinson
Lieutenant, United States Naval Reserve

Published and Printed by
River Park Press, Inc.
www.navywingsofgold.com

Printed in the United States of America

I.S.B.N. 0-9710795-0-1

Table of Contents

Preface

The opening chapters of *Wings of Gold* were written so my family would have a personal record of those dramatic years. These chapters include my memoirs, and those of my brother, Charles W. Robinson, Lt. USNR. He served as engineering officer on the heavy cruiser USS Tuscaloosa during the attacks on the German gun batteries above Utah Beach at Normandy on D-Day.

Another member of our family, whose story is included, is my brother-in-law John Jaqua, USMCR, a pilot with Marine Squadron VB-233. Pilots of VB-233 flew throughout the fight for the Solomon Islands, the most costly aerial campaign of the entire Pacific war.

Joan Robinson, my loving wife and closest friend, wrote the final chapter. She lived the historic years and knew all of the men of whom I write.

As my work progressed, I decided to expand it to recapture the stories of some of my flying associates. This, I realized, would give the manuscript a valuable historic and heroic dimension. Their stories were not easy to recover. I had lost contact with some of these navy pilots for over a half century. Through various searches I was eventually able to locate all of them and gather the information I sought. None were willing to write in great detail. But, through visits, notes, telephone calls, and some tape recording sessions, I finally was able to prepare the material. I eventually was assured of the completeness and accuracy of their accounts. There has been reward in the telling of their stories, for they were true heroes, who miraculously survived the deadly contest. I know that even though their time in history has passed, their personal stories will not now also pass into that vast pit of lost memories.

*　　　　*　　　　*

The World War II generation experienced more technical and social change than any other generation in history. From World War I, when the United States matured as a world power, to a few years later when the trauma, upheaval and sheer despair of the Great

Depression hit, the people struggled for equilibrium. Unprepared, this generation was called to fight for the preservation of America's freedom, a freedom being challenged by the dictatorial powers that sought control of the world. Men and women imbued with patriotism and courage, embarking on their foundation of traditional values, went out to meet the enemy. Along with the pain, suffering and loss, an element of adventure, a community of purpose, an optimism, and a discipline were all carried to the engagement. These are values to which some in the following generations are taking a new look. It is my hope that these memories will contribute in a personal way to their understanding.

F. Willard Robinson

Acknowledgements

I give acknowledgment for support and help in the preparation of this manuscript to:

• Joan L. Robinson, my wife, for continued encouragement, and for writing her perspective of a wife who was left at home when our flight squadron went off to war.

• Charles W. Robinson, Lieutenant, USNR, my brother

• John E. Jaqua, Major, USMCR, my brother-in-law

• William Barnett, Lieutenant, USNR

• Albert K. Earnest, Captain, USN

• Leonard Muskin, Lieutenant, USNR

• Arnold Erickson, Lieutenant Commander, USN

• Fred Dungan, Lieutenant, USNR

All of these men share their personal stories of strategic involvement in World War II.

• And to Don Dutcher of Boise, Idaho, for his editing and tireless computer assistance in the preparation of this manuscript.

"Robbie" Robinson, January 2001

1

LIFE DURING THE FAR OFF RUMBLES OF WAR

I sit here on a portion of the old Corona del Valle ranch in northern Los Angeles County, looking out over the west end of the Antelope Valley to the snow-covered Tehachapi mountains to the north. The year is 1995. It is time for me to begin this record of my memories as they relate to World War II.

*   *   *

It all began for me on a troubling night in 1931. My father, at the dinner table right here on the old ranch, announced that Japan had gone to war with China. Pop had heard the news on our massive battery radio, just before the dinner hour. It took me a long time to go to sleep that night. I did not understand what this war news meant, but somehow I inherently knew that in someway beyond my comprehension, we as a family would eventually be touched by this far away turmoil. I was twelve years old.

In retrospect, this was the actual beginning of World War II for the United States in the Pacific, a war in which I would eventually be involved. Within six months of that invasion in 1931, the Japanese Army seized control of Manchuria. This was their first aggressive step that within the next ten years would lead to their economic, political and military control of the Far East, culminating with their disastrous attack ten years later on the American forces at Pearl Harbor on December 7, 1941.

*   *   *

Eight years passed. In the summer of 1939, in search of adventure, my high school friend, Jim Dyer, and I left Seattle, Washington in our little eighteen-foot sailboat for the Territory of Alaska. It was an adventurous summer. We completed the trip, and in September 1939, I enrolled at the University of Alaska in Fairbanks. I mention this date for at daybreak, September 1, 1939 the German Panzer Divisions began pouring across the Polish frontiers from north, south, and west. Although it was reported as just a regional invasion, in reality World War II had begun. This news hit me with a personal impact. I remember going for a walk through the wooded hills behind the University of Alaska with my friend Charles LeFebre. In the distance, across the Tanana Valley the massive snow covered ridges buttressed the towering peak of Mt McKinley. "It's just a matter of time now," Chuck said, "until all of Europe will be involved and when that happens, the United States gets involved too." I guess I knew that what he said was true, and that I would not escape the results of this action.

*   *   *

That fall, an Army Air Force pilot, Lieutenant Richard E. Ragel, flew his biwing red cabin Waco airplane into Fairbanks. He landed with precision on the old dirt strip at the edge of town. He had come to recruit and train pilots for the Civil Aeronautics Authority. We gathered in a large room on the University of Alaska campus, and listened with fascination as this well-built, close-cropped, handsome, blond army pilot in his leather flight jacket outlined the requirements of this new training program.

> *We will select twenty of you—only the very best. The United States Government has established this civilian training program to prepare a pool of future military pilots. This is a part of a nation-wide program. We are facing uncertain times. If you are selected for this program, and selection will be based on your academic standing and physical condition, you will be enrolled in courses including ground training, meteorology, parachutes, mechanics, and navigation. In addition you will get thirty-five hours of flight time. If you pass your courses and the final flight test, you will qualify for a Limited Commercial pilot license.*

Wow! That sounded exciting to me. I was cleaning the University classrooms at night to pay for my room and board while I attended classes. There would be no way that I could get this kind of training, unless I qualified for the CAA program. How excited I was when a few days later the names of those selected for the University of Alaska flight-training program were posted outside the administrative offices. There was my name, right there on the list of those selected. I was launched on a program that would eventually lead to my becoming a Naval Aviator and eventual assignment as a carrier pilot in the Pacific War against the Japanese forces. All I knew then was that I was going to get a chance to challenge the skies and enter a whole new dimension of human experience.

*   *   *

I was busy during the fall of 1939 with my studies. Now I pursued them with more purpose than I had during my first two years at the University of Southern California. I continued working at nights, cleaning the classrooms for the next day; earned the lead in the school play, and completed forty-two units of work during the 1939-1940 school year. I also edited the school yearbook and completed the aviation ground school classes for the Civil Aeronautics Authority. It was a busy time and I was hardly aware of the short winter days. In the month of December the daylight hours lasted less than three hours.

Sometime during the latter days of January 1940, Lt. Ragle had us report to the Fairbanks airport to start our flight training. I took a bus into Fairbanks, as the school was located four miles out of town. It was a short walk from the end of the bus line over a snow-covered street to the airport. That was far enough to walk in the thirty-degree below zero weather. There were no hangars for our planes. Lt. Ragle had three airplanes, a Waco biplane, a Rearwin Sportster, and an original Taylor Cub. The Cub was our primary trainer. Later the Piper Aircraft Company took over this original design and many future pilots were trained in the reliable and classic Piper Cub airplane. Along the snow-covered dirt runway, there was a little plywood shack where some of the tools, parts and records were kept. A small wood stove heated the hut. We needed this protection from the bitter Alaskan winter. All of the planes were equipped with skis.

"Well are you ready for your orientation flight," Lt. Ragle said.

"Yes sir." I tried to sound assured, as I replied, but I was nervous and excited.

"Your first step is to learn how to start the engine. To do this, get in the cockpit and turn on the gas. I will get in front of the plane and turn over the propeller by hand. While we do this, make certain that the skis are blocked, so the plane will not move forward. Make certain the magneto switches are not turned on." Ragle rotated the little wooden propeller several times. "Switch on", he yelled.

I turned the switch on; replying, "Switch on." Again he rotated the prop and the little plane came alive. With the engine started, Ragle got into the front seat and with ease taxied out to the runway; a feat I later found could not be taken for granted. Skis have no brakes, and if one ski hits a pocket of soft snow, the plane veers in that direction. The only way to correct it is to apply power and work the rudder to bring the plane back into line. Taxing on skis was definitely a skill to be learned.

When we reached the takeoff position on the runway, Lt. Ragle took me through the routine I was to follow before takeoff. It was really quite simple, because there were few instruments in the Cub.

4

All that it had were a needle and ball to show the plane's attitude in flight, an airspeed indicator, and a simple compass. A cork in the gas tank, with an indicator on top, that went down as the gas was used, served as the gas gauge. He checked the magnetos, lined up on the runway, and with ease moved the throttle forward. The plane picked up speed over the packed snow and we soon broke free, climbing into the clear sky.

"I'll just show you a few things today," Ragle said, as we flew over the vacant land, the scattered stunted pines of the Arctic, and the spaces of tundra broken by the sloughs that traced the turns of ancient and abandoned rivers. It was a vast and uninhabited land over which we flew. My training as a pilot had begun.

*   *   *

Several days and seven hours of flying time later, Lt. Ragle declared that I was ready. He left the plane and said, "Take it around the field and show me a good landing." I was on my own and too thrilled to think of being frightened. Although I have made hundreds of landings since, I shall never forget that first return to earth as that little plane, with skis for landing gear, crunched onto the snow-covered runway. My first solo flight had been accomplished with a "thumbs-up" from my watching instructor.

For the next several months I practiced the maneuvers required and gradually honed the skills needed to pass my final flight test. My first solo cross-country flight was to a small Indian village on the Yukon River. In 1939 there were no radio navigational aids in Alaska. So, like all pilots on that frontier, the rivers and mountain ranges, as confirmed on the navigational chart, guided us. It was primitive, but worked well as long as the weather was clear. My most vivid memory of that flight was the little Indian children running out when I landed. With smiles and laughter they surrounded my plane. The landing was as much of an event for them as it was for me.

My elation was only tempered by the news that came over the radio. The powerful Panzer divisions of the German army had moved with devastating force on May 10, 1940, outflanking the

French Maginot Line and blasting into Holland, Belgium, France and Luxembourg. In less than a month the German occupation was complete and Hitler's brutal and notorious new order was in control.

This all happened within a month of my final flight check. The clock was ticking, and the events that would eventually lead me into front-line air combat in the greatest conflict in the history of the world were established and irrevocable. I sensed then that the lessons I was learning in the Alaskan skies were deadly serious and I was embarked on more that just a lark of high adventure.

I finished my class work at the University of Alaska at the end of May and took a job driving a dump truck for the U.S. Government. We were building the Ladd Field military airbase on the outskirts of Fairbanks. This airfield would become a staging place for the ferrying of military planes to Russia. I worked nights, so I could continue my flight training during the daylight hours.

Then on a June day in 1940 Lt. Ragle informed me that I was ready for my final flight check. A Civil Aeronautics Official flew in from Anchorage, Alaska to put me through those final checks that I would have to pass before I could be approved for my commercial rating. I felt some pressure, as I was the first one of the twenty trainees ready for that final test. If I passed, I would be the very first government-trained pilot in the Territory of Alaska. This would be a high honor, and an event that would be quite newsworthy throughout the Territory of Alaska.

The local radio station, KFAR, assigned news anchor Bud Foster, later a renowned national newsman for NBC in the lower 48 states, to broadcast my final flight test. He followed me in another plane, piloted by Lt. Dick Ragle, and described all of the required maneuvers that Flight Check Officer Gentry gave me. Although I felt some pressure, I was so busy concentrating on the instructions given me by the check pilot that I thought of little else. All went well and I was confident. Then Gentry cut the engine and I knew that I had to make a simulated forced landing. What breeze there was came up the valley, so while looking over the terrain, I turned in that direction. There was one small meadow ahead, but two large pine trees guarded the entrance. This was my only possibility, so I headed in anyway, keeping a little more altitude than I needed. Then, at about 400 feet above the ground, I cross-controlled. This set the little plane up on its wing and we sideslipped precipitously between the two trees through a space hardly wide enough for the plane had I been level in flight. Between the trees we went. Just above the ground, I recovered, and was in a safe landing position. Mission accomplished! Gentry said, "Fine, let's go back to the field."

I was grateful to Instructor Ragle for giving me confidence in this maneuver. He had said, "You might need this sometime. There are not a lot of places to land in Alaska if your engine cuts out. This sideslip maneuver just might come in handy." I had never dreamed I would have to cross control and "slip" an aircraft on a first flight check, however. The flight was broadcast on the evening news and they gave me a recording of the event, which I kept for many years.

*   *   *

During that summer of 1940 the Battle of Britain was under way. The German Luftwaffe (German Airforce) struck British shipping and the Channel ports. The Germans had three air fleets, together comprising more than a thousand fighters. On August 13 the Germans flew more than a thousand sorties over England. They made the attack with assurance and self-confidence. Goering, the German air commander, believed that within four days they could eliminate all the Royal Air Force fighters and that within two weeks the air war over England would be finished. It did not work out that way. The RAF Fighter Command had fewer planes than the Germans, but the *Hurricane* and *Spitfires* were good fighters and the aircraft plants were turning them out at a satisfactory rate. The RAF had another advantage. Since the fight was over England, pilots who parachuted out of their damaged planes were saved and could be in the air again the next day to continue the fight.

The most critical two weeks of the battle opened with a massive raid on August 24th. The Luftwaffe flew more than a thousand sorties. One English airfield was knocked out of action. Two others sustained serious damage. The British Fighter

Command lost twenty-two planes. The intense battle continued and the RAF had resources to sustain the fight. They had lost 300 fighter planes in just a few days. Though the German's total losses were higher, their fighter losses were lower than the RAF's. Attrition in men was severe. Between August 24th and September 6, 1940, Fighter Command lost 103 pilots to the German attacking force and another 128 were wounded. Newly trained replacements were not sufficiently battle-tried to hold their own in aerial dogfights, and the experienced pilots were wearing down from the constant strain. But those that were left rallied, and on September 15th, when Goering planned to finish the British off with a massive daylight raid, Fighter Command rose to the contest, knowing that their government expected a German land invasion to follow. That day the Luftwaffe lost sixty planes to the RAF's twenty-six. The Germans could not continue to take such losses, and the large-scale daylight missions were abandoned. The blitz would go on, however. Night after night German planes continued to bomb in a prolonged attempt to break the British morale and induce surrender. It didn't happen. Although the United States maintained their position of neutrality, many American pilots, inspired by the bravery of the English in defending their land, went to England and formed the Eagle Squadron under the command of the Royal Air Force.

*   *   *

Subsequent to completing my basic flight training, I wrote the RAF volunteering my services for further training and qualification for the Eagle Squadron. I soon received an official letter thanking me for volunteering. However, they also said that their billets were full, but I would be hearing from them in the future. Of course I did not know then that Pearl Harbor would be bombed the following year, that the United States would enter the war, and that all of my plans would be changed.

Another significant event for the young men of the United States happened in that summer of 1940. Congress ordered the first national draft since World War I. I duly registered for the national draft in Fairbanks, Alaska and received my official draft card. It was important, for the United States was beginning to marshal its forces, should war come to our country.

There is an interesting sidelight. A year and a half later I would, as required, notify the Fairbanks Draft Board of my enlistment in the U.S. Navy. Several months after that, the draft board wrote back that they had no records for me. Apparently they had misplaced my papers. If I had been so inclined, I would never have been called to participate in World War II. I would have been free, because I continued to carry my official draft card.

*   *   *

By the end of summer of 1940, I knew it would be best to return to my home in Long Beach, California to complete as much of my senior year at USC as possible. It was apparent that was my best course of action in those uncertain months. Not wanting to spend any of the $700 I had saved from my summer's earnings driving dump truck for the new army air base the government was building in Fairbanks, I hopped the empty Alaska Railroad train back to Seward. These trains came into Fairbanks a couple of times a week loaded with cement and supplies for the construction of the airbase. It was a train ride I shall never forget, because it was unique. I rolled out my sleeping bag on an empty flatcar. As night came, a glorious full moon lit the passing landscape. About two o'clock in the morning the train passed through Mt. McKinley National Park. The great mountain came into view, its shimmering snow covered crests towering over 20,000 feet into the clear night sky. I lay in my sleeping bag taking in the full vista of this majestic sight.

*   *   *

Late the following afternoon I arrived in Seward, Alaska, a seaport town nestled at the end of a deep inlet protected from the storm-tossed waters of the Gulf of Alaska. The main street of the little hamlet ran to the dock area where the U.S.A.T. Etolin, an army

9

transport unloading war supplies, was docked. I watched as two disassembled P-40 fighter planes were lifted by crane off the ship to a train flatcar. These were the first combat fighter planes to come to the Territory of Alaska. The sight of these two metal planes with their powerful engines was awe-inspiring. I had only flown small fabric-covered planes. I had never seen flying machines like these. What would it feel like to have that kind of power under my control? Someday I would know.

I needed to get back to California without spending most of my summer earnings for passage, so I hustled a job. I went aboard the Etolin and asked to see the Chief Engineering Officer. The seaman on duty told me his name was Griffin and that he was on shore leave for the evening. There were half a dozen bars along the main street of Seward. I figured I would find him in one of the bars, so I started making the rounds, looking for an officer in the ship's uniform. About the second bar I went into, I saw a person that looked like he filled the bill. I went up to him. "Excuse me," I said, "Is your name Griffin?"

"That's it. What do you want?" He was blunt, but not unfriendly.

"Well, my name is Robinson, and I'd sure appreciate a chance to work my way back to San Francisco."

"Are you willing to scrape paint in the engine room? It's hot as hell, and three levels below water line, but if you want it, the job is yours. Bunk and grub is all I can give you."

"That's great," I said. "I'll take it."

Then he added, "Don't expect me back to the ship before morning. This is my night in town."

I was elated. Here it was night, the streets were wet with that oppressive Alaskan drizzle that shrouds the coastal inlets for weeks at a time. But now I had a dry place to go, a bunk where I could sleep and a job that would take me home. I was thankful. "San Francisco, here I come!"

The next morning I went to work. I joined two other members of the crew who had been assigned to the paint scraping detail. Soon the ship was underway, the giant pistons driving the massive screws, pounding the engine room and blasting us with an

10

incessant roar. The heat soon reached 115 degrees as we worked. When we hit the open waters of the Gulf, the ship began to roll and pitch with great intensity. I felt trapped. It was three flights up the steep ladders to the fresh air, and here I was with the heat, the smell of fuel, and a stomach that rolled with the intensity of the ship itself. I kept working, and somehow made it without vomiting.

The next day I felt better and made it up to the galley for something to eat for the first time. It was in the ship's mess hall that I first experienced the hierarchy of the military. This was a whole new experience for me. The officers sat at a separate table with tablecloths and silverware. Even the Second Lieutenants were addressed as "Sir". I realized right away, that as a crewman, I was the lowest of the lowest. It didn't upset me, but it was apparent to me that it was better to be an officer in a military organization—just a fact of life to be put into my memory bank.

*   *   *

A week later we entered San Francisco Bay. It was a clear early September evening in 1940. The city on the hills was majestic and sparkled in the sunset as the ship moved with power and grace, gliding under the awesome span of the Golden Gate Bridge. I would some day experience other such passages, sailing in and out on missions of war, to and from the far side of the Pacific Ocean. None of this mattered on this afternoon. It was the final day of the San Francisco World Fair. I left the ship and went to Treasure Island in San Francisco Bay and marveled at the exhibits and the fireworks display that marked the closing of the Fair. What a contrast this was to the fifteen months I had spent in the Territory of Alaska. I still had a year and a half of college work to accomplish before graduation. So, it was back to the University of Southern California.

*   *   *

In November 1940, Franklin Roosevelt was elected to an unprecedented third term. For some time he had wrestled with the problem of how to aid Britain. In December he introduced the

11

concept of lend-lease. It was a way of producing war supplies for England, and no one really expected that we would ever be paid back. As the United States started shipping the supplies to England, the Germans stepped up their submarine attacks on shipping in the Atlantic, for war materials sunk were of no value to Britain. This battle in the Atlantic was almost as important to the United States as it was to England. As long as the English could control the Atlantic Ocean we could keep the bulk of the fleet in the Pacific Ocean where we were facing a threat from the growing military power of Japan. On March 11, 1941, the Lend-Lease bill was signed. America was committed. Britain would not go under. I was in the middle of the first semester of my senior year at USC.

*   *   *

As the war pressures mounted, the United States began to gear up for production. I had never seen such industrial energy come to life. After all, we had been through ten years of the greatest depression in the history of the country. All of a sudden the Long Beach shipyards and the airplane manufacturing plants in the area had hiring signs posted.. For the first time since 1929, any able bodied person could get a job. I was getting short of money, so I decided to go to work while still attending classes at USC. Douglas Aircraft Company was building warplanes at their Long Beach plant. I went to their employment office. It was alive with activity, but I finally negotiated the lines and sat down with an employment officer.

"We have openings for typists," he said. "Can you type fifty words a minute?"

"I doubt it. I haven't taken typing since Junior High School, and then I could only do thirty words a minute."

"Go into that room and give it a try," he said.

Actually, I had always typed my high school and college papers, so I wasn't out of practice. I took the test, and to my surprise came up with fifty-seven words a minute. I had almost doubled my speed since taking that typing class without ever realizing that I had made such an improvement.

I reported to the Douglas plant at the Long Beach Municipal Airport and was assigned to the Tool Planning Department. The department designed the tools needed in producing the A-20 attack bomber. My job was to keep all the blueprints in order and disperse the needed prints to the engineers as requested. I got paid $2.20 an hour, a lot more money than I had made up until that time. I took the swing shift, working from 5:00 PM until 2:00 AM. It was a forty-five minute drive from the Douglas Aircraft Plant to USC, so I only had four hours sleep before my 8:00 AM classes. It was a tiring schedule.

*   *   *

I was able to keep current on my flying by renting a Piper Cub at the Long Beach Municipal airport on the weekends. It was during this time that I made my one-and-only forced landing. I had a fraternity brother, I don't remember his name, but he was a 220-pound reserve fullback on the USC football team. He had never been up in an airplane and he kept asking me to give him a ride. I did not know of another pilot at USC at the time. We drove down to Long Beach and took off. I climbed to 3,000 feet and went through a few mild maneuvers. He seemed to enjoy the flight, so I cut the engine, pulled up the nose, kicked left rudder and went into a controlled spin. As we recovered, I pushed the throttle forward, but the engine had stopped. I couldn't get it started. I yelled, over the sound of the wind, that we were going to make a forced landing. We were just north of where the Long Beach State College is now located. But in those days it was just cornfields and plowed ground on the old Bixby Ranch. I got squared away into the gentle breeze that floated in over the coast, and glided down toward a freshly plowed area I had spotted. It was all that was available, unless I wanted to land in a field of six-foot corn. We made the approach OK, and I held the little plane off as long as possible, stalling it nose high just above the ground. The tail hit first, and then the wheels. The tail came up, and for a moment I thought we were going to nose over. Then, after a brief moment of suspension, the tail came down again without the propeller hitting the ground. If I hadn't had a

13

220-pound fullback in the rear seat we would have nosed over in the soft dirt! We landed safely without any damage to the plane. From the spot we hit the ground to the place where the plane came to rest was only a distance of twelve feet. I walked to the old Bixby ranch house on Anaheim Avenue and called the dispatcher at the airport. A team came and trucked the undamaged craft back to the airport. That was a first flight my fraternity brother would not forget. In a sense we had made a simulated carrier landing without power or an arresting cable, not a recommended procedure. Little did I know then, that I would experience many of these so-called controlled crashes on the deck of a United States aircraft carrier.

This forced landing taught me a much-needed lesson. It never occurred to me that the plane's carburetor could freeze up in the mild temperatures of Long Beach, California. After all, I had flown in fifty-seven degrees below zero in Alaska and I had never had a problem. Never again would I cut off my engine in a humid climate without first pulling on the carburetor heat.

*   *   *

On June 22, 1941, the German army, after bringing central Europe under control, struck east. Russia was the target, and this began the largest battle in the history of warfare. For sixteen months after the first blitzkrieg had struck Poland, the Germans experienced one military victory after another. Except for the battle of Britain, in which the armies had played no part, not one major defeat had slowed the German advance. Now on this June day, Hitler moved his forces with 2,700 tanks and 6,000 heavy guns against the Russian defenses. In that first forty-eight hours Russia lost more than two thousand aircraft. Spearheaded by four armored divisions, the Germans advanced as much as fifty miles into Russia that first day.

Those of us working in the Douglas Aircraft plant in Long Beach talked of little else. Some even set up a little betting pool, wagering whether or not the Germans would be in Moscow by Christmas day. Not many would bet against that without steep odds, for by early fall the Germans had taken a million Russian prisoners, and another million had been killed. But as the Russians died by the thousands, the living retreated, forming new lines of resistance until the German advance stalled in the winter snows within sight of the Russian Capitol. Moscow held.

*　　　*　　　*

One November afternoon, when these battles between Russia and Germany were raging, I came to work as usual. As I entered the Douglas plant, I saw soldiers on the roofs of the buildings. They were placing sandbags in circles, protecting large guns that were pointed toward the sky. I approached one of the security officers.

"What's going on up there?" I asked. "Why the guns?"

"They think the Japanese are going to bomb us," he volunteered, as if I should have known. In retrospect, I have often tried to relate this incident to the surprise attack on Pearl Harbor that would come in less than thirty days. Why, if our military forces were preparing for a Japanese attack on our airplane plants in Long Beach, had they not been prepared in Hawaii. A lot of what happened didn't make sense.

*　　　*　　　*

I wasn't aware at that time that in July 1941, Japanese troops had moved into Indo-China. Our country had responded by freezing Japanese assets in the United States. This had made the Japanese government angry, especially the military party that was gaining more control in the Japanese Cabinet. Then in August, President Roosevelt warned Japan that the United States would take steps if she did not cease her policy of military domination. All that fall the Japanese delegates and the United States officials negotiated, but I don't think our general population was aware that all oil imports had been cut off to Japan by our embargoes. With that, the Japanese militarists were urging their country to go to war with the United States. The Washington talks deadlocked, and on October 16th the former War Minister, Tojo, took over and became the Premier of Japan. The militarists were in control and war was

15

imminent. As far as most of us knew, legitimate negotiations were going on in Washington with the Japanese ambassadors. But the negotiations later proved not to be legitimate, and so were doomed for failure. The Japanese were simply using the talks to stall for time, while their task force of aircraft carriers moved undetected out of Japan toward Pearl Harbor, under the protection of the north Pacific weather. Thus they moved successfully to a position for their attack on the island of Oahu in the Hawaiian Islands.

In Japan the last peacetime Imperial Conference convened on December 8th Tokyo time. A final message to the United States, declaring that the talks were at an end, would be delivered to our Secretary of State at 1:00 PM Washington time, some twenty minutes before the Japanese planes would dive with their bombs and torpedoes on Pearl Harbor. Anyone who was alive on that Sunday morning when Pearl Harbor was bombed, remembers exactly where they were and what they were doing. I was at my parents' home at 858 Linden Avenue in Long Beach, California. I usually came home on the weekends to catch up on all the sleep I had lost during the week. Working full time and going to school full time demanded that I get this added rest.

I remember the exact moment I heard the news that Pearl Harbor had been bombed. I was seated in a little breakfast nook on the second floor of our Long Beach home. Mother had prepared a breakfast of pancakes and eggs. The radio was on.

"Pearl Harbor is under attack! Japanese planes are bombing the ships and facilities in Hawaii," the radio blasted. Throughout the day the amazing news continued. We were in a state of shock and disbelief. Gradually the gravity and reality of what had happened sunk in. The tragedy and seriousness of the situation became apparent. A total of 363 Japanese planes, organized into two waves, had attacked. Shining in the clear early morning sunlight, Pearl Harbor presented a perfect target. A hundred warships were riding quietly at anchor or tied to the docks. The Americans were so surprised that they could muster little resistance. The primary target for the striking force was the seven battleships moored in a tidy row along the southeastern shore of Ford Island, in the middle of the harbor. Within half an hour after the first torpedo struck, the Arizona had blown up, the Oklahoma had capsized, the West Virginia was sunk, the California was sinking, and the Tennessee, Nevada and Pennsylvania were damaged. These were all of our best battleships. Their fighter and dive-bombers hit the planes on the ground, so there was little air resistance available. American casualties were high. The navy lost about three times as many men in that one brief action as it had in the Spanish American War and World War I combined. The total dead or missing numbered 2,280. More than a thousand more service men were wounded. Oahu's air strength was almost wiped out. And Pearl Harbor was just the beginning. The main Japanese assault fell in the Far East from the Philippines to Singapore.

Naturally, Mother and Pop were shaken. They had three boys and a prospective son-in-law in the prime age for military service, but they did not say too much as they listened with amazement. I drove back to USC later that afternoon. My mind was spinning

The sequence of my actions the following day, Monday, December 8th, 1941 are still clear. I was on the USC campus in morning. Students were in little groups engaged in subdued conversations. Then the word came over the radio. President Roosevelt was asking Congress to declare war: "Since December 7th, a day which will go down in infamy, a state of war exists between the United States and the Empire of Japan!" That was the way the President put it.

That day, December 8th, 1941 I made the decision to apply for navy flight training. I got into my 1934 yellow Cadillac convertible and drove to the Long Beach Naval Air Station. It had been a long time in coming, but the die was now cast, and my commitment was clear.

ALASKA
1939 - 1940

"In the summer of 1939, in search of high adventure, my high school friend, Jim Dyer, and I left Seattle, Washington in our small 18-foot boat and sailed to Alaska."

Willard Robinson

Fairbanks, Alaska on a Mid-winter Day

December 21, 1939. Time-lapse photo shows the sun at 15-minute intervals from 10:15 am to 1:00 pm.

Main Entrance (above) to the University of Alaska (impressive don't you think?). The girl's dorm is on the left and the senior men's dorm is on the right. This is where Robinson lived for a year.

"In September 1939, I enrolled as a student at the University of Alaska."
Willard Robinson

Flying in Alaska

"In June, 1940, I became the first United States government-trained, certificated pilot in the Territory of Alaska. It was a high honor and an event that was newsworthy. KFAR, the local radio station in Fairbanks, broadcast my final flight check throughout the Territory."
Willard Robinson

Left to right:
Willard Robinson, pilot
Bud Foster, NBC announcer
Mr. Gentry, CAA official
Lt. Dick Ragel, instructor

Ski-equipped planes for winter travel at the Fairbanks Airport.

2

PILOT TRAINING BEGINS

The Long Beach Naval Air Station, where I would begin my training, was located at Daugherty Field, which was also the municipal airport. In those days it was just a large dirt area between Cherry Avenue and Lakewood Boulevard, north of Signal Hill. Today it is a giant municipal airport. I was well acquainted with the field. My father had been a good friend of Earl Daugherty. They had gone to Long Beach Polytechnic High School together. Earl Daugherty was a town hero, because he had flown against the Germans in Europe during World War I, and came home to Long Beach to establish his flying facility at the airport. Earl and Pop had remained good friends, and I spent many wide-eyed weekends at the airport with them. I was fascinated with the planes he kept in an old open hangar and wondered at the brave man who flew them. In 1926 our entire family took a flight over Long Beach with Earl Daugherty. He had just taken delivery on a six-place Stinson Travelair plane that he wanted my father to buy. The whole family, my mother and father and the four children, went out to the airport to see the new plane. Earl Daugherty was at the controls. We took off in an easterly direction and soon were above the sloughs and marshes east of the airport. All of this wasteland has been reclaimed and today it is filled with beautiful homes. We soon turned toward Long Beach and Pop pointed out familiar landmarks for us. It was quite an adventure for a young family in those early days. I was eight years old and this was my first flight.

A tragedy put a damper on my father's interest in flying. I vividly remember the day. I was at the beach when I saw Earl Daugherty's new black biplane, with it's golden wings glistening in the sky, fly out over the ocean just south of the Pine Avenue Pier. The sleek plane spun and rolled and looped in a thrilling display of aerobatics. I suspected it was my father's friend, because no one else in Long Beach could fly with that precision. It was confirmed later that it was Earl Daugherty and his passenger, a Press Telegram reporter, who had requested the thrill of flight. On the way back to the field, just east of Cherry Avenue, Earl decided to put the plane into one last dive before he landed. A wing collapsed and they never came out of the death plunge. In the last light of that afternoon, Pop drove me out to the crash site, and we looked into a gaping hole in the earth and the scattered debris left by the crash. The entire city was in shock. Their hero was dead. In his honor, the Long Beach Municipal Airport was christened Daugherty Field.

*   *   *

Now I was driving to the Naval Air Station, located just east of the Daugherty hangars, to enlist in a program that would start my own military adventure in the air.

"Where is the recruiting office," I asked the sentry on duty at the entrance to the base. He directed me to a building on the small base. As I entered the main hall a large poster caught my attention:

CADETS FOR NAVAL AVIATION
IF YOU HAVE THAT EXTRA SOMETHING, APPLY HERE.

A short line had formed, and soon I faced the recruiting officer.

He explained the requirements and the procedure for qualifying for "Elimination Training" at the Long Beach Naval Air Station. "First, do you have two years of college?", he asked.

"I graduate with a degree in Economics from USC in February."

"Good! Now of course there is a demanding physical exam you will have to pass. Do you have 20-20 vision?"

" Yes, I'm sure I do."

" If you pass your physical, you will receive orders that will give you a date to report. Remember, Long Beach is an 'E' Base. That means Elimination training! The navy doesn't want to waste time on those that don't have a natural aptitude for flying. You washout here and you remain a Seaman 2nd Class." The officer was direct. I could have been intimidated. "Do you want to go ahead?"

I took the lengthy forms and signed the formal agreement with the United States Navy. The physical examination was scheduled for the following Monday. The recruiting officer addressed me, "Enjoy the few weeks of freedom you have left. It will be all work after that!"

As I drove back to the USC campus that afternoon, several significant thoughts stirred in my mind. I had taken a major step in my life one day after the Japanese attack on Pearl Harbor. In a sense, I had demonstrated a control over my life. I was naïve, assured and certain. Frankly, I never thought of dying; it is a gift to the young. I had met a deep felt obligation to my country, with the added bonus of prospect for high adventure. Secondly, I knew I could fly. This assurance was so important. I knew, too, that it had been best not to mention my previous flying experience in Alaska and my current rating as a commercial pilot to the navy recruiting officer. Was my instinct right! Later I saw the trouble an instructor could give a cadet who came into training with prior flying experience. The cadets were to learn to fly the navy way. So as a matter of principle, an instructor might degrade anyone who had previous flying experience. Fortunately, I kept my own counsel, and as a result moved through all of my flight checks without the "down" failing mark on my record.

A week later I reported back to the Naval Air Station for the rigorous physical examination that would now determine whether of not I would be accepted in the flight-training program. About thirty-five of us were in the line-up for the examination. All the fellows looked in great shape to me, and I suspected that we would all pass. This didn't prove to be the case. It was my turn to get on the scale. A gruff old corpsman took my weight. The reading was 129 pounds. I should have been at least ten pounds heavier. "You should be applying at Santa Anita race track," he said. "We're hiring pilots here, not jockeys." With a pleased smirk on his face, he let me proceed with the examination.

I met the 20-20 requirement on the eye examination. The next test was one they called the Snyder, and this became a major hurdle for a lot of us. It produced a combination score that took into consideration the heart rate, both before and after exercise, blood pressure, and several other indicators that I don't remember now. I just made the cut-off score and passed. Another test a month later was recommended, and in that test I earned a perfect score. I suspect that my demanding schedule of work and school had taken its toll, affecting my weight and the marginal score on the Snyder test, but I did pass.

By early afternoon, fifteen of us had passed and twenty had failed for one reason or another. The physical examination was a major hurdle, one that I had not expected to be so rigid, and I was relieved. "Congratulations on passing the examination," the supervising officer said. "You will now get orders for Elimination Training and a date to report. That will be early in February."

*   *   *

During the final weeks of December and all of January, I concentrated on my studies. It was fortunate that I could do this, for a whirlwind of activity and emotion engulfed the USC campus. There was a lot of "hype" going on over the war. Military personnel were busy at the recruiting tables, hastily put up on campus, enlisting students. By January, fifteen of us at the school had been accepted as prospective navy pilots. Navy recruiters called us together at the USC Student Union for a publicity picture. This group picture of those of us who had been selected for navy flight training appeared in the Daily Trojan, our student newspaper and in the Los Angeles Times. The headlines read, TROJAN NAVY FLIGHT SQUADRON GOES TO WAR. It was a recruitment gimmick, because after we finished E-Base, we all went our separate ways, and some of them I never saw again.

In January I received my orders. I was to report for duty the first week in January, just two weeks before I was to finish the work for my degree from USC. Because of the pressure of the time, the University agreed to give me full credit without taking my final examinations. That qualified me for graduation, but the diploma would not be awarded until the official ceremony the following June. By that time I would be in Texas.

The navy base did not have barracks for the trainees, so Ed McNeil, a Phi Kappa Tau fraternity brother, and I went to Long Beach to live with my parents while we were in training. The routine and requirements at the base drastically changed our lives. We were issued plain khaki uniforms, given a shaved-up haircut, and put under the tutelage of a Chief Petty officer by the name of Murphy. He would march us by the hour around the dirt airfield and then admonished us when we had dust on our shoes. Beside the twelve of us from USC, there were another dozen recruits from other schools in the area. I was surprised to find one of my old friends from high school in the group. Dale Tillery had just graduated from the University of Chicago. Dale, Ed and I were soon dubbed the Three Musketeers. We had a good friendship at the time we needed it the most.

Elimination training lasted for less than three months. Besides the drastic change in life style, it was a time of extraordinary tension and apprehension. We seldom missed a day in the air, and not a week passed that a young flyer would not be cut from flying status and sent to the regular navy as a seaman second class. That kept us always wondering who would be the next one to be cut. The ground school was a test too. We spent many hours in the classroom learning blinker, code, navy regulations, the use of a military rifle, close order drill, mechanics, mathematics, and the recognition of enemy ships and aircraft. At the end of each week we were tested. If we didn't pass in a subject, we were restricted to the base for the weekend. I did fine until I got into logarithms. It was so foreign to me. I failed the test and was restricted to the base for the weekend. This restriction never did make any sense to me, because all I did was to walk around at night on guard duty with a rifle on my shoulder.

We had been assigned flight instructors and were scheduled for our flight times. The planes were old fabric biplanes manufactured exclusively for the navy. The official designation of the plane was N2N. It was a forgiving aircraft, a little slow on any abrupt maneuver, but rather easy to fly. It took the required seven hours to solo. My instructor was Ensign Lockridge. When I was ready to solo, he flew me to a vacant field at Los Alamitos and climbed out of the cockpit. "It's all yours. Show me a good takeoff and landing."

"O.K., I'm ready," I tried not to sound too excited. I made that first solo flight in a navy plane around the field without incident, another major step completed. Later this grass area became the location of the new Los Alamitos Naval Air Station, from which I would fly following the war with a naval reserve squadron. On the flight back to Long Beach, Ensign Lockridge performed a victory slow-roll in celebration of my successful solo flight. It was the first aerobatic maneuver I had experienced. What an eventful and memorable afternoon it had been.

Periodically, I was assigned sentry duty on the base at night. My orders from the officer in charge were, "If anyone moves, yell who goes there? If there is no response, fire off a shot in that direction." Everyone was edgy in those early days of the war. I never did have a problem, but there was never a night, when I had patrol duty, that I did not hear a distant yell, "Halt!" Then a shot from a 30-06 military rifle might echo through the night. I never knew the result, because it was so dark. But I did hear reports that there were periodic deaths.

An incident happened during the first week of March 1942 that gives insight into the hysteria and fear people felt. I was sleeping at my folk's home in Long Beach. Shortly after midnight the wailing sirens awakened me. From dozens of anti-aircraft gunnery

28

positions, searchlights laced the night sky. There were orange bursts from the exploding shells thrown up by the artillery. As an unidentified object slowly moved across the northwest sky, the guns and searchlights converged on the moving target. The city shook from the concussion of the Ack-Ack guns that coughed steadily as they spewed out hundreds of shells. All of a sudden a rain of shrapnel hit the city, puncturing the hoods of several cars in our neighborhood. One jagged fragment hit the sidewalk next to where I was standing. I ran back into the house to escape the falling metal. I had no doubt that we were under attack. The morning extra paper confirmed the raid. The Los Angeles Times reported:

> *Roaring out of a brilliant moonlit western sky, foreign aircraft, both in large formation and singly, flew over southern California. At 5:00 AM the police reported that an airplane had been shot down near 185th Street.*

There were casualties and damage, but not from the bombs. Three people had been killed in automobile crashes fleeing from the area. Windows were smashed, and shell fragments struck several who ventured out to see the shattering of the night sky. The following morning I found the jagged piece of shrapnel that had taken a chunk out of the sidewalk next to where I had stood. I have kept it as a souvenir from this memorable night. We found out later that there wasn't an attack at all. It had all been just a false alarm. Japan occasionally released incendiary balloons during the war that floated over the Pacific Ocean to harass the jittery Americans. Apparently, that was the unidentified target upon which our gunners fired.

Within the next few days I would be taking my final Elimination flight check. If I passed, it would be off to Texas for further flight training. The anxiety was building up in all of us as we approached the day of our check flight. I realize now that the pressure was deliberately put on us to see how we would respond. The navy knew that when we got into combat there would be tremendous pressure. Now was the time to determine whether or not we had the emotional make-up to perform well when that occurred. It was a necessary, but unpleasant aspect of our training.

But, too, there were moments of great exhilaration. Every hour at the controls of the N2N yellow biplane brought new confidence and a basic feel for the air. I was so thankful for the training I had received from Lt. Dick Ragle in Alaska. That valuable experience enabled me to move ahead with more confidence than some of the other students experienced. I actually developed that basic sense of being a part of the airplane. I loved to fly alone. There was a new freedom when I became airborne—soaring, zooming, diving, spinning, and rolling. To fly the sky, and hear the wind singing through the wing struts was an ethereal experience. The Long Beach skyline and Signal Hill clustered with oil wells had been the familiar sight of my childhood, from the ground. Now I was seeing it from a new perspective.

There was great speculation among the students as to which instructor we would get for the final test. Some of the instructors had the reputations for being easier than others, more compassionate and understanding. We all had our preconceived opinions, much based on nothing more than scuttlebutt, but we were all in agreement about down-check Dietrick. Lt. Senior Grade Dietrick had washed out more cadets than any other instructor. The schedule was posted, and wouldn't you know it, I got down-check Dietrick! My flight was scheduled for 9:00 AM, Easter Sunday morning.

The morning was calm. A few cumulous clouds floated through the clear California sky. The base was relatively quiet. Only a few service men were on duty as I checked out a parachute, put on my helmet and prepared for the flight. Shortly, Lt. Dietrick, his ruddy face showing little emotion, strode to the flight line.

"Are you ready for your check flight?"

"Yes sir, I am ready."

"Here is the procedure I want you to follow. Once we are in the plane, taxi us out to the takeoff position and go through your flight check. There isn't much wind this morning, so take off to the west. At one thousand feet begin a 180-degree climbing turn, and continue on an easterly course until we reach 3000 feet. This should take us somewhere out over the vicinity of Los Alamitos. When we get there, I will tell you the maneuvers that I want you to make."

He was matter of fact; no pleasantries were exchanged. This was all business. Ours was the only plane in the sky that morning. Dietrick never said another word to me until I reached the designated area for the test. Then his voice came through the gasport, a flexible rubber tube that connected his mouthpiece to my leather helmet. It was through this rubber tube that I could hear him speak. This was our only means of communication, and the helmet, fitted to the rubber speaking tube, did muffle the roar of the rotary engine in the open cockpit. I flew through each maneuver just as he instructed. When he finally cut the engine for a simulated forced landing, I was near the area where I had dead-sticked an emergency landing in the Piper Cub several months before. I took it as a good omen.

Finally, he said, "That's it, take it home."

I thought I had done O.K., but you never know, so I was a little apprehensive on the flight back to the base. I landed, taxied to the flight line, cut the engine, and climbed out of the cockpit.

"Good flight. Congratulations! You will do fine. Good luck." He shook my hand.

"Thank you sir, thank you very much."

It had been as pleasant an experience as I would ever have with a navy flight instructor, He was quite a nice man, and the fear of E-Base was behind me.

By the end of the next week the flight checks had been completed and a few more than half of our class would qualify for further flight training. Our graduation celebration was held at the Coconut Grove at the Ambassador Hotel in Los Angeles. We were served a wonderful meal and danced to the familiar music of Freddie Martin and his band. The male vocalist was Stewart Wade. Following the war, Joan and I became friends of Stewart and his wife Virginia. His actual last name was Groshong, and we have kept in contact over the years. Among other memories, I will always associate him with that special night when we celebrated our graduation from the Long Beach Naval Air Station Elimination training. We were on our way to new experiences and adventure.

Ed McNeil and Dale Tillery had also passed E-Base and we all received orders to report to the Grand Prairie Naval Air Station out of Dallas, Texas. It was the holding base for us until the next class of aviation cadets was open at the Corpus Christi Naval Air Station.

Ed had a 1940 Ford V8 and offered to drive Dale and me to Texas. We left Long Beach on an April evening. There were no freeways in those days. We just drove on and on through the night on a two lane highway out through Blythe, and on to Phoenix. By daylight we were in the Arizona mountains on our way to Globe, a working mining center rich in copper. We had left a place that was familiar, and now we were in a new land that was fascinating and strange. Was it symbolic of the continued change we would experience in adventure ahead? Little did we know then that each of us would be destined for a vastly different wartime experience. Ed McNeil would be trained in multiengine aircraft and would fly transports. Dale Tillery, following his commission, would spend the war as a navy flight instructor for new cadets. I would be assigned to the Pacific Fleet as an aircraft carrier pilot flying torpedo planes. All of this did not matter, for now we were bound together on a common course.

At noon we arrived at my Uncle Phil Gould's ranch in Safford, Arizona. He and his wife Gen were there to meet us. "You must be hungry," Gen said.

"Great! We have been driving all night and a meal sounds wonderful. We have a couple of hours, and then we're on our way to El Paso for the night."

Soon she grilled steaks for us, and prepared the most wonderful farm grown food. Phil and Gen were so welcoming. Over the years, I have remembered that impromptu visit with great warmth.

By mid-afternoon we were on the highway again, and before midnight we were checked into a hotel in El Paso, Texas. We needed rest before the final twelve-hour drive to Dallas. We were off again the next day, hour after hour across the lonely wastes of west Texas. The names of the infrequent towns were not familiar to me: Pecos, Odessa, Midland, and Abilene.

As we approached each town we turned on the car radio to get an update on the war. We needed some diversion to break the boredom as we passed through the barren and endless land. The war was not going well for the United States. Japan, we learned, had opened a devastating bombardment on Corregidor, our last stronghold in the Philippines. "This marks the beginning of the now inevitable disaster for our brave soldiers isolated so far from home," the announcer said. "The defenders are too ill and too weak to resist." I don't remember that Dale, Ed or I even commented. We were deep in our own thoughts.

Later in the day we heard the news that German submarines, within sight of the East Coast, had sunk three more ships. Since January the German U-boats had taken a terrific toll on our shipping. More than 360 merchant ships had been sunk in United States coastal waters. Americans suffered a shortage of airplanes for coastal patrol, and we had few pilots for flying over water or hitting small moving targets such as submarines. The news was not encouraging. We drove on as night spread over the vast prairie land.

The Grand Prairie Naval Air station was small. A single runway allowed all but the largest planes to land. The base was partially surrounded by a lake where an occasional seaplane could land and dock at the base. A number of wooden barracks had been recently constructed to house the cadets waiting for openings at the Corpus Christi Naval Air Station on the gulf in southern Texas.

Long lines of double-decker bunks gave us a place to sleep. Each of us had a small locker for our personal belongings. It was my first experience with limited privacy and twenty-four hour military supervision. It was not the happiest of experiences, and the month we spent on the base had its lonely and boring times. The instructors tried to keep us busy with basic ground school classes and physical fitness training, including hours of marching and close order drill. I did become more proficient in sending and receiving code, and I learned to communicate by blinker. That was the only skill I would ever use. Blinker code flashed from the carrier would give us our landing instructions when we were flying over the carrier. I also learned semaphore, the art of communicating with flags. It was an interesting diversion, but we never used this means of communication.

I retain two clear memories of my time at the Grand Prairie

Naval Air Station. One day a new plane landed and taxied to a large service hangar on the base. I went to look at this giant single-engine bomber and marveled at the pilot who had stopped on his way to deliver the plane to the Pacific Fleet. I learned that this was the new TBF Grumman Torpedo Bomber, one of the first off the assembly line. The pilot let me climb up behind the folded wings of the plane and sit in the cockpit. I was overwhelmed by the complexity of the instrument panel and the gadgets that surrounded the pilot. I gripped the control stick and worked the massive ailerons, elevators and rudder controls, and marveled at the huge two thousand horsepower radial engine that powered the beast. How could anyone land a plane like this on the pitching deck of an aircraft carrier? This was my first introduction to the airplane that in less than ten months I would be flying as a navy pilot.

The second memory I have is of a relaxed evening with a number of prospective cadets. We were sitting around a long table in a screened area at one end of the barracks. The balm of a humid Texas evening engulfed the base. Towering white clouds colored in the sunset sky. Expectant trainees talked and shared. The day had been another milestone. The next morning we were on our way to Corpus Christi, Texas for the demanding months in primary and basic training.

*   *   *

Our elation was dampened by news broadcasting from the loudspeakers. A huge naval aerial battle was underway in the Coral Sea northwest of Australia. United States carrier planes were engaging the Japanese attackers, though the radio reports confirmed that the two opposing naval task forces were not in sight of one another. The naval aviators were carrying the fight beyond the fighting ships in the fleets. U.S. pilots had attacked and sunk the Japanese carrier Shoho. Reports indicated that the Japanese had inflicted a higher loss than they had sustained, for their aircraft were being credited with damaging the aircraft carriers Yorktown and Lexington. Later the discouraging news came that the Lexington had sunk. This was terrible news. The cadets were

34

subdued.   But not all was lost because, although crippled, the American navy flyers had stopped the Japanese advance for the first time in the war.

*   *   *

Ed, Dale, and I left the next morning for the huge training base at Corpus Christi, Texas with an unstated resolve and a new sense of the seriousness of the mission we were to undertake.

Elimination Training
Long Beach Naval Air Station

Wind her up! Our *Yellow Perils* were started by inertia. A machinist mate would crank her up so we could start the engine.

Flight Board. This is where we got our directions for the day's flight schedule, plane assignment, weather conditions, and the area in which we were to fly.

3

CORPUS CHRISTI AND
"WINGS OF GOLD"

The Corpus Christi Naval Air Station was a newly constructed airbase, located on the Gulf of Mexico, 130 miles north of the Mexico border. The northern end of Padre Island, a hundred-mile long sand barrier, created a protected bay for the base and the city of Corpus Christi. Here in this ideal location, the largest flight-training center in the world had been constructed in less than one year. Besides the main base, there were four auxiliary airfields. In this massive base were the hangars, barracks, repair shops, subsistence buildings, power plants, warehouses and the many auxiliary structures needed to support this complex. The Secretary of the Navy said, "This powerful naval air training center will breed and school the best pilots in the world for the most essential task which has ever confronted our nation."

I arrived at the Corpus Christi Naval Air Station on the afternoon of May 14, 1942. This was the "University of the Air". I was now one of 3,000 navy-flying cadets in training to take the power of the United States into the far reaches of the world. I was excited, overwhelmed, and, yes, a little apprehensive.

Our days soon became full of new and demanding requirements. We were each assigned to what they called "wings". One wing would attend ground school for half a day while the other wing flew, and then the schedule would be reversed. Ground school included classes in aerodynamics, the theory of flight, aircraft engines, navy rules regulations and customs, and identification of enemy ships and aircraft. Most importantly we learned navigation, both celestial and dead reckoning. I studied very hard, not only because I found the classes difficult, but also lessons learned could very well be the key to survival. This hard work, both in the classroom and in the air, was what we needed to reach our goal to become the best-trained pilots in the world.

I was assigned to Class 5A-42-C. There were 170 of us in this class, and Ed McNeil was selected as our commanding cadet officer. I don't know how the selection was made, but Ed was a good choice. He was smart, big, handsome and most important, he was all business. There was no fooling around with Ed. He projected a bearing and presence that the other cadets respected. The cadet class lived in the same barracks, ate together in the same mess hall, marched and took physical training, went to class and flew on the same schedule. We were always together. We developed an esprit de corps. This was important because we were being rushed through flight training in six months, a program that was originally designed to take fourteen months. The war demanded pilots, and the government needed us as soon as possible. The commander of the base said:

> You are still going to have to measure up to the high standards set, before you will be commissioned as a navy officer and a navy pilot. What you are about is deadly serious. Some of you will not make it through the war. Those of you who do will be awarded medals for heroism. Continue to work hard and we will prepare you.

This was hyperbole, but it does demonstrate the atmosphere

which surrounded our regulated lives. We marched in formation everywhere we went, to breakfast, to ground-school classes, and to the flight line. The navy believed that formation marching was a useful exercise in our indoctrination, for it helped break down our individual inclination to "go it alone". Later, our attacks would not be successful unless they were coordinated and we could fly in close formation. Aviation ground school provided the foundation for our flight training. A person could learn to fly an airplane without understanding the physics involved, but all great pilots have knowledge of what makes the airplane fly. They also understand navigation, map interpretation and communication. Skill in all facets of military flight only increases a pilot's probability of survival. I found the study even more demanding than what had been required while working on my college degree.

I often worried about passing the final examinations in flight school. We could not study after hours, for in the regulated life we were living, the lights had to be turned out on schedule. I had a little hand flashlight and sometimes I would go into the lavatory at night and study the material until I had some assurance that I could pass the test the next day. These first days in ground school, although I knew they were important, became tedious. It had been over a month since I had flown and I was anxious to get back in the air. I longingly watched the sky as the advanced students flew through their maneuvers, the drone of their planes' powerful motors resounding in the clear Texas air.

Then one day in late June, Class 5A-42-C was marched to the main hangar on the base. Row after row of N3N Stearman biwing yellow trainers awaited our arrival. What wonderful planes they were, about as steady and reliable as they come, forgiving and yet they had enough power and pep to fly us through the basic aerobatic maneuvers of military flight. I met my instructor and he prepared me for my first indoctrination flight. The first ten-hour phase in the "Yellow Peril", as the N3N was dubbed, started with a basic flight in which the instructor evaluated our skill. He wanted to see if we really had the "right stuff". There were rigid rules to follow, important because the air was filled with planes piloted by new students with varying ability, talent and skill. The field from which we flew did not have a runway; rather it was a huge asphalt circle with a large yellow wind tee at the edge. Flyers were to take off directly into the wind as indicated by the wind tee. This sometimes led to a free-for-all, as the wind did have a tendency to shift. We learned a quick lesson; keep your eyes open in all directions. I saw several smash-ups on the pad, but to my knowledge no one was seriously hurt. There was no radio contact with the tower, so we were all on our own. A number of the cadets were washed out and sent home, but the percentage of failures was not as high as it had been at the Long Beach E-Base.

I soloed in the required time, and was then allowed to fly to the extremities of the sprawling base to hone my skill in all of the basic maneuvers. For the first time I learned the snap roll, the slow roll, the Immelman, the split S, and how to go into a tailspin and recover on a predetermined heading. The giant white cumulous clouds, so typical of the Texas sky, provided a spectacular playground in which to fly.

The procedure for landing at the end of each session was to fly to a pylon about a mile from the landing pad. The flying cadets would race to the pylon, which determined the order of landing. It became quite a game. During this time the class suffered our first fatality. Kurt Schaefer, a fellow cadet from Bakersfield, California crashed into another plane as he raced for the pylon. Fabric, parts and debris blew apart and scattered to the ground. Both pilots died in the Texas wheat field. There would be other crashes, and other losses, but the death of Kurt, the first one to go in our class, put us in shock.

*   *   *

News, especially concerning the war in the Pacific, kept drifting into the base. On June 4, 1942 a United States search plane spotted Japanese carriers 240 miles northwest of Midway. This, we found out later, did not come as a surprise. The Japanese code had been broken and our limited forces had been sent out to intercept the Japanese. Admiral Nimitz could pit only seventy-six ships, no battleships, and only three carriers, the Hornet, the Enterprise, and

42

the Yorktown, against the enemy. While the three American carriers set an interception course, the unsuspecting Japanese began attacking Midway Island. Having completed their strike, the Japanese planes came back and landed on their carriers. Then to their surprise the first American planes appeared. They were torpedo planes, and the Japanese fighters who had been circling at altitude came down to attack the American flyers. This left the American dive-bombers free to come in a bit later and make their successful attacks on the Japanese carriers. Of course the enemy devastated the low-flying American torpedo bombers, but the American flyers sacrifice enabled the American victory.

The story of Torpedo Squadron 8 became history. Out of the twenty-four planes and seventy-two men who made the attack, only one plane and two men returned; all shot down in less than twelve minutes. I relate this, because the one pilot who returned to crash land on Midway was Albert K, Earnest. Seven months later Bert joined Torpedo Squadron VC-7, where I, too, would be assigned. We would fly together in squadron VC-7 for a year, and during that time would participate in the attack on Kwajalein in the Marshall Islands. Bert tells the story of his participation in the Battle of Midway in a later chapter of these memoirs.

In the Battle of Midway, four Japanese carriers were sunk, three in the initial attack by the American dive-bomber pilots. Only the Hiryu remained, and in the desperate effort by the Japanese to recover the initiative, their Admiral ordered his planes to attack the U.S. carrier Yorktown. The Yorktown was so badly damaged in this attack that it was later abandoned. But before the Japanese hit, the Yorktown launched their dive-bombers. The American flyers, in the course of the melee, sunk the Hiryu, the fourth and last Japanese carrier. It was the turning point in the war. Japan's westward advance had been stopped. The United States could perhaps, even with their limited force, hold the enemy until our new ships, planes, and replacement pilots could be provided. This is why the Battle of Midway had such an impact on those of us who were in training at Corpus Christi. They were waiting for new pilots.

*　　　　*　　　　*

The next big milestone in our primary training was the dead-stick landing check. A cadet had to land, after his engine's power was cut, within a fifty-foot circle marked out on the ground. It was a simulated emergency landing that took a lot of skill and a cool head. One could approach the target circle straight in, but the better technique was to make a large S turn, keeping an eye on the circle and adjusting the tightness of each turn as the wind velocity changed. In this way the pilot had a chance to adjust so he would not come up short or coast over the circle. One could also cross-control and slip off excessive altitude, if necessary. I was comfortable using this technique. I would get five shots at the circle. If I landed within the circle three out of the five times, I could go on with the training. If I didn't, I would get a ticket home. That's why we felt a lot of pressure when taking the dead-stick landing check.

On the day of my check, I flew my instructor out to a dirt field, which was some distance from the main base. When we landed he got out of the plane and joined several other instructors whose students were also flying the dead-stick landing test. The instructors sat or lounged on the grass around the chalk-lined circle that was the target. My first two landings hit the circle and I felt some of the pressure lifted. The cadet in front of me had hit the circle twice, but he had overshot twice. This was his fifth and final try. If he hit on his fifth try he was in. If he missed he was washed out. As I watched from my safe landing interval behind him, I could see that he was a little high on his final approach. When he reached the circle he just pulled the nose up, stalled the plane, and pancaked right into the center of the ring. The wings collapsed and one of the wheels broke loose, rolling into the area where the instructors were waiting on the grass. You should have seen those instructors scatter! I landed a short distance away and walked over to where the action had taken place. The cadet crawled out of his plane unhurt and said, "Well I hit the target anyway!" I didn't know the cadet, but I thought his reaction was amusing. The instructors didn't think it was funny and I presume they washed him out. When the damaged plane was removed, I made my final

44

two landings and was on my way. I credited Lt. Ragel and the training he had given me in Alaska with helping me through this test, but of course I didn't mention this to my navy instructor.

In primary training we had our introduction to aerobatics. It was not just a matter of doing the required maneuvers, but to do them in a prescribed sequence with precision. For example, when told to do a tailspin I lined up on a highway or some object on the horizon, stalled the aircraft on that line, did three complete revolutions as we headed for the earth and hopefully recovered on the exact heading that I had started the spin. It was the same with the snap roll in that it was also a stall maneuver. However, in the snap I kept full power, raised the nose slightly above the horizon, kicked full rudder and pulled the stick back into my gut. If done precisely the plane would snap roll in a horizontal position. The trick was to come out of the snap on precisely the same heading and altitude that the maneuver was started.

Another requirement was the slow roll. Here I actually flew the plane through the maneuver, keeping full power, dropping the nose slightly, and then pulled up gradually as I dropped the wing, keeping increased pressure on the rudder. If done correctly the plane rotated on a horizontal axis and recovered in level flight on exactly the same heading as it started. I liked the falling leaf maneuver. In this maneuver I would begin just as in a tailspin, but this time instead of letting the plane fall off into a complete turn, I kicked opposite rudder on the half turn. This created the falling leaf effect as the little plane, falling back and forth, headed toward the ground in a lazy rocking motion.

The split-S is a one-half snap roll. It is a great maneuver that required to change 180 degrees in direction with some violence. Here again, it is a stall maneuver that became useful in combat. On the other hand, the Immulmann is a coordinated, powered maneuver, a climbing 180-degree turn to reverse direction and gain altitude. The basic cartwheel and wingover are just variations of the other basic maneuvers.

I practiced many times before I felt comfortable enough for my final primary check flight. I did begin to feel a new freedom as I lost my tenseness. The experience was exhilarating; just me with a responsive airplane flying around the lazy clouds in a blue Texas sky. I pretended I was a World War I ace seeking out the Germans. I listened to the wire struts as they vibrated in the air, and felt the coastal air as it washed through the open cockpit. It could not get any better. This was a new taste of life.

The aerobatics phase of flight training was not a happy experience for a few of the cadets in our class. Great athletes and otherwise fine flyers could develop a staggering problem with equilibrium. This manifested itself in gripping stomach pains and nausea. For some there seemed to be no solution. I remember talking with Bill Dudley, the All-American football player from Virginia, and later a national star when he played for the Washington Redskins. "I've never been so sick in my life," he told me. "If this is what flying is all about, I'm out of here." Bill Dudley was one cadet who had no regrets over terminating his flight training. Bill finished out the war happily as a navy physical fitness officer.

In due course, I was scheduled for another flight with my instructor. He wanted to check on my progress in properly executing the maneuvers and within the required sequence in which I was to fly them. When I finished he said, "Good! Let me take over." I couldn't speak back to him through the communication tube, so, as we were trained to do, I patted my head and pointed to him. That was the sign that he would be flying the plane. I think he was a little bored with instructing and decided to take out his frustration by wringing out the stout little plane. What a ride he gave me. He put me in positions I had never before experienced. "I'll bet you have never flown through an outside reverse Immulmann", he said. I shook my head.

Over we went into a powered downward outside loop. As the G forces built up, my feet came off the floor and the seat belt drew tight. The belt was all that was holding me from catapulting out of the cockpit and into the air. At the bottom of the outside half loop my eyes felt like they would pop out of their sockets. There was a moment of excruciating pressure as the blood was forced into my head. Then as he rolled the plane back from the outside position, the strut wires and the wings vibrated violently. When the plane recovered, I realized we had lost a thousand feet before we had regained straight and level flight. I was never tempted to try that maneuver. That's a good way to tear the wings off an airplane.

*   *   *

On August 7, 1942 the 1st Marine Division landed on Guadalcanal. This was the U.S. Navy's first amphibious assault since the Spanish American War in 1898. The operation was hastily planned and executed under far-from-ideal conditions, but our forces did establish a beachhead, overran the Japanese encampment, and captured the airfield. After this initial success, a desperate and grueling war of attrition began. The planes from the Wasp, Saratoga, and Enterprise covered the Guadalcanal landings. Navy aerial fighting was vigorous, and large numbers of planes from both sides were shot down. The marines were able to put the airfield on Guadalcanal in operating order so the navy and marine pilots could begin flying to protect the continuing landing operation. The plan was to move on up through the Solomon Islands and eventually neutralize the Japanese stronghold and staging base at Rabaul.

It was generally accepted that many of the current cadets at Corpus Christi would eventually be involved in the bitter coming aerial battles. I knew three who would be killed. They were Pat Patterson, my friend from USC and flight training, Jim Boyden, best friend of my brother-in-law, John Jaqua, and Bill Hater, a Sunday school classmate from Long Beach. Marine pilot, John Jaqua, who did survive the long battle in the Solomon Islands, tells his own story later in this manuscript. Many others did lose their lives in this eighteen-month struggle in which over 5,000 Japanese planes were shot down, thousands lost their lives and countless ships were sunk. The lessons we were learning at Corpus Christi did save many of those who were later flying in the navy and marine squadrons that were ordered to the Pacific war so many miles away.

*   *   *

We experienced night flying while in advanced training. The instructor took us up on our first night flight, mainly to get us oriented to the lighting on the base and the runways. It would have been easy to get disoriented at night, because all the familiar landmarks were gone. Once the instructor was assured we could find our way back to the landing field, we were on our own. I was always apprehensive during these night flights. So many planes were in the air, and it was difficult to see the other flyers. Green and red lights kept flashing by; that was all you could see of the other planes. Running lights were going in every direction, right, left, above and below. It was with great relief, when at the end of each flight, I felt the ground once again under the rolling wheels of the plane. It was important training, for I would be required to do many hours of night flying when later attached to a designated night flying squadron. These training hours would eventually be culminated with the experience of all experiences, landing on the dark deck of an aircraft carrier in a heavy and powerful torpedo bomber.

After the least talented cadets had been washed out, we did our first formation flying. This became one of my favorite experiences in military flying. All the maneuvers in formation flying demanded our coordination, smoothness and alertness. The join-up with the other planes had to be done with precision and timing, each pilot relying on the skill of the other. We started in the three-plane, basic "V" sections, working slowly up to echelons and crossovers. Eventually we took off and landed in formation.

I remember one incident in formation flying when my friend, Pat Patterson from USC, was leading a three-plane section in take-offs and landings. I was in another three-plane section flying above him. The three planes landed together in good formation, but somehow Pat got a little out of line on his take-off. The three-pane section flew at an angle that did not give full use of the little auxiliary square field to which we had been assigned. Off they went, and before they could get three feet in the air, all three planes, one after the other, hit the top wire of the fence and flipped over in the adjoining cornfield. The pilots all walked away unhurt and I flew back to the main base to report the accident.

Before we left Corpus we did a lot of formation flying in the SNJ North American advanced trainer. Almost all of our military flying from then on was in formation. With increasing skill and assurance we gained pride in flying wing to wing with precision.

Corpus Christi Naval Air Station had three auxiliary air stations, Rodd Field, Cabaniss Field and Cuddihy Field. These naval air stations were used for basic training, the second of the three phases we needed to complete before qualifying as a commissioned officer with the rank of Ensign. Kingsville Auxiliary Naval Air Station, some thirty air miles away from the main base, was used for advanced fighter pilot training. Cadets eventually assigned to fighter training were moved to Kingsville, following basic training. That was the only auxiliary station that had barracks, so the cadets stayed there during the final phase of their training.

Our group was assigned to Cuddihy Field for the first part of our basic training. The naval air station bused us to this base every day for our flight instruction. It was there that I got my first experience in a fleet operational scout plane. It was a Vought-Sikorsky OS2U, a rather slow plane, quite solid in the air, and relatively easy to fly, but a major step up from the Stearman primary trainer.

The SNV *Vultee*, which we also flew in basic training, took a little more skill, I thought. Take off and landing speeds were higher than in any other plane I had flown. The approach for landing had to be thought out and planned with more care. It was important to gain skill and confidence in the SNV, for this was the airplane we would fly in our critical instrument training.

We returned to the main base for instruments and blind flying. The first hours in instrument training were simulated blind flying. We were assigned to a Link Trainer that was a mock-up of a regular cockpit with all the instruments and controls of a regular plane. Instruments and radio range finders were very primitive in those days. We learned to fly under the hood, keeping the mock plane in control and finding our way back to a base without any reference other than the panel instruments. This single training aid, the Link Trainer, probably saved many young flyers' lives. If a cadet were disposed to vertigo, panic, or claustrophobia, it was better to confront it in the Link Trainer than in the air. I hated being enclosed, but I did learn how to follow a radio beam as the dit-dash signal sounded in my ear. When the steady hum came, I honed in on the beam that guided me to the field marker. I learned to make the steady one-needle turns and the let-downs that would later bring me back to a weather-obscured runway.

The emphasis on perfection in the earlier phases of our flight training culminated in the hooded hours spent in the rear cockpit of an SNV instrument plane. The instructor sat in the front cockpit, screaming in protest if we varied in altitude in straight and level flight, or if we did not hold a steady descent in our turns. Fortunately, I drew an instructor who was utterly forgiving of my minor transgressions.

Ed McNeil was not so lucky. He drew a cocky little ensign for his instrument instructor. The dynamics between the two were volatile, because a pretty little girl in the photographic laboratory had taken a shine to Ed. We had gone to this lab to have our pictures taken for the Yearbook. The instructor claimed the girl was his territory. He gave Ed, an excellent flyer, nothing but trouble during instrument training. Every time Ed drifted just a little off direction while flying under the hood, his instructor grabbed the control stick in the front cockpit and slammed it from side to side. As the controls were synchronized, the control stick in the back cockpit hit Ed in the knees with some force. In one of the required drills, the instructor intentionally put the plane in an out-of -control position. This might be upside down, in a spin, or in a dive. Then the cadet had the responsibility, while still flying blind under the hood, to bring the violently tossing plane back into level flight on a prescribed heading and air speed. When Ed got this maneuver, the instructor banged Ed's knees again with the control stick. Ed got so mad that he shoved the stick forward, forcing the plane into a dive. The panicked instructor grabbed the control stick and tried to recover, but could not over-power Ed who was bigger and stronger. Before losing too much altitude, Ed pulled the plane back into level flight. "Now take me back to the base, you S.O.B.," Ed yelled over the radio. When they landed, Ed went straight to the squadron's commanding officer and told him what had happened. The whole unfortunate situation apparently died, because no one heard any more about it. That was fortunate because Ed's navy flying career could have ended right there. Ed had a top academic and flying record and was the head cadet officer in our class. I know that carried a lot of weight.

All of us dreaded the instrument check flight. If we passed, we would receive the instrument rating required of all navy flyers. If we failed we would go back for additional time in the Link Trainer and eventually another check in the air. But if we got a second down-check, that meant failure and a washout.

It was time for my instrument flight check. At my scheduled time I met the instructor in the main base hangar. " Good morning," he greeted me. "I'll do the flying until we get squared away. Then I'll turn it over to you. Check into the Beeville radio range and fly that heading until you get over the marker. Once you hit the marker, start your turns and let down to the runway." He was pleasant and matter of fact.

Beeville, Texas was located about sixty miles northwest of Corpus Christi, so it was only a half-hour flight. But for me, flying blind under the hood, it was an endless time of concentration. The radio pulse sounded through my earphones, giving me the bearing and direction through the dot and dash code that would direct me to my destination and final approach course to the Beeville field. My check instructor was a fine person and did his best to keep me focused and relaxed. The flight seemed to be going well and I made my destination. "Good job. Open the hood," he said. I looked, and there dead ahead was the Beeville airstrip. I felt a great sense of achievement, for now I was cleared to proceed to advance training, the last hurdle in my quest for the "Wings of Gold."

*   *   *

It was sometime during the summer of 1942 that our class marched into the main hangar at Corpus Christi. As we stood at attention; a senior naval officer stepped forward:

The time has come to make a decision for the type of advanced training you want. Up until this time there have been three possibilities: fighters, dive-bombers, or multi-engine. Now for the first time we will be commissioning a special torpedo squadron that will train right here at the main base, Squadron 13. As you are all aware, the fleet has lost an undue number of torpedo plane pilots in the engagements against Japan. Because of the situation we face, I'm going to ask right now that if you are willing to be trained as a torpedo pilot, will you step forward.

Over the years, I have tried to reconstruct the gymnastics my mind went through. I have never felt that my decision was impulsive, but on one level it didn't make a lot of sense. Regardless, I did step forward with thirty of the 160 cadets who were in our class. We had committed to flying in the very first specialized torpedo class in the history of the United States Navy.

Let me explain the tactic of the torpedo plane in combat. On a torpedo attack against a warship, the plane approaches the target low over the water, reducing speed to 200 knots just 200 feet above the water. This straight and level flight enables a 2,000-pound torpedo to enter the water at exactly the right angle and direction for a run at an enemy ship, enabling the torpedo to explode just below the water line. This is where a ship is most vulnerable. Of course, this attack technique puts the bomber in a position for the enemies direct fire. It was understandable why so many torpedo planes are shot down in the battles where they had been deployed. Now we were to replenish the greatly depleted ranks of the navy's torpedo pilots. It was a sobering development.

*   *   *

Ed McNeil went into multi-engine training. That was his first choice. Dale Tillery commuted to Cuddihy Field for advanced training and was later assigned as an instructor. However, we all continued living together in the barracks on the main base.

I reported to the new torpedo training Squadron 13. This was the last of the three phases of flying required at Corpus Christi before being qualified as a Naval Aviator. My new instructor took me out to the flight line and introduced me to the plane I would fly. It was a beautiful new silver SNJ. This was the navy's designation for the famous AT-6 advanced trainer used to teach thousands of military pilots during World War II. Over 10,000 of these planes were produced during World War II. The SNJ had a 550-horse power Pratt & Whitney engine, and flew up to 212 miles per hour. I mounted the wing, got into the cockpit and looked over the controls. The instructor explained the procedures to me, how to set the throttle, adjust the gas mixture and get the landing flaps up and down. It would be the first time for me to fly a plane with retractable landing gear. There was much more information for me to absorb in a short time and I was doing my best to keep it all in my mind. What later became routine was very complicated for me at the time.

"Get in the front cockpit. I think we are ready to go," he said. "I'll take you out to one of the practice fields and let you shoot a few takeoffs and landings so you will get the feel of the plane." There was awe and anticipation as he sped down the runway and smoothly vaulted the plane into the air. I had never experienced such power.

"Now, go ahead and take over," he said through the radio intercom after we had climbed to a sufficient altitude. His voice was calm. "See how she handles. When you are comfortable go over the landing procedure and shoot a landing."

The time had come! Wheels down, mixture rich, flaps down, air speed under control; my mind whirled. I made three landings and three takeoffs and flew through a few basic maneuvers, that's all. And then we returned to the main base. The instructor climbed out of the back cockpit. "You're ready. Go out and make a few more landings and just fly it around for a while. Enjoy the flight," he said in almost an off-hand way.

I panicked! I didn't believe what I was hearing. "Do you really think I am ready to solo in this plane? I don't think I am."

"You're in advanced training now. It's up to you to learn to fly these new planes on your own. When you get into the operational planes in the fleet, there won't be an instructor in a back seat to help you. Go ahead. You are on your own." I thought I could detect a smile as he left and went back to the hangar.

There was another cadet getting ready to takeoff in the plane next to mine. "Do you feel ready to take this thing up by yourself?" I asked.

He looked at me in a rather cocky way and said, "Sure, no problem. Follow me out."

This didn't help my state of mind, but the die was cast. I had to go, shaking knees and all. So I took off, following the other cadet (I don't remember his name) to the practice strip some distance from the base. As we approached the landing pattern I meticulously went through the landing check-off procedure; wheels down, landing flaps set, gas mixture rich, altitude and air speed under control and the proper interval established behind the lead plane. Now I was squared away for my first solo landing in the SNJ. But to my amazement, I saw the cadet that I was following belly in his plane on the runway. Sparks and smoke streamed out from the rear of his skidding plane. He had forgotten to put his wheels down!

I learned another important lesson. Never become overconfident. Always respect your airplane. Never take anything for granted and always go over the checklist for takeoff and for landing, no matter how experienced you are. Nonchalance in the air is the formula for disaster.

As my skill in flying the advanced trainer became honed, I enjoyed a new exhilaration and freedom in the air. The loops, the spins, the rolls and the snaps eventually came with an ease that negated any initial tension I had experienced. I was ready and passed my final aerobatics check.

Now that we were senior cadets, we were given more freedom. For the first time we were allowed off base on the weekends. There wasn't a lot to do in Corpus, but just being free from the regimentation of our lives was a tremendous relief. Dale Tillery, Ed McNeil and I decided to take our first liberty together.

"All I want is a good meal, a little music and a quiet night's sleep in a good bed," Dale said.

"Why don't we rent a room in the Driscoll Hotel? I hear they have a good dining room, too," Ed suggested.

"Sounds fine to me. Anything to get off this base for a while." So we got into Ed's car and took off for our first quiet weekend in weeks. The drive along Ocean Boulevard to downtown Corpus Christi was a joy. Soon the towering white hotel on the bluff overlooking the city and the bay came into sight. It had just opened and was the pride of Corpus Christi.

We registered for one of the spanking new rooms, took a warm and relaxing shower and reserved a special table in the plush dining room. All was complete for the evening we had only dreamed about for weeks. Dale beamed as a classical violinist played while we ate. This was real class. Our evening was complete. Then, at about ten o'clock, we retired for the sleep to which we had looked forward.

There was a banging on our hotel room door! "Let us in," a voice boomed.

"Who is it," Ed yelled back, with some irritation.

"Jay Perrin," was his drunken reply. "Sherman and Patterson are with me. We can't get a room so we're coming in and spending the night with you." The three cadets had been members of that first Trojan Squadron, and we had all gone through flight training together.

"Like hell you are," Ed responded to Jay's demand.

With that, Jay went back down the hall, turned around and ran back toward our room with some speed. As he hit our door, the force of his body tore off the hinges and the door crashed into the room. Jay came crashing in, too. Ed met Jay with a fist straight to his face. Two teeth flew out of Jay's mouth and blood spurted all over the plush hotel carpet. Now we were in a real mess! Dale rushed into the bathroom, grabbed a towel and stuck it into Jay's mouth in an attempt to stop the spurting blood. Sheridan and Perrin were drunk, but Pat Patterson who never drank and had just tagged along with them on their first liberty, volunteered to drive Perrin back to the base hospital. That seemed the best course of action, because if we called the police we would all be restricted and in a lot of trouble.

The three of them left, and we placed the door back on its hinges as well as we could. The carpet was a mess. We took wet towels and cleaned the room as best we could. But, our peaceful night had been shattered and the sleep we had looked forward to did not come easily. The next morning we told the manager of the hotel what had happened. He was not happy! Eventually, we settled the damage for $80.00. It seemed like a huge sum of money to us then, but today after almost sixty years later, the settlement would be more like a thousand dollars. Between us, we scraped up the money and returned to the base, somewhat despondent, but relieved that none of us had been put on report.

There is another episode to this story. Pat Patterson became even a closer friend. He attended our wedding in Seattle. We were in San Diego together in the summer of 1943 and said goodbye as he left for the war in the first navy *Hellcat* fighter squadron sent to the Pacific. Later we were saddened to learn that Pat was missing in action during the battle for the Solomon Islands. The last anyone knew, he had a Japanese *Zero* on his tail. He was never heard from again. Gene Sheridan and Jay Perrin became carrier fighter pilots and got kills in the famous Mariana *"Turkey Shoot"* off the Mariana Islands. The Japanese, in that one-day engagement lost over 300 of their planes to the U.S. Navy Fighter Pilots. This again raises so many questions about the unfathomable mysteries of life.

*　　　　*　　　　*

Late in the summer of 1942 I had another experience that related to the Driscoll hotel. My sister, Robin, an American Airline stewardess, received leave and came to Corpus Christi to see her fiancé, John Jaqua. He was a cadet in basic training at the base. That weekend a hurricane formed out in the Gulf and a hundred-mile strip along the coast was put on alert. No one was sure where the storm might hit. The planes on the base were flown north to inland airports and people were busy everywhere boarding up windows with plywood. All liberty leaves were cancelled, except for the very senior cadets. It was into this emergency situation that my sister flew into Corpus Christe for her visit with John. She registered at the Driscoll Hotel, and under the circumstances, I was the one to meet her. I knew I was a poor substitute for John, but I did take her to dinner and we had a welcome visit, which I at least appreciated. I have always been sorry that Robin and John did not see each other that weekend. How lonely military life can be. Separation during this period of our history was something most would experience. The hurricane veered away from Corpus Christi, and as a result we only had a few rainsqualls and a wind that did not exceed forty miles an hour.

*   *   *

America was badly in need of heroes. Up until this time, especially in the Pacific, the U.S. forces could do little more than organize a holding action against the Imperial military strength of Japan. That had changed somewhat a couple of months earlier in the Battle of the Coral Sea, and a few weeks later at Midway. We had one true naval hero at that time. He was Butch O'Hare. This aggressive navy fighter pilot, on February 20, 1942 shot down five Imperial Navy *Betty* twin-engine bombers as they came in to attack our carriers in the Battle of the Coral Sea. Flying an F4F *Wildcat* he made five passes into the enemy formation and with each pass shot down an enemy plane. In that one flight Butch O'Hare became the first navy ace in World War II. That was how he became an American hero.

During the summer that I was a cadet at Corpus, Lt. O'Hare visited the naval air station. All of us were marched to a large parade field on the base. There we stood at attention as the Commander, Rear Admiral Montgomery, took the reviewing stand that was backed by red, white and blue bunting. Behind the platform, an American flag fluttered in the gulf breeze. He began:

> *It is my great honor to introduce to you Lt. Butch O'Hare. Lt. O'Hare is here to receive the highest award that can be bestowed by the United States Government. As a result of his heroic action in shooting down five attacking planes at the battle of the Coral Sea on February 20th 1942, thus contributing substantially to the retreat of the enemy, he is hereby awarded the Congressional Medal of Honor*

We all cheered and clapped. It was a ceremony I shall always remember. I know there wasn't a cadet among us that did not fantasize that he, too, would someday come home with such an honor. It seldom happened that way, but the dream was there. Soon after, Lt. O'Hare returned to the Pacific to fly night fighter missions. Tragically he was shot down by a gunner in one of our own TBF bombers who saw the flashing exhaust from O'Hare's plane, thought an enemy *Betty* was approaching, and tragically made the kill. At least that was the general speculation after O'Hare never returned. O'Hare airport, in Chicago, was later named in his honor.

*   *   *

I flew the SNJ all through the final senior phase of our training. I loved formation flying, honing our skills in joining up and flying as a single unit. I was a member of a team, each one of us dependent upon the skill of the other, each of us training for the common mission of striking the enemy in coordination and force. The break up of the formation was always a thrill for me. At the end of each flight, back to the base we would come, the leader moving us out in echelon as we flew down-wind along the side of the runway. Then at the right moment the lead plane went into a wingover, dropping and turning smoothly but aggressively to the runway. Then each following plane at the exact interval would duplicate the maneuver, one after another, touching down on the runway at the same spot. There were no long drawn out approaches. We flew the navy way, precise, exact and with authority. I loved it!

Near the end of the training we were sent off in three plane divisions for our first cross-country flight. We flew south over the vast King Ranch to Brownsville, Texas on the border between the United States and Mexico. It was only a little over a 150-mile flight, but it seemed a long way and an adventure to us. South Texas is a flat, dry land covered with large patches of mesquite. Although there is a ranch outpost on occasion, I saw no sign of habitation on the flight. There were no land bearings, so we just flew our compass

58

heading over the desolate land to Brownsville. Just before noon, the country below us became greener. We surmised we were approaching the Rio Grande Valley. Soon the border town of Brownsville came into view and we landed at the airport. There was time for a sandwich before the flight home.

On the way back we flew a hundred miles up the coastal barrier of Padre Island. The island then was nothing more that a narrow deserted string of rolling sand dunes; the gulf washing the clear beaches on the seaward side and a lagoon waterway on the other. It was the perfect place to practice low flying, and we zoomed all the way home up and down over the rolling sand dunes.

My flight training at the Corpus Christi Naval Air Station was coming to a close. The last test was the advanced aerobatics check. We would fly a set sequence of maneuvers, coming in over the main base at 3,000 feet. After each maneuver we were to reverse our flight course, so that the instructors could judge our performance from the reviewing stand. I thought of it as a ballet in the sky. I don't remember feeling a lot of pressure on my final check, because by this time I knew I could fly the airplane well. The SNJ North American was a trustworthy and steady platform in the sky, always responsive to the aileron and rudder. The final check went well. I was qualified. Graduation would follow.

*　　　　*　　　　*

On October 26, 1942 the aircraft carrier Wasp was sunk and the Saratoga hit and put out of commission by an enemy attack in the Solomon Islands in the South Pacific. This left the Hornet the only American carrier in the South Pacific. Our land forces on Guadalcanal were now unprotected. This happened just before my graduation as a naval officer and aviator. The news created a pall over the base. The battle for Guadalcanal would rage on, a sobering note to the cadets who would graduate and soon go on to the fleet.

*　　　　*　　　　*

During the first week of November 1942, my parents drove

from California to Corpus Christi to attend my graduation and commissioning. This was an amazing thing for them to do in wartime, for we were on gas rationing and other restrictions. Regardless, they were there and I was thrilled to have them share in my graduation. On November 6, 1942, I was commissioned an Ensign USNR, and a U.S Navy Pilot. How touching it was to have Mother pin the Wings of Gold on my uniform. My experience as a navy flight cadet was over. With this step behind me, came my new orders:

> *From: The Commandant*
> *To: Ensign Franklin W. Robinson Jr. A-V(N) USNR*
> *Subject: Orders to active duty (VTB)*
> *You will consider yourself detached November 7, 1942 And will proceed and report to the Commanding Officer, Opa Locka Naval Air Station, Miami, Florida for Operational training.*

I said good-bye to Ed McNeil and Dale Tillery. Their orders sent them on different routes. I would not see them again until long after the war was over. It was the closing chapter of the experience that we had shared.

Mother and Pop drove me to the railroad station in Corpus Christi and then left for the long drive back to Long Beach on the West Coast. I rode silently on the train, bound for my new assignment near Miami, on the East Coast.

Corpus Christi Naval Air Station
"The University of the Air"

N3N Stearman *Yellow Perils* on the Flight Line

"Then one day in June, Class 5A-42-C was marched out to the field on the main base. Row after row of N3N Stearman biwing yellow trainers awaited our arrival. What wonderful planes they were, about as steady and reliable as they come, forgiving and yet with enough power and pep to fly us through the basic aerobatics of military flight."

Flying Cadet F. W. Robinson Jr.

Primary Trainers

The N3N yellow Stearman was the plane that we flew in primary training at Corpus Christi.

"We flew the SNV Vultee trainer for our instrument training at Corpus Christi. On the final check flight, I flew the radio beam from the main base to the flight strip at Beeville, Texas. All of this was done under a hood. I relied only on instruments for this final flight test."

Lt. F. W. Robinson

Advanced Training Cross-Country Flight to Brownsville, Texas
August 1942

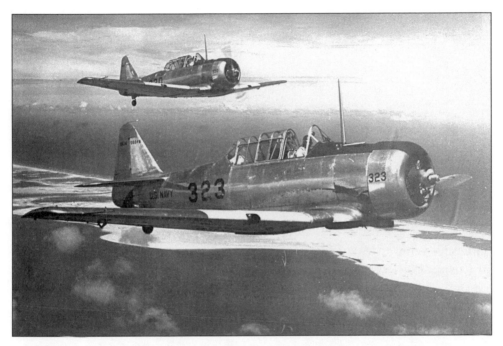

"On the way back from Brownsville, Texas, on our first cross-country flight, we flew our SNJ's up the coastal barrier of Padre Island. The island was a narrow 100-mile deserted strip of rolling sand dunes with the Gulf of Mexico washing the beach on the seaward side. On the western side there was a protected waterway between the island and the mainland. For most of the way home we zoomed up and down over the undulating sand dunes."

Flying Cadet F. W. Robinson, Jr.

Advanced Formation Flying
Corpus Christi, Texas

"I loved formation flying in the SNJ Trainer; honing my skills in joining a formation of planes and flying together with them as a unit. I was a member of a precision team training for the common mission of striking the enemy with coordination and force."

Lt. Willard Robinson

Flight Class 5A-42-C(C)
U.S.N.A.S. Corpus Chrisit, Texas

Edwin F. McNeil
Los Angeles, California
University of Southern
California

F. W. Robinson, Jr.
Long Beach, California
University of Southern
California

Harry D. Tillery
Long Beach, California
University of Chicago

M. E. Patterson, Jr.
Hollywood, California
University of Southern
California

Robert W. Koontz
Auburn, Nebraska
Peru Teachers College
(Nebraska)

Leonard G. Muskin
Omaha, Nebraska
University of Nebraska

Special friends who are mentioned in these memories. . .

F.W. Robinson, Jr.
Naval Aviator

Commissioned Ensign USNR
Corpus Chrisit, Texas
1942

Ensign Robinson's
Naval Aviator Certificate

United States Naval Air Station
Corpus Christi, Texas

Know all men by these presents that

Ensign Franklin W. Robinson, Jr., A-V(N), USNR

has completed the prescribed course of training and having met successfully the requirements of the course has been designated a

Naval Aviator

In Witness Whereof, this certificate has been signed on this   6th   day of November 1942, and the Seal of the Naval Air Station hereunto affixed

Rear Admiral, U. S. Navy
Commandant

Commander, U. S. Navy
Superintendent of Aviation Training

4

OPERATIONAL TRAINING AND QUALIFYING AS A NAVY AIRCRAFT CARRIER PILOT

The train ride from Texas to Florida was a unique experience. I had never seen this part of the United States and I was fascinated as I passed through the country. It was heavily forested and this was a surprise. Through the swamplands and the lakes the train made its way over miles of viaducts to New Orleans where we had a two-hour layover. This gave me time for a hurried visit to Basin Street and an opportunity to listen to the famous "blues", so distinctive of New Orleans music. This was a short and welcome respite from the togetherness of military life.

A vivid memory still remains from the trip through Mississippi and Alabama. The endless miles of shacks along the route with black people loitering in the rocking chairs and on the porches of their unpainted abodes, waving at the train as we passed was disturbing. I had read about the South, but this was the first time I had seen the poverty in which so many of the people lived. It was apparent that they were still not free from the results of the slavery their ancestors had endured.

On November 10, 1942, I reported to the commanding officer at the Miami Naval Air Station in Opa Locka, Florida. It was a busy base with several large hangars and a new Bachelor Officers Quarters to house the ensigns who had come for their final training before their assignments with the fleet. The housing that was provided for us was a welcome upgrade from the community barracks life to which we had been subjected as cadets. Also, as navy officers our schedule now was much more relaxed. We were on our own from 5:00 o'clock in the afternoon until 8:00 the next morning. It was only then that we had to report to muster in the main hangar. Our weekends were free and we could relax in the plush Officers Club. We had been so regimented as cadets that I found it strange, no matter how enjoyable, as I adjusted to this radical change in our military life.

My first interest when I arrived at the air station was in the planes that I would be flying, so I went directly to the flight line. With the exception of the SNJ, in which we would begin training for aircraft carrier landings, I had not seen the operational aircraft we would also fly. On the line were the few remaining Douglas TBD torpedo planes that had survived the early carrier battles in the Pacific. These *Devastators*, now obsolete, because of their light armament and slow speed, had been easy targets for the *Zero* pilots in the battle at Midway. I was fascinated in seeing for the first time the F2A *Buffalo* fighters; flying buckets of bolts we called them. This barrel-shaped plane, underpowered with a 1200 H.P. Cyclone radial engine, had not been reliable enough to be used in combat. Now they were being employed as the starter plane for the new Ensign fighter pilots at Opa Locka. The F2A's were not used for very long, for in the month of November, when I was in Florida, three pilots had engine failure and were killed. The planes crashed in the swamps of the Florida Everglades. These losses did put a damper on

70

an otherwise pleasant time we had in Operational Training.

The Curtis SBC *Helldiver* was the first plane I flew at the Opa Locka Naval Air Station. It was a biwing dive-bomber, obsolete for combat, but a legend in naval flight history. What a thrill it was to pop the diving flaps, roll the plane over on its back and come down in a vertical dive on the target to release the bombs. I made several flights in this historic plane out over the Bahamas, looking for German submarines that were operating with such devastating results on our coastal shipping.

I had an interesting experience in the Curtis *Helldiver*. The tail wheel lock broke, just as I left the ground on takeoff. This was the only navy plane I ever flew that had this type of tail wheel, one that had to be locked to keep it from ground looping upon landing. Fortunately, there was a large open dirt field on the base and I decided it would be best to land the plane there, rather than on the main runway. On landing, I kept my heading as long as I had enough speed for the rudder to keep the plane in line. However, as I slowed, the wind over the plane's rudder decreased and the plane started to ground loop. To regain control, I hit opposite rudder and applied full power. This temporarily brought the *Helldiver* back into a straight heading. However, as I slowed again, the plane started to ground loop in the opposite direction. Each time the plane started to ground loop, I applied power and managed to recover, but that huge biwing plane was all over the field before I brought it to a complete stop. I kept from damaging the SBC, but it was a close call. One little locking pin had broken and that had caused the problem with the freewheeling tailwheel.

*   *   *

I spent several hours flying the TBD *Devastator* torpedo bomber. One day several of us were assigned to participate in a simulated torpedo attack on a target ship off the Florida coast. A very sharp instructor who had survived the Battle of Midway led us. Before we took off he prepared us for the attack.

We are going to be opposed by a training flight of fighters. Their

71

instructors are preparing the pilots to fly full overhead deflection runs on us, but we will give them a lesson to learn. (He was getting a real kick out of his plan to frustrate their attack). Follow my directions. We'll string out in a line as we fly abeam the target ship. The F4F Wildcat fighters should be directly above us in their position to begin the attack. Instead of increasing our speed, I will slow us down to about eighty knots, hanging there at just above our stalling speed. Then when I see them roll over we'll turn ninety degrees toward the ship, diving to increase our speed to about 200 knots before pulling out just over the water. He laughed. That will foul up all their timing. Instead of a deflection shot, they'll fall in behind our tails where our gunners can get a dead on shot at them. (It worked out just the way he said.)

*   *   *

I never did get to know any of these instructors, because they always flew in their own planes and rotated, flying with our formations for brief periods of time. Whether it was in teaching us to dive-bomb or to launch a torpedo attack, there was a specialized discipline for them to share. I was sorry that I did not get to know these instructors, for they all had stories to tell about their experiences in the Battle of Midway. They had been tested under fire and survived to pass on their valuable lessons that would save many of the new Ensigns that would be going into combat.

It was a privilege to fly some of those old historic planes, the last of their line, planes that had been so important in the development of naval aviation. When we were ready for night formation flying and simulated carrier landings, we got back to our familiar SNJ North American trainers that we had flown during advanced training in Corpus Christi.

One night I was assigned to a formation flight in a SNJ. It was an experience that still remains a vivid memory. I was flying in a three-plane section out over the vast Florida Everglades. It was a black moonless night. For some reason, that I do not remember, there were two pilots in each plane. The pilot in the rear cockpit was an observer and this was not a desired assignment. I was in the front cockpit, and as such the designated pilot. About an hour out on the flight, the red fuel pressure warning light began to flash and the previously smooth running engine began to miss. All of us were familiar with the stories of pilots who had made forced landings in the alligator infested swamps of the Florida Everglades. A downed flyer had only a slim chance of survival. A faltering engine on a dark night was a good reason for panic. Over the intercom came the alarmed voice of my passenger, "I'm bailing out!"

This was not a solution to our predicament. A forced landing in the dark with a dead engine was not a good prospect either. "Don't bail out! Get on the manual wobble pump and keep the gas flowing. That's our best chance. We don't want to go down out here." The hand-manipulated pump brought our fuel pressure back to normal. My frightened passenger kept it going all the way back to the Opa Locka Naval Air Station where we were cleared for an emergency landing.

I never did get over the anxiety of flying a single engine aircraft over hostile terrain or the vast expanses of the ocean, often alone and for hours at a time. I was always alert for any little sign of a faltering engine that could signal disaster. Navy carrier pilots especially lived with this tension, as many of their missions were at night and in inclement weather.

The final phase of our operational training, in the latter part of December 1942, was in the advanced SNJ trainer. In this plane we would qualify on an aircraft carrier. To prepare us for this culminating event of our training in Florida, there was a painted area that simulated an aircraft carrier's deck on an outlying practice field near the base. Around and around we would fly, getting the feel of maneuvering the plane near the ground at just above the stalling speed. Then we would make the required turn toward the spot we were to drop the plane to the ground; all of this under the guidance of the Landing Signal Officer. With the LSO's outstretched arms and his yellow signal paddles, he guided us to the painted landing deck. If his hand held signal paddles were stretched directly out from his body, we knew we had the correct airspeed and attitude for landing. If the paddles were a little higher, we knew we were too high. Likewise, if the Landing Signal Officer dropped his paddles a little, we knew to raise the nose. If he flashed one of the paddles with one hand in any of these positions we knew we were either too fast or too slow to make a successful drop to the deck. If both signal paddles were moved up and down emphatically, that was a mandatory wave-off. When the LSO brought the yellow paddle across his body with authority that was the signal to cut the engine. Once the engine was cut, in concert with his direction, the plane would drop with precision onto the runway. After several hours of this training, the procedure became more natural.

*   *   *

By Christmas 1942, I had completed operational training in Florida and received orders to report on January 1st to the Norfolk Naval Air Station in Virginia to qualify as a U.S. Naval Carrier Pilot. I had a couple of extra days, so I boarded the train to Washington D.C. and spent the time with my brother Charles Robinson who was teaching steam engineering at the U.S. Naval Academy in Annapolis. He gave me a tour of the Academy and then we went to Washington D.C. where I would catch a bus to Norfolk. It was a cold December night in the nation's capital. The frozen snow crunched under our feet as we walked the Mall and viewed the lighted memorials. I remember this as a special night; the only time I saw Chuck during all the years of World War II. He later served on the USS Tuscaloosa in the Atlantic. This assignment eventually went into the history books. Chuck was the Engineering Officer on the heavy cruiser, USS Tuscaloosa, when his ship was sent in to knock out the German batteries above Utah beach on D-Day in Normandy. My brother relates their duel with the German batteries in a subsequent chapter.

*   *   *

The two weeks in January 1943 that I spent at the Norfolk Naval Air Station was a lonely, painful and anxious time. I got off the bus early in the morning after an all night trip from Washington D.C. It was chilling and oppressive. The thermometer was in the teens and the humidity was high. The light flight uniforms that I brought from Florida were inadequate for the freezing winter in Virginia. It was a week before the weather cleared enough for a familiarization flight around the area in the SNJ airplane I would fly to qualify on the aircraft carrier. All that first week I sat in one of the hangar ready-rooms waiting for our orders to be posted. I met no one who seemed to be in charge. It was very impersonal. Often it is said, "In the navy there are moments of terror, separated by long periods of boredom." This describes my waiting and flying experience while in Norfolk.

I did meet one pilot I knew. He was Bob Koontz, a member of our graduating class at Corpus Christi; a Nebraska boy who was also waiting to qualify on the carrier. We spent a lot of this waiting time together and I got to know more about him. His lifelong girl friend had come from their little rural hometown of Auburn, Nebraska to Florida three weeks before and they had married. They had managed to find a place to stay in a Norfolk rooming house. It was a terrible place for a honeymoon, but at least they could be together before Bob would be assigned to a squadron and leave for the war.

About ten days later, Bob and I found our names posted on the day's flight schedule. In an hour we would be flying out with twelve other ensigns to the British aircraft carrier HMS *Attacker*, operating in the Atlantic. There we would make the eight landings that would qualify us as aircraft carrier pilots. I never did understand why American pilots were assigned to a British ship for carrier qualifications. But it was not for us to question.

I checked out a parachute and located my assigned plane on the flight line. There were no service personnel working around the planes. This was a concern to me, because it had stormed during the night and there was a thin layer of snow on the wings of the SNJ that I would be flying. I went back to the hangar and obtained a broom to clean the wings of the plane. The cleaning was difficult because under the snow there was a thin layer of ice that needed to be removed. We also had to undo the ties that secured the planes to the parking ramp. This, too, was unusual, because even as cadets, service personnel always prepared our planes for flight.

There were twelve of us that flew out that cold morning to the aircraft carrier, HMS *Attacker*. Bob Koontz was the only one of the twelve pilots that I knew.

No one at the air station had given us directions or a briefing on what we were to do. There were just the posted orders, giving us the location of the ship and the time of the rendezvous. In retrospect, I know I should have realized that this morning was a prelude to disaster. The cold was bearable on the flight out to the ship, but when I opened the canopy, a required procedure in landing, I thought I would freeze right there in the cockpit. It was that cold. Whether my shaking knees were a result of the cold or of anxiety I don't know. I suspect it was a little of both. Anyway, we located the English carrier, which upon our approach flashed in blinker code, the "prep-Charlie" signal from the ship's command tower. That was the command, "prepare to land". I broke off from the formation, made my turn—mixture rich, wheels down, flaps down, canopy open, tail-hook down, and came up the groove for my first landing. The Landing Signal Officer picked me up as I approached the deck and I followed his signals in for my first cut. Boom—I hit the flight deck, caught the arresting wire with the tail hook—my first carrier landing completed. Except for the intense cold, which caused my legs to shake, the second and third landings were completed with ease. However, after the third landing, the tail-hook would not come back up and catch in the flight position. One of the deck crewmen wired it up and I was told to fly back to Norfolk a get another plane. Back at the air station I made a quick switch of planes and returned to the HMS *Attacker* to make my final five required landings.

As I took my place in the landing pattern, I noticed that Bob Koontz's plane was just ahead of me. I followed him in on the downwind leg. As he began his final approach turn, the plane stalled. Just before it hit the water, I saw Bob try to jump out. The front corner of the cockpit caught him across the ribs and he went down with the plane. I continued my approach, got the cut signal and landed on the deck. I was ordered to stop my engine. Then the ship made three circles around the area where Bob had spun in. There wasn't anything to be found. He was gone. Another British crewman jumped up on the wing of my plane and told me to start the engine. "Keep up your bloody speed, matey. We have lost three pilots already this morning."

Two other pilots had been launched, before enough pressure had been built up in the catapult for a successful take-off. As a result they flopped into the water just ahead of the carrier and were killed. The aircraft carrier had run over them. I had not known either one of these pilots. At this point I was more terrified than at any other time in the entire war. How I made the next four landings, I will never know. I was shaking all over. It was a combination of fear and cold. I was the fortunate one who drew a reliable plane, except for the tail-hook failure, and the catapult operated correctly when it was my time to be launched. Fortunately, I completed the eight required landings without a wave-off. A major milestone was behind me, but there was little joy because of the tragedies of the morning.

When I returned to the flight office at Norfolk, a navy chaplain came up to me. "You and Bob Koontz were classmates?"

"Yes," I said, "and you know he had only been married for twenty-nine days."

"I knew it could only have been for a short time," he responded. "There are too many of these," he sighed. "Have you ever had to notify a next of kin?"

"No, I haven't."

"It's no fun, believe me, but I would appreciate it if you would go with me.

We got in his official navy car and went to a rooming house in an older section of Norfolk. The chaplain took the lead and I followed. The lady, who appeared to be the manager of the house, came to the door.

"I'm looking for Mrs. Koontz." The chaplain said. "Does she live here?"

The lady sensed this was not good news. "I'll get her."

The chaplain had told me that there was no easy way to break tragic news to a loved one. " You best be direct." He told me.

A young Nebraska farm girl, with a dismayed and questioning look appeared. I hesitated for a moment and then shakily said, "Bob was killed this morning. It was a crash at sea and they were not able to find him." I couldn't go on. She looked at me for a moment, shaking her head as if in disbelief, wanting me to say that it wasn't true. Then she fell to the floor, sobbing uncontrollably. I wanted to console her, but there was nothing I could do. That was the afternoon of January 14, 1943.

"We need to get this girl back to her folks in Nebraska as soon as possible," The compassionate chaplain said. "Can you take her?"

I had been issued orders in Florida: "Upon completion of carrier qualification in Norfolk, Virginia, report to the North Island Naval Air Station in San Diego for duty involving flying. You will be assigned to a fleet squadron."   These orders also entitled me to two weeks travel time and a two-week leave, the first I would have since joining the navy. "Yes, I can leave tonight," I answered the chaplain.

"Good, I'll make arrangements for you and Mrs. Koontz to leave on the train tonight. Under the circumstances I think I can at least get a Pullman sleeper for her tonight."

In a daze the stricken young wife agreed to go with me. As the last rays of that eventful and tragic winter day waned, we embarked on the train for the long and slow transit to Nebraska. There was no bed available for me, but we were able to get a bunk for Bob Koontz's wife on that first night.

As the train lumbered northwest through the Cumberland Gap, I reconstructed the events of the day. Why had the SNJ that Bob was flying stall and crash? He was a good pilot, and had experienced no difficulty throughout his entire training. No one will ever know for certain, but I am convinced that the thin layer of ice that had formed under the night's snow had not been completely removed when he swept the wings of his SNJ. This almost invisible film could have restricted the flow of air over the airfoil. That could be just enough to cause the plane to stall in the low speed power approach to the carrier. I had been trained, while first flying in Alaska, that this could be a problem.

Early in the morning, after a third night on the train, we arrived in Omaha, Nebraska. Family and friends were there to meet the grieving widow. Again shaken, I told her goodbye and continued my weeklong trip to Los Angeles. Seven days was a long time to sit on a crowded train, but I was so elated to be back home that I felt little weariness.

In twelve pressure packed months, I had successfully completed all the requirements to become a fully qualified United States Navy pilot. Now I would be ordered to a combat squadron.

Opa Locka Naval Air Station
Miami, Florida
Planes Flown by Lt. F. W. Robinson
November - December 1942

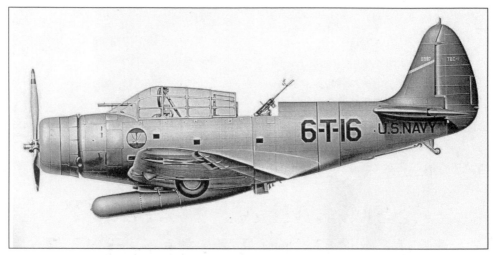

Douglas TBD-1 *Devastator* Navy Torpedo Bomber

Curtis SBC-4 *Hell Diver* Navy Dive Bomber

5

ASSIGNMENT TO NAVY SQUADRON VC-31 & VC-7

The two-week leave I enjoyed during the last of January 1943 and the first week of February was special. My grandmother, who had lived on the family ranch, died when I was in Corpus Christi, Texas. My eighty-year-old grandfather was living alone now and it was important to me to visit him at the ranch. This was not easy because a heavy rain had washed out the bridge on old Highway 99 north of Saugus at the entrance to the L.A. County Prison. My father suggested that he drive me from Long Beach to the point of the road closure. There I might find a way to cross the swollen river. This he did and I started hiking north through the mud until I found a large cable-held gas line that suspended the river. I tenderly worked my way across and walked on to Castaic, a small truck stop at the foot of the Ridge Route grade. There were no trucks or vehicles there because of the washed-out bridge. However, a highway maintenance truck soon drove in from the north and the crew offered to take me the twenty-five miles to the summit at Gorman. I guess my plight and my navy-winged uniform made this special passage possible. By mid-day I was in Gorman, still some fifteen miles from the ranch.

My good fortune still held. Claude Barnes, a member of the well-known Antelope Valley Barnes family, drove in from Lebec and offered to drive me to the home of his brother, Roy Barnes. Roy and his wife Mattie lived in a little cottage at the intersection of Old Ridge Route Road and Highway 138. This would put me within five miles of the old ranch. Mattie and Roy Barnes greeted me with surprise and warmth. Mattie gave me a hand-tooled belt she had made. It had replicas of all the brands used by the various ranches in the area. There was a wallet to match and I used them for many years. I changed into Levi denim pants and hiking shoes and made the long walk across the country, through the foothills, around the sagebrush and past the oak-lined lanes to the ranch. Dad Gould had a supper prepared and a warm fire burning when I arrived. The old ranch has always been a place where my spirit could be restored. I looked forward to a respite and a time of reflection. No longer could I take my life for granted. Life was a temporary gift, precious now in a way that my adventurous spirit had not always perceived.

The thought of going into combat without experiencing all the joys intended in a marriage commitment, were becoming unbearable. Could I balance this reality with the reality of the war and all that potential painful consequence? I wanted someone to love and someone who would care. Within me, a God-given dimension said, "Go home again. Find Joan, your true love, and promise your life to her."

In the final days of my leave, I went back to Long Beach and found Joan working in a small branch of the Security First National Bank. Joan recalls: *They would hire anyone during the war. I knew nothing about banking and I had to learn fast. My salary was $18.00 a week and I was fortunate to have the job. There I was a twenty-one year old teller when this navy flyer walked in. Robbie, what are you doing here? I exclaimed. Then he asked if I would go to dinner with him?*

Joan had to work until 7:00 o'clock that evening when the bankbooks reconciled. When she finished we went for a quiet dinner. We had a lot of catching up to do. Much had happened in each of our lives, since we had last seen each other some two years before. Joan recalls, "When it was time to go, Robbie became very serious and looked directly into my eyes."

"Joan, I'm going to ask you a question. I don't want you to answer me now. I am leaving in the morning for Seattle to join my squadron." There was a pause.

"What is the question?"

"Will you marry me?"

"Robbie!" Joan hesitated a moment to catch her breath. "This is a very unusual proposal. I can't think about marrying you. I haven't seen you in two years."

I didn't hesitate a moment. "I understand, that's why I don't want you to give me an answer now."

The next morning I left for Seattle, Washington to join the newly formed Composite Squadron VC-31. In those days the drive from Long Beach to Seattle was over a two-lane highway that went through every town along the route. The highway twisted and turned endlessly over the mountain passes of California and Oregon. I drove my yellow Cadillac convertible I had bought in 1941. Norma Shearer, a famous Hollywood film star, had previously owned this beautiful automobile. Three days later I arrived at the Sand Point Naval Air Station, a spectacular facility on the shore of Lake Washington. It was like being quartered in an exclusive club. The lounging areas were handsomely furnished and the dining room featured linens, fine dinnerware and a menu from which we could select our meals. I called Joan as I had promised.

Joan recalls: *My mind was made up and I was sure. When Robbie called, I said, Yes, I will marry you. I do love you and I think I always have. I will come.*

A week later her parents took her to the train station in Los Angeles, the center of activity and the place of many emotional farewells and reunions during the war. Joan had never been away from home before. "I was scared to death," she recalls. "Here I was headed for Seattle to marry a man I loved and admired, but did I really know him?" Joan has shown a lot of courage over the years, and this first decision was only the beginning of the fortitude she would demonstrate.

*   *   *

My orders to the Sand Point Naval Air Station read:

February 11, 1943: You are to report for temporary active duty in connection with the fitting out of Escort Scouting Squadron 31 and for active temporary duty involving flying in that squadron when commissioned.

I met our squadron commander, William R. Bartlett, Lieutenant, USN. He was a soft-spoken, wonderful man whom I would always respect. Later, he selected me as his wing man, a special honor of which I have always been proud.

"Welcome to the squadron," he said. "Check out one of the SNJs on the line and familiarize yourself with the area. You need to feel comfortable with the base and the territory before you fly the *Avenger*.

It had been a month since I had been in the air. My last flight had been on that tragic day I had qualified on the aircraft carrier HMS Attacker in the Atlantic. This was a new day and it was time to fly again.

I filed my flight plan with the control tower, checked out a parachute and walked out to a new silver North American SNJ. As I prepared to climb into the cockpit, a young sailor approached, "Could I go along with you as a passenger?" he said.

"Sure, check out a chute and hop in."

I went over the preliminary flight checklist. All was in order with but one exception, there was no communication with the passenger in the rear seat. The young sailor could not hear me. This was not unusual, as we often had some radio and intercom problems. So, with hand signals, I asked if he was ready to go. He responded with a "thumb up," so we took off..

84

It was a beautiful day in Seattle for flying. Towering cumulus clouds floated over the blue water of Puget Sound. Exhilarated and free we dove and spun with precision and grace in aerobatic flight, ending in a controlled slow roll. I looked back to see how my passenger was enjoying the flight. To my amazement and concern all I could see was a leg hanging out of the open cockpit. Soon a white-faced sailor popped up. I returned immediately to the airfield. When we landed he was still shaking. This is what I discovered. The sailor was on leave and had come to the Sand Point Naval Air Station from the destroyer base at Bremerton to see if he could get a flight. He had never been up in an airplane before and wanted a chance to fly for the first time. Our flight had been a new experience for him. He hadn't hooked up the intercom or the seatbelt and shoulder straps in the cockpit, because he didn't know how. I asked him if he knew how to pull the ripcord on his chute, if he had fallen out of the plane when we were upside down. His answer terrified me. "What's a ripcord?" This was a valuable lesson! I never again took any situation for granted. I have often wondered if that sailor ever flew again. Not only was it a close call, but also it shook me up. I knew that as the captain of the plane, I was responsible.

*   *   *

New TBM *Avenger* torpedo planes were delivered and assigned to our Squadron. The following morning I was given a manual that explained all about the new aircraft. It covered every detail, takeoff and landing procedures, dials, levers, gauges, circuits and flight controls. It was important that I assimilate this knowledge in a few hours, for I was scheduled to fly the *Avenger* that afternoon. I read every page in the manual. I riveted the particular information in my brain that dealt with the starting of the engine, the takeoff and landing procedures, and some of the basic instructions that were outlined. Then I sat in the cockpit, touching every control that I would need, going through every procedure with my eyes closed, until I was assured that I was ready. The act of taking-off in a two thousand horsepower military bomber was not a minor step for me. I would be alone and on my own.

By late afternoon, with my knees shaking a little, I took off for the first time in the plane that I would eventually fly from an aircraft carrier and into combat. The TBM responded with a firmness that later would become assuring and familiar.

The series of clear days that followed were unusual for Seattle. We experienced a month without rain and we took advantage of the beautiful flying weather. During this time other pilots arrived and joined the new Squadron. Sometimes we would fly in formation to the Canadian border where P-40 fighters flown by the RAF pilots would swoop down on us in mock attacks, and we would take evasive action. It was all great fun and worthwhile practice for us.

One of the fighter pilots on the base flew his plane under the bridge at the north end of Whidbey Island. He did not see the high-tension wires strung beneath the span and hit one of them. The wire tore through the *Wildcat's* right wing before it broke. The plane kept flying with the remnant of cable trailing behind. When he made a forced landing at the Whidbey Island Naval Air Station. This cut all of the electrical power on the base. Fortunately the pilot, whose name I do not remember, was not injured, but he was restricted to the base for a prolonged period of time. He did not get to leave with his squadron when his fellow pilots left to fly from the aircraft carrier Liscombe Bay. Several months later the Liscombe Bay exploded during the assault on Tarawa in the Gilbert Islands, killing most of the pilots with whom we had flown in Seattle. The pilot who had broken the high-tension wire was still confined at the Sand Point Naval Air Station. He had escaped the tragic end of his fellow flyers. During the time he was at Sand Point he married the Commanding Officer's daughter. The vicissitudes of war are never to be understood.

On March 1, 1943 Joan arrived in Seattle. A new friend, Arnold Erickson, who had joined the Squadron, went with me to meet Joan. I had asked him to be the best man at our wedding. Lt. Erickson, who later was assigned as the Landing Signal Officer on the USS Franklin, tells his story in a subsequent chapter.

On March 4, 1943 Joan and I were married at the University Methodist Church in Seattle. It was unusual because she was the only woman, besides the organist, who was at the wedding. Joan was beautiful in the powder blue suit her mother had made for her. All the new members of Squadron VC-31 were there, handsome in their dress blues, adorned with braid and "Wings of Gold."

"I felt like a queen," Joan recalls. "It was a truly special and a beautiful wedding."

There were several others in the squadron who were married in the following weeks, but ours was the first and that made it special. We had a month together, marred only by the death of Tom Wylie, a graduate of Southern Methodist University in Dallas, Texas. He was taking off in a F4F *Wildcat* fighter when it veered slightly and hit a piece of heavy equipment carelessly left along the runway. The impact exploded the plane and instantly killed Tom.

* * *

During the first week of April 1943, Squadron VC-31 was transferred to the U.S. Marine Air Station in El Centro, California. The morning Joan and I left Seattle it was raining, the first storm we had experienced during the time we were there. We drove to Portland in our yellow 1934 Cadillac convertible, and then down the spectacular Oregon coast to California. This was our delayed honeymoon trip and we were given a week to make the long drive. Because of gas rationing, the roads were almost deserted. We had thirteen flat tires that had to be changed and repaired before we reached San Francisco. This was a frustration in an otherwise spectacular trip. We finally arrived in Berkeley and the University of California for a short visit with my brother Ted. He was a student there and held the honored position as Cadet Commander of the Naval ROTC at the university. We left early the next morning for the old family ranch in northern Los Angeles County.

At 9:00 A.M. we arrived in Fresno. I was in search of a large tire that would replace the one that continued to give us trouble. Getting tires of any kind during the war was a major problem, but a helpful agent in Fresno was able to locate a truck tire that would fit the Cadillac, so by noon we were on our way again, free at last of the tire trouble we had experienced.

After overnight visits with Granddad Gould at the ranch and

our parents in Long Beach, we headed south again on our way to El Centro, California. By mid-afternoon we were driving along the western side of Salton Sea below Palm Springs. To our surprise we saw a TBF torpedo plane on its fuselage in the sand near the shore of Salton Sea. I ran to the crash and to my surprise, standing on the hulk of the *Avenger* was Bob Nash, a pilot in our Squadron VC-31. He looked like a trophy hunter on top of a downed elephant. "What a surprise to find you out here. What happened?"

"Oh, my motor just quit, so I bellied her in here," he said.

Soon emergency equipment arrived, and Joan and I resumed our trip to El Centro. It was later determined that the plane had run out of gas and Bob had forgotten to switch gas tanks, an unforgivable error.

I shall always remember Lt. Bob Nash as an unusual and tragic person. He was a pilot who could manage the actual flight of an airplane with skill but with a mental carelessness that put the plane and those that flew with him in jeopardy. Here are three incidents that will illustrate what I mean.

The first incident came later in the spring of 1943. Bob Nash flew me from El Centro to the North Island Naval Air Station in San Diego to take delivery on a new TBM *Avenger* for our Squadron. We left the marine base in a SNJ for the flight over the mountains. The weather was marginal, but there appeared to be a gap between the cloud cover and the 8,000-foot ridge of mountains through which we could fly. Bob flew us into this opening, but soon the clouds closed in and our visibility became extremely restricted. I was helpless as a passenger in the rear cockpit, but I did express my concern to him over the intercom. "Let's turn around and get over this stuff!"

"I know this country and we will make it through." He responded with some nonchalance.

He was the captain and had command, so I just hunkered down and kept my mouth shut. It began to snow heavily and Bob flew lower and lower in an attempt to keep visual contact with the terrain. A mountain flashed by our port wing and I caught sight of a rocky cliff on our right. It was panic time as far as I was concerned, but it was no time to open my mouth again. Without

88

any embarrassment or concern he came over the intercom. "Any idea where we are?"

"No. When we get out of this canyon, keep a 270-degree heading with as much altitude as you can so we can still keep contact with the ground. When I pick up a familiar landmark I'll let you know."

In a few moments I spotted a four-lane road I suspected was Highway 101. There were no paved highways south of the border so I guessed we were somewhere north of San Diego. "Fly south and follow that highway."

Soon I saw the racetrack at Del Mar. I knew then exactly where we were, and in a short time we were safely on the ground at the North Island Naval Air Station.

The saga of Bob Nash did not end with this incident. A couple of months later we were practicing night field carrier landings at Ream Field just north of the Mexican border. Several of us were rotating in the landing pattern, flying our TBM planes. The landing signal officer was using his lighted signal wands to direct us to a precise landing spot on the runway. I was following Bob in our rotational pattern when he hit the runway in a shower of sparks. I knew immediately that he had forgotten to put his wheels down.

The final tragic incident came after Nash had left our Squadron. He led a three-plane formation of TBM's one foggy morning out over the ocean. To keep his perspective he flew just over the wave tops a few feet above the sea. Tragically he was on a direct course to the southern end of Catalina Island. The planes disintegrated on the rocky cliff and the remains fell to the beach below. Three pilots and six crewmen were dead.

I had never mentioned my harried flight through the snowstorm with Bob Nash to our commanding officer Bill Bartlett. Was this a dereliction that eventually led to the death of nine men? I have often wondered.

*   *   *

All of us continued to watch the progress of the war with intense interest during the spring of 1943. There were some bright

89

spots for the United States as the tide of the conflict began to change. Large numbers of troops reached England and newly constructed naval ships were being deployed to the Pacific. However, the overall situation was far from secure. Moving vast quantities of war supplies as well as personnel across the Atlantic for an assault on Europe, in the face of the continued attack by German submarines, was a major challenge. German Admiral Doenitz had as many as a hundred U-boats operating in the Atlantic to stop the allied supplies from landing in England. The United States lost over a hundred ships during the two months we were in El Centro.

*   *   *

Finding housing for married couples, whose wives traveled with their husbands during the war, was always a major problem. Joan and I moved thirteen times during the first year we were married, usually living in a hotel or renting a room in someone's house who lived near the base. Joan was resourceful and lucky enough on occasion to find an apartment or little house where we could live. While we were in El Centro all of the married couples rented rooms in the Barbara Worth Hotel and the new wives became good friends.

In the evenings, Joan would take the wives in our yellow Cadillac convertible out to the air station. Joan could get all the gas she needed, ten miles from El Centro in Mexicali, Mexico. We could eat at the Officers Club more reasonably than in town. All of us were broke by the end of the month, but these were carefree days and we had a lot of fun. On occasion while flying we spotted our yellow Cadillac and would make simulated torpedo runs on the girls as they drove across the desert. This always created a stir!

While we were at El Centro the squadron began night formation flying. One night Andy Anderson led our six-plane division. About 1:00 o'clock in the morning he dove us down over El Centro and the Barbara Worth Hotel. We were strung out abreast in what we called a "crack-the-whip" formation. Down we roared with full power and maximum propeller settings. It rocked the town! By the time we got back to the base all of the authorities were out to meet us. We all looked shocked and innocent. Andy Anderson did the talking for us. Andy was such a mild-mannered man that the commanding officer of the base let us off with nothing more than a reprimand. Everywhere we went in El Centro the next day the people buzzed about the night attack and it made headlines in their local paper. People in those days were edgy because they always feared an attack by the Japanese, as unrealistic as that was.

One night Joan and I went to dinner at a restaurant in town with several other couples in the squadron. While we were there, two shore patrol officers came in to the restaurant where we were eating, "Report immediately to the base!" they ordered. Word had been received that a group of unidentified planes had flown in "at altitude" over the coast and the mountains. They were expecting an attack from the Japanese. We jumped into the car and sped out to the base. The pilots assembled in the Ready Room. Commander Bartlett hurriedly made the assignments and gave us orders for the intercept. He was deadly serious. The problem was that the pilots were all smiling because he had a big smear of lipstick on his face where his wife had kissed him in a hurried goodbye. We thought this was pretty funny. Long after this night passed, the incident remained as a favorite squadron story: "Bartlett smeared with lipstick as he leaves to attack the enemy". What made it more amusing was that the whole incident was just a big false alarm. When the intercept was made it was established that the "bogies" were nothing more than paper balloons to which some incendiary bombs had been attached. The balloons had been released in Japan to harass the Americans and keep us off balance. All the incendiaries ever did was to set off a few forest fires and that was no threat to anyone out there on the desert. They were harmless. So ended the great defense of the United States by Squadron VC-31.

*   *   *

Early in the summer of 1943 the squadron was transferred to the North Island Naval Air Station in San Diego. Joan was able to rent a bedroom in the Coronado home of a marine colonel and his wife. Charles and Marge Mulligan, another couple in the squadron, rented a room in the same home.

Soon after we made this transition, Squadron VC-31 was disbanded. The fighter pilots were assigned to new squadrons and left immediately to bolster the Solomon Islands campaign, flying the new F6F *Hellcat* Grumman fighter planes. I never saw any of these fighter pilots from VC-31 again. My special friend from USC, Pat Patterson, was last seen with a Japanese *Zero* on his tail and was reported, "Missing in action." He was never heard from again. Later I went to see his mother in Hollywood for a very sad visit.

*   *   *

The torpedo pilots, with Bartlett still as our skipper, formed the nucleus of a new squadron, VC-7. We were to be trained in the latest techniques for night attack and air-to-ground rocket launches. The pilots were not aware at that time of what would be involved in this specialized training. We were transferred to the U.S Naval Auxiliary Air Station east of Holtville, California for the initial phases of night attack flight. This practice included simulated torpedo runs on flare-lighted targets in Salton Sea, night formation flying, and night bombing runs.

Holtville blistered under the summer sun. The naval air station had no air conditioning and I saw temperatures as high as 122 degrees in the pilots' Ready Room. Pilots needed to wear gloves to get into the planes to keep from burning their hands on the heated metal. It was difficult to fly at night and then get any sleep during the day because of the heat. For this reason we would fly for three nights and then return to Coronado for rejuvenation. Our wives continued to live in Coronado during this time.

In September, with our night flying attack skills honed, we returned to the North Island Naval Air Station. For the next several weeks we launched dummy torpedoes at target ships in the ocean off San Diego, fired our guns at towed target sleeves over the Pacific, and dive-bombed targets on San Clemente Island.

Squadron VC-7 made a night, simulated torpedo attack on a United States cruiser a hundred miles at sea. This was the first such attack ever attempted, and made possible only because of the newly installed radar in our planes. That experience still remains as a vivid memory. Our entire torpedo squadron took off from North Island at 10:00 o'clock that night. How glad I was to be flying on the wing of the skipper. The attack had been well planned. Commander Bartlett had gone over every detail with us.

We will take off and fly without any running lights. I will put the Squadron on an intercept heading and then we will fly up into the dense overcast reported over the coast. Keep the formation tight because you will have only the light from the engine exhaust of the plane next to you to hold position. When we break through the overcast at about 2,000 feet, we'll keep our heading until the radar screen indicates that we are about five miles from the cruiser. When we reach that position, I'll change course ten degrees to the port, and (Lieutenant) Long, you break off with your flares and fly ten degrees to the starboard. Take that heading for two minutes and then release your flares at ten second intervals. Now the rest of the formation will string out behind me. When I come abreast of the target as indicated on the radar screen, I'll turn for the attack and you will turn with me. Each of you will be on instruments and on your own as we dive through the overcast. We should come into the clear at 500 feet.

I knew this attack would take a lot of precision, but we had enough training by this time that there was a good chance for success. Nevertheless, just as I emerged out of my dive and leveled out over the dark ocean for my run on the cruiser, I saw the flares drop through the overcast. Dead ahead was the illuminated silhouette of the massive hull, and towers of the ship. In we came for the launch, lower than the superstructure, at the last moment swooping up to clear the ship. What a thrill! It could not have been a more successful attack. The captain of the cruiser radioed Commander Bartlett and expressed his amazement that we had located his ship in such inclement weather and carried out the attack with such dispatch.

I wasn't worried about getting back to North Island. After flying back up through the overcast I emerged into a brilliant moonlit night. If the fog had rolled into San Diego, as it often did, I still had plenty of gas to fly on over the mountains to El Centro. I tuned in the North Island radio beam. I was on the N quadrant. When the A and the N quadrant merged, the beam became solid. With assurance, I made the left turn that put me on the correct heading to the North Island Naval Air Station. The fog broke at the coastline. Below me was the San Diego Channel and ahead were the lights of the landing field.

Today, with our sophisticated weapons, the story I relate is archaic; but in the early days of World War II, the things that Squadron VC-7 was trained to do were quite impressive. The irony is, we were never given the opportunity to use these skills against the Japanese. We were destined for support missions, mostly in daylight, for our landing forces on small Pacific atolls.

U.S. Navy Flight Squadron VC-31
Marine Air Station
El Centro, California 1943

Front Row, left to right: Ted Keller, Torpedo Pilot; Willie Fisher, Supply Officer; Hal Myers, Torpedo Pilot; Andy Anderson, Torpedo Pilot; Laverne Peck, Fighter Pilot; Skipper W. R. Bartlett, Torpedo Pilot; Al Long, Torpedo Pilot; Robbie Robinson, Torpedo Pilot; Paul Tangas, Torpedo Pilot; Burr Williams, Fighter Pilot.

Middle Row, left to right: Ed Luck, Torpedo Pilot; Del Karr, Torpedo Pilot; Arnold Erickson, Torpedo Pilot; George Flinn, Personnel Officer; Bob Nash, Torpedo Pilot; Buddy Pepper, Torpedo Pilot; Lloyd Nickols, Torpedo Pilot; Tom Burton, Fighter Pilot; George Morris, Fighter Pilot; Jim Miller, Fighter Pilot; Jim Farley, Fighter Pilot.

Back Row, left to right: Charles de Brettville, Communications Officer; Bob Jones, Torpedo Pilot; Chuck Mulligan, Torpedo Pilot; Smokey Schrader, Torpedo Pilot; Leonard Muskin, Torpedo Pilot; Gene Breen, Fighter Pilot; Stub Meyer, Fighter Pilot; Albert K. Earnest, Torpedo Pilot.

THE "JO-DO"
With Plane Captain Stella (Chief Mechanic)
and Lt. F.W. Robinson

"Jo-Do," a TBM Grumman *Avenger* Torpedo Bomber, at the North Island Naval Air Station, San Diego, California. This was prior to leaving on the aircraft carrier USS Manila Bay, January, 1944.

6

THE DEVELOPMENT OF AIR-TO-GROUND MISSILES

The torpedo plane division of Squadron VC-7 was given an unique assignment during the fall of 1943. We were assigned to work with the California Institute of Technology in Pasadena, California to test and fire a new rocket developed by that scientific and research institution.

It was not until fifty years later that I was able to put all of this experience in perspective. We took so much for granted in those war years, as we moved from one new adventure to another. So much of what we did was top secret and I know that I had only a very limited understanding of air-to-ground missiles. The limited participation by our squadron gave me little understanding as to how this contributed to the rapid weapon development of the era.

Many years later I realized that our squadron had participated in the very first experiments in air-to-ground rocket launches. They were primitive shots compared to today's guided missiles, but a major step in the amount of explosive power a single aircraft could throw against an enemy target.

In preparing for this manuscript, my wife Joan and I went to Cal-Tech in Pasadena in January 1997. Our initial exploration for historical information about the 1943 rocket project was discouraging. However, we were later referred to Jean Anderson, Head Librarian at the Fairchild Library of Aeronautics, a position she held for many years. How fortunate we were to make this timely contact, for she was retiring the following week. Without her memory and her help, much of the story I now relate could never have been told. She alone, of all the professional help at Cal-Tech, had any inkling as to the material for which I searched.

Now I can tell the rocket testing experience of Navy Flight Squadron VC-7 during World War II within an historical perspective that is, to me, fascinating and significant. Some of this information comes from *The Wind and Beyond, Pioneer in Aviation and Pathfinder in Space*, a book written by Theodore von Karman. Jean Anderson located this rare manuscript, for which I was deeply appreciative. With this material, combined with my own memory and other data I was able to retrieve, I can relate this story with assurance.

*   *   *

Dr. von Karman, a German Jew and renowned rocket scientist, had a terrible foreboding in the later months of the 1920's for the future of Germany. "The advance of the Nazis toward domination of Germany was great and the situation for non-Aryan teachers at the universities was, to say the least, delicate," he said. These were anxious days for von Karman as he became tormented with the idea that someday he might have to leave his beloved Motherland.

Goering, head Nazi of the German Air Force, suggested that von Karman join the Air Ministry as a consultant. Goering once said, "Who is or who is not a Jew is up to me to decide." This did not persuade Dr. von Karman. In October 1929, Dr. Millikan,

President of the California Institute of Technology wrote the renowned space scientist and offered him a teaching position. Dr. von Karman accepted.

In the early 1930's Cal-Tech's reputation in scientific teaching and research was on the rise. The institution attracted highly qualified and inspiring teachers and this, in turn, attracted dynamic and talented young men. They were called rocketeers. The skies, and then the universe, were their goals.

But rocketeering was a new and novel idea and at first not even Cal-Tech was interested. The school turned down the initial proposals on the basis that rocketry was not practical or even scientifically interesting. Cal-Tech considered it to be just a fad, a Fourth of July lark. John W. Parsons was one of the men who made an initial proposal in rocketry that was turned down. In desperation he went directly to Dr. von Karman, "My project is not harebrained!"

Dr. von Karman was impressed. The earnestness and the enthusiasm of this young man immediately captivated this easy-going professor from Germany with a reputation for being interested in unconventional ideas. "It was the unusually strong background and drive of this rocketeer that interested me," Dr. von Karman recalled. "Jack Parsons was not a student. He was a tall, handsome, dark-haired, self-taught chemist with considerable innate ability. He was a rocketeer to whom rocket engines were as familiar as automobile engines were to many young tinkerers."

Parsons had corresponded and exchanged ideas with the early German and Russian rocketeers. His backyard in Pasadena was pockmarked from the effect of rocket explosions. "He was just ahead of his time," Dr. von Karman said, "but he captured my imagination so I decided to let him have at it."

Two others joined Parsons, and together they developed the first rocket program at this distinguished institution. One was Frank J. Malina, an outstanding graduate student in aeronautics who had proposed a Ph.D. thesis on rocket flight and propulsion. The third man in this group was Edward S. Forman, who, like Parsons, was not a student, but was an ardent rocketeer. Under the tutelage of Dr. von Karman, Malina, Parsons and Forman became the team that brought the use of rockets to the United States military.

In the 1930's, when these men began to bring their vision into reality, there was little general knowledge about rockets. But by 1941 these pioneers had developed the dry-extrusion process of making explosives, and they used this method to provide appropriate fuels to power their rockets. The hand-held Bazooka developed by this Cal-Tech team, was used in the invasion of North Africa. This was the first time that rockets had ever been used by the United States military.

These men next began to develop the means for launching aerial rockets from diving military aircraft against an enemy target. The visionaries at Cal-Tech were almost ready. Here in the story I digress.

*   *   *

Squadron VC-31 was disbanded in the summer of 1943. The fighter pilots were sent off in the new F6F *Hellcats* to participate in the fierce battles that were to rage for months as the allies moved up through the Solomon Islands to neutralize the Japanese stronghold at Rabaul. Those of us who were flying TBM *Avengers* in the torpedo division were sent to Ream Field, a naval air station just south of San Diego. There the new squadron VC-7 was commissioned under the leadership of our original skipper, Lt. Commander Bill Bartlett. A group of new fighter pilots joined the squadron and began their training. These new flyers would eventually provide us with an air combat patrol and protection during the torpedo, bombing, and rocket missions while in combat.

Commander Bartlett called the torpedo bomber pilots into the Ready Room at Ream Field and addressed us.

> *Men, we have just received some very special orders. For the next few months we are going to be trained to fire a new weapon, an air-to-ground rocket. These missiles are not fully developed yet, so we will be working with some of the scientists from Cal-Tech. They will need to test this weapon. Our planes are undergoing modifications so that we will be able to mount and fire these rockets. It should be an interesting assignment.*

The project is secret. We will be flying to a remote dry lake out near Death Valley where the work on this project has been proceeding. The scientists will brief us there. This is a top-secret assignment, so act accordingly.

For some of the pilots, this just seemed like another delay before they could engage the Japanese in combat. The realization that I would have a few more months with Joan mollified any slight frustration I might have felt. I certainly had no real understanding of what was involved in the air-to-ground rocket project.

*   *   *

On a bright October day in 1943, three of us took off in our Grumman bombers from Ream Field. We were bound for Goldstone Dry Lake where the scientists were working on their rocket project. Today Goldstone is a part of the vast China Lake Naval Weapons Center.

Our three-plane division led by Commander Bartlett climbed out of the San Diego area on an almost due-north heading. I could see the majestic peak of Mt. San Jacinto looming off to the starboard, guarding the shimmering desert from the creeping coastal haze. Soon the vast desert, clear under the October air, studded with dead volcanic peaks and rock outcroppings, brought a fantasy to the land I had learned to love. The drone of the powerful motors in our planes brought back the reality that, yes, in all this vast tranquility this was a mission of war. In an hour the Muroc dry lake bed, some years later to become Edwards Air Force Base and the landing area for the space shuttles, passed under the port wing of my plane. Away to the west was the southern granite rift of the towering Sierra.

Goldstone Dry Lake soon came into view. Routinely we flared off to establish our landing intervals and dropped to the earth, bringing up clouds of alkali as each plane touched down on the smooth surface of this ancient lake bed. A jeep sped out to meet us. We climbed aboard and soon we arrived at a little group of Quonset huts that had hurriedly been constructed on a rise of land overlooking the dry remains of the ancient lake. This was our first contact with the wild visionaries who would be among those who would lead the world into the space age. For now, a few of us from Navy Squadron VC-7 were at Goldstone, in an isolated desert hideaway between Death Valley and the High Sierra, to help bring their vision of air-to- ground rockets to reality.

We did no firing on this first trip to Goldstone. Rather we received a briefing on the project and met the team in charge, including John Parsons, with whom I would have a number of interesting contacts. I was immediately attracted to his easy-going personality and unassuming way. It was several weeks before I began to detect the creative fire within John Parsons. We became acquainted, when on occasion, I flew him back to a little airfield in Monterey Park just south of Cal-Tech. From there it was just a short drive to his home in Pasadena. I was selected for this duty because I was the only pilot in the squadron from southern California. There were days when the smog was so heavy in the area that visibility was difficult. When this happened I would locate Atlantic Avenue and fly at less than 500 feet north along the boulevard until the small field came into view. It took a nose-high, powered, carrier approach over the Eucalyptus trees to negotiate a safe landing on the short airstrip. John Parsons appeared relaxed and undisturbed on these air commutes. I admired this quiet, impressive man.

*   *   *

It was not until fifty years later that I gained any understanding of the dimensions of this complicated scientist. Before I had met him, John Parsons, along with Madina and Forman, met in Dr. von Karman's living room in Pasadena to lay the foundation for their first rocket company. It was a serious decision for them! Each man agreed to put up two hundred dollars to found the company. This was a considerable gamble in those days for a theoretical professor, a former graduate student and a rocket tinkerer, all who had limited resources.

Dr. von Karman writes, "John Parsons was an excellent chemist, and a delightful screwball that loved to recite pagan poetry to the sky while stamping his feet. He stood six-feet-one, had dark wavy hair and penetrating black eyes that appealed to the ladies and he was the son of a one-time tycoon."

When John Parsons wasn't working with explosives, for which he had an uncanny talent, the story goes that he headed a local chapter of a religious sect called the Thelemites. Strange tales have been told about this sect. An English ex-mountain climber named Aleistar Crowley, who was once labeled by the press as the world's most wanted and evil man because of his strange practices, had founded the Thelemites in Europe. The members met in a mansion on Millionaire's Row in Pasadena in a room with walls of carved leather. The members were sworn to obey the law: "There is no law beyond, do what thou wilt. Do what thou wilt shall be the whole of the law." In practice this translated into among other things, sex rituals. Dr. von Karman learned all of this later when the FBI questioned him about Parsons.

What strange lives we live. One of the now-forgotten geniuses in the birthing of the space age had many facets to his personality, certainly never known to me at the time. John Parsons worked for several aerospace firms immediately following the war and left his imprint on the development of solid fuel rockets. But he was restless, always searching for some private gate to happiness. In 1947, he became involved with arms for Israel. Some years later the Mexican government commissioned him to set up a factory south of the border to make explosives. The Mexicans furnished him a seventeenth-century castle in which to live. But Parsons never entered it. His unique life was snuffed out through an explosive creation of his own genius. While he was packing a trailer with explosives in front of his home in Pasadena, a bottle of fulminate of mercury slipped from his hand and exploded. A few hours later he was dead.

Fifty years later when Joan and I visited Cal-Tech to get additional information, not a person on that prestigious campus, with the exception of Jean Anderson the retiring librarian, could identify this pioneer in rocket development. John Parsons was among the select few who enabled man to venture into space and into a new age. From the little rocket company they founded with two hundred dollars each, emerged the Aerojet Engineering Corporation and later the Jet Propulsion Laboratory (JPL).

This little group of pioneers was the first in the United States to prove by mathematics that escape from the earth was possible with a multi-staged rocket. They also provided practical criteria for the design of such rockets. America's first satellite, Explorer I, which was launched in 1958, carried the exact amount of payload proposed by this Cal-Tech group, of which John Parsons was an important member. A new age was born.

Now, as I sometimes drive the 210 Freeway near the Rose Bowl in Pasadena, California, I look at the massive Jet Propulsion Laboratories and remember with wonder the small group of eccentric men whose dreams made it possible to escape the bounds of our earth.

*   *   *

In August 1943 the navy became so interested in the Cal-Tech air-to-ground rocket project that scouting began for a suitable site for a testing facility where the actual firing could be done. A deserted little aircraft landing field west of the inconspicuous village of Inyokern and about fifty miles from Goldstone was selected as an appropriate site. On November 8, 1943 the U.S. Naval Ordnance Test Station, located at the Inyokern Naval Auxiliary Air Station, was officially established.

Throughout the following weeks of November and December, I made several flights to Inyokern to fire the rockets that Cal-Tech had developed under the leadership of John Parsons and other members of the team. After landing, an ordnance crew would attach four five-inch high velocity aircraft rockets under each wing. This gave me a salvo of eight Holy Moses missiles fitted with explosive heads to fire. The explosive head on each rocket decreased the velocity of each missile to about 700 feet per second. When launched from a diving *Avenger* the rocket's velocity at release was already approaching 200 miles an hour and the tail fins were effective. Thus their accuracy was about eight times greater than that of ground-fired rockets and quite comparable to a cannon.

At first we used launching rails mounted under the wings that were about as long as the rockets. It was felt that this was needed to give stability to the rocket in the first few feet after being fired from the plane. It was soon discovered that these rails were unnecessary, and by the time Squadron VC-7 took the rockets into combat the rails were replaced with zero-length launchers. This guided a missile for only the first inch of travel after launch, but that was enough to keep it on line. These new launchers decreased the aerodynamic drag that had initially cut the maximum speed on our planes, and this, of course, was an improvement.

I clearly remember my first firing of these primitive rockets. I had flown from San Diego to this quiet little auxiliary naval air station at the base of the towering Sierra range. Not another military plane was on the field. It was a welcome respite from the busy air bases in the San Diego area. I climbed out of the plane and was met by a naval officer who introduced himself as the Project Director. He took me in his Jeep over the undulating terrain of rock, sagebrush and juniper to a clearing in the desert several miles north of the field. "Here is your target. It isn't much but it will do the job."

A twenty by twenty-foot target of mesh and boards had been hung between two salvaged telephone poles. "Do you think you can hit that?"

"I've never fired these rockets before," I said, "but I'll give it a try."

By the time we returned to the airstrip at Inyokern, eight rockets had been mounted under the wings of my plane. I got into my old TBM *Avenger*, "Jo-Do," fired up the massive 2,000 horsepower rotary engine, and felt reassured as the familiar old plane came alive with a deep and pulsating roar. I was on my way making the first air-to-ground rocket launch in the history of naval aviation!

A mild wind was coming down over the Sierra slope and the air was rougher than it had been earlier in the morning. The 200-mile an hour dive through the turbulent and bumpy air made it difficult to keep the electric gun sight on the target. I had another problem. The drop, or trajectory, of the rockets, after being fired from the plane beyond the 1,000-yard range from the target, was significant. This necessitated a correct calibration from the launch position to the point of impact. Our planes had just been installed for the first time with a primitive radar system for night attack work. The thought hit me that perhaps we could utilize radar to accurately determine the distance to a target during the dive. Before the flight I talked with George Driesback, my radioman about this possibility. George suggested that he calibrate each one thousand-yard mark on the radar screen. Then he would call out that distance to me throughout the duration of the dive on the target. It was worth trying.

We were ready. George called out over the intercom as I brought the diving plane on target: "2,000 yards, 19, 18, 17, 16, 15, 14, 13, 12, 11, Fire!" His rhythmic call gave me the pattern I needed. This quickly designed technique worked well. The eight charged heads hissed off and exploded through the target breaking the desert silence with a roar.

This now gave us the same firepower as a full salvo of shells from a light cruiser; a tremendous jump in military might. Torpedo Squadron VC-7 was destined to be the first in the history of warfare to take air-to-ground missiles into battle.

*   *   *

When we arrived at Pearl Harbor several months later on the carrier Manila Bay, our rocket-equipped *Avengers* became a source of interest to the navy brass. The Flag Admiral was assigned to our carrier. On the way to the invasion of the Marshall Islands, he ordered a demonstration of these new aerial rockets.

Commander Bill Bartlett, our original skipper, had been assigned to the Admirals staff after we had reached Pearl Harbor. Now, speaking for the Admiral, he ordered our new skipper, Lt. Gene Breen, to launch a three-plane division for the demonstration. I was selected to lead the flight.

In mid-afternoon we were catapulted into the clear Pacific sky. A cable-attached spar had been rolled out astern of the Manila Bay. We could see the white wake of the spar, moving as a porpoise in the blue water. "Ready to fire," the report came. I thought the target was too close to the carrier, so I radioed back that I thought it best to let out more cable.

"No. The Admiral wants a good view. Go ahead and make your run," the answer came.

I started my dive, increasing speed until making the fire at the one thousand-yard range. The eight rockets hit around the target spar with a giant thump exploding shrapnel high into the air. Some of the fragments fell onto the flight deck of the carrier, causing no damage but considerable dismay.

"That will be enough. Cease Fire!" The orders came clear and distinct over the radio. That was the first and last time we ever put on a demonstration. I was told later that the Admiral was duly impressed.

I have related these events in some detail, because although it was routine for us at the time, VC-7's involvement in the development and employment of air-to-ground missiles was important. Put in historical perspective, I realize now the significance of what we did. The use of air-to-ground missiles, for the first time in the history of military aviation, occurred when Navy Flight Squadron VC-7 participated in the attack and occupation of the Marshall Islands in March 1944. It was a primitive start, but this rocket project contributed an important step for the scientists who eventually put America into space.

Grumman TBF *Avenger*
Firing Holy Moses Rockets

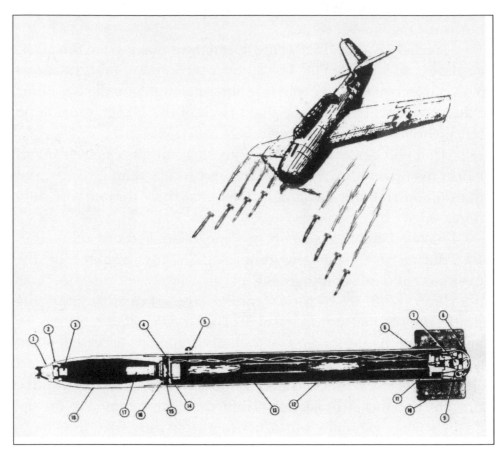

1. Fuse	10. Fin
2. Fuse Liner	11. Grid
3. Booster Cap	12. Motor Tube
4. Igniter	13. Propellant
5. Lug Button	14. Front Seal
6. Suspension Mount	15. Felt Seal
7. Wire and Plug	16. Fiber Seal
8. Rear Seal	17. Base Fuse

Cockpit of TBM *Avenger*

Lt. Franklin W. Robinson Jr. USNR
in the cockpit of his TBM *Avenger* torpedo plane.
Navy Torpedo and Bombing Squadron VC-7
North Island Naval Air Station
San Diego, California 1943

Original Team of Cal-Tech
"Rocketeers" at Work in the Field

**John W. Parsons
at Rocket Test Site**

Project Number 1 at Rocket Test Site. From left to right: unidentified, Frank Malina, unidentified, Edward S. Forman, John W. Powers

Founding Fathers and Early Directors of Aerojet Engineering Corporation

Persons from left to right:
   Second from left; John W. Parsons
   Third from left; Edward S. Forman
   Sixth from left; Theodore von Karman
   Seventh from left; Frank J. Malina

In the background is a Douglas A-20 attack bomber, installed with a rocket power plant. The picture was taken at Muroc Air Force Base, California, in January 1943. This was the same type of installation that was made on the Grumman Avenger, flown first into combat by United States Navy Torpedo Squadron, VC-7, during the invasion of the Marshall Islands, flying from the aircraft carrier Manila Bay.

7

COMPOSITE SQUADRON VC-7 AND THE AIRCRAFT CARRIER MANILA BAY

By the late Fall of 1943, our squadron was stationed at the U.S. Naval Air Station at Ream Field south of San Diego making preparations to board the escort carrier Manila Bay. The ship was a new little jeep carrier built in Vancouver, British Columbia and commissioned on October 5, 1943. The Manila Bay came to San Diego with its new crew for training and the important initial shakedown cruises necessary to prepare us for combat.

Our torpedo squadron had been joined with a young fighter group who had been equipped with the new FM-2 *Wildcat* fighter planes. These new planes looked like the original F4F *Wildcats* but were 500 pounds lighter and had increased horsepower. This was the only plane I ever flew that could do continuous loops and still gain altitude. It was a very maneuverable airplane. These young fighter pilots were a bright bunch and we were glad they would be flying cover for us.

The autumn days of 1943 were busy as Squadron VC-7 prepared to embark on the aircraft carrier Manila Bay. Our landing signal officer, who would guide us aboard the little carrier, worked with the squadron at the Ream Field Naval Air Station as we practiced simulated night carrier landings. A make-believe deck was outlined on the runway. Around we would go, honing our skill in following the directions from the bright neon paddles of the landing signal officer as he brought us to the position of the "cut" that would land us, bang, on the precise spot we were to hit. This was the ultimate skill in precision flying, and we needed to learn it well.

Once again the reality of what we faced struck home. "Bloody Sunday" as it was reported in the Los Angeles Times, brought news that a young fighter squadron out of San Diego had crashed twenty-three of their twenty-four planes in landing exercises off the coast. Only a couple of pilots had been killed, but the wreckage of one of the planes had catapulted onto the bridge of the carrier, tragically killing the ship's chaplain. I don't remember all of the particulars of this tragic event, but it did impress all of us with the imperative that we learn well the art of landing on an aircraft carrier.

Actually, when it was our turn to fly out and land on the Manila Bay for the first time, it was deceptively easy. The sea was calm and the day was clear. There was enough wind over the deck to give us ample time in the "groove" to prepare for a safe approach to the deck and a cable catch with the tail-hook that would bring us to a stop before hitting the barrier. We all made our five landings and returned to Ream Field, our mission accomplished. I say "deceptively easy" because later we would, at times, experience rough seas when the little carrier's deck would roll and pitch as we came in to land. In the equatorial regions where we would later operate, there were often tropical squalls that hindered visibility, and zero wind conditions that, combined with the low speed of the ship, meant that we would be hitting the deck at around ninety knots. All of these factors combined, along with our heavy bomb loads on occasion, made the operation much more hazardous.

It has often been written that landing a heavy plane on a heaving escort carrier in the dark is "all part of the job, and the risk, of being a navy pilot." Some flyers say, "It's even more frightening than combat." First, the pilot must spot the carrier, nothing more than a pinpoint of moving unsteady light, muted for security on a black sea. Sometimes clouds obscure even these small reference points. In seconds the pilot must find the proper approach angle, pick up the directions from the landing signal officer, look around the massive rotary engine in front of him, and all the time keep the plane steady in the groove, just above the stalling speed. Most pilots do report that it is difficult to keep their nerves under control and their heart steady in that final approach. The landing signal officer directs the pilot up the groove and gives the final signal to "cut" the engine. If all goes well, the plane bangs to the deck at ninety knots, catches the arresting gear with the tail-hook, and comes to a neck-snapping halt just short of the crash barrier. In one respect, every successful carrier landing is a controlled crash.

There were other dangers on these little escort carriers that were brought home to us in November 1943. The landings on the Gilbert Islands on November 20th marked the beginning of a new Central Pacific offensive. In the invasion of the little atoll of Tarawa, a thousand Marines, a fifth of the invasion force was killed. The battle for Tarawa greatly shocked the American people for they began to see how costly the defeat of Japan could be. Nor was it a shock confined to statistics because for the first time newspaper photographs of American corpses floating in the tide, or piled up on the beaches next to burned-out landing craft were widely circulated.

Even more devastating to the pilots of VC-7 was the news that in this action off Tarawa a Japanese submarine had torpedoed the escort carrier Liscombe Bay. In one violent explosion the carrier was blown apart. There were 644 men killed, including most of the navy pilots who had bunks right above the high explosive gasoline tanks on the ship. We had trained with this navy squadron during the time we were in Seattle and now they were all dead, including my friend Robert W. Wyatt, from Riverside, California. I had trained with Bob Wyatt in Long Beach when we first joined the navy. Later we had been together as we trained in Texas and Florida. When I reported to the Sand Point Naval Air Station in Seattle, Bob was there too, joining his newly formed Composite Squadron. The deadly submarine torpedo attack had come before daylight and all of the pilots were still in their quarters on the Liscombe Bay. From that day on I think all of our pilots felt safer in the air than sleeping on the ship loaded with explosives and high-test gasoline. Later these little unprotected carriers would become prime targets for the diving Kamikaze bomb laden planes.

On another shakedown cruise off San Diego for the Manila Bay, we watched as the gun batteries along the flight deck fired at a target sleeve towed by a utility plane out of the North Island Naval Air Station. As the target sleeve came into range, all the guns on the ship started to fire. We could see the stream of fire tearing the canvas target to shreds, and this was just a little carrier with limited firepower. How could any attacking plane make a successful run on an enemy capital ship? That was the unspoken question on the mind of every VC-7 torpedo pilot, as we watched with dismay the firepower that the ship displayed.

*   *   *

Christmas 1943 was our last visit home before my scheduled departure for the war. Joan and I spent time with our parents in Long Beach. There were many good-byes during wartime, and none of them were easy. For all we knew it would be the last time we would be together. Later, as I became a parent, I appreciated the bravery of those left at home wondering and waiting for any scrap of news that might come and knowing how helpless they were to effect any part of the outcome for those who were gone. In my parents' case there were four blue stars in their window for their three sons and a son-in-law who were in World War II. They prayed always that none of those blue stars would have to be replaced with gold ones.

*   *   *

In January 1944, the Manila Bay was docked at the southeast corner of North Island in San Diego harbor. The dock crews scurried about, busily loading the carrier with bombs, ammunition, torpedoes and the various supplies needed to sustain action for a period of time. Day after day the little tractors brought their loads and the cranes were busy.

Those of us in the torpedo squadron, now flying from the North Island Naval Air Station, were finely honing our gunnery and torpedo launching skills. On one of these flights my brother Ted, who was the commanding cadet in the naval ROTC on the University of California campus at Berkeley, flew with me. I was flying my Grumman *Avenger* Torpedo plane on gunnery runs out near San Clemente Island. Ted rode in the belly of the big plane. Our three-plane formation peeled off, one at a time, for an overhead run on the target sleeve, firing the fifty-caliber guns. I am sure it was not the most pleasant experience for a first flight, but Ted was a good sport and didn't complain. He told me he could hear the chatter of the guns but that there was little he could see from the confined area in which he rode.

In that final week before going aboard the Manila Bay, we made several dummy torpedo attacks on a target ship off the coast of San Diego. The practice torpedoes were defused, so they would not explode, and were set to run deeper than the shallow keel on the target ship. The torpedoes weighed 2,000 pounds and were launched at a thousand yards, 200 feet above the water. The flashing of a battery of colored lights from the bridge of the target ship signaled a hit. It was always a thrill to see that your launch had been successful.

*   *   *

Eventually it came time to taxi our planes from the airstrip at North Island down the streets to the loading dock. The huge cranes lifted our planes up to the flight deck where they were secured for the passage to Hawaii. The time had come. Our torpedo squadron had been given the unusual opportunity for extensive training before being sent to combat. We had logged a thousand hours in the air. We had been trained in torpedo, rocket, bombing, gunnery and night flying attacks. Now we were ready.

I shall never forget that January morning in 1944 when we left on the Manila Bay for Pearl Harbor. The wives of those of us who were married came to the dock to see us depart. Some were in tears and others were in emotional distress. This was all understandable. Joan, as usual, was her strong, controlled self. I have always admired her courage in times of crisis. On this day she displayed an inner strength as we said goodbye; a trait I would see many times in the years ahead as we met new and different challenges. I turned, climbed the ship's ladder, saluted the officer on duty, and came aboard. There were last-waving farewells as the Manila Bay was slowly moved away from the dock and was turned by the assisting tugboats. Soon the carrier was under her own power, sailing out through the harbor channel, past Point Loma and on into the open sea. We were on our way.

On the sixth day at sea, word was passed that soon we would get our first glimpse of the Hawaiian Islands. I stood on the flight deck searching the horizon with several other pilots in the squadron. The Manila Bay continued to move through the tranquil sea. I remember standing beside George Flynn, the Personnel Officer for Squadron VC-7. George came from a wealthy New York family active in the construction business. He was rightfully proud, that among other noted projects, his father had built the Holland tunnel in New York that connected Manhattan with Jersey City. Over the months George had flown with me on many training missions and I had enjoyed our numerous conversations. He was a highly educated and informed man. "See that line on the horizon that looks like a cloud bank," he said. "That's the eastern shore of Molokai Island." Sure enough, soon I could make out the island in the distance.

"We'll proceed northwest along the coastline to the southern end of Oahu and then on in to Pearl Harbor," George continued. It was all an exciting experience to a bunch of young ensign navy flyers that had never before been out of the continental United States. By early afternoon we reached Pearl Harbor. As the carrier slowed and proceeded into the channel, the massive half-submerged hull of the battleship USS Arizona came into view. It still partially blocked the entrance to Pearl Harbor. Our ship eased by. Somewhere down within that blasted hulk there would forever be trapped the remains of over a thousand dead crewmen, killed when the forces of Japan had bombed Pearl Harbor on December 7, l941. Not a word was spoken between those of us standing on the deck of the Manila Bay. I experienced a strange feeling of unreality. A sense of sacredness engulfed us. This was Holy. Here was a unique and historic cemetery upon which we looked. Silently, the bubbles of oil rose and burst on the water, as the old warship continued to die in what seemed to be its own bloodletting.

The Manila Bay came to dock on the western side of Ford Island. Pearl Harbor surrounds this little island that is just large enough for an airfield, several hangars and a number of large storage complexes. It is a confined anchorage and naval center that had provided a concentrated target for the attacking Japanese planes. Now the dock area was alive with little tractors pulling their trains of trailers loaded with boxes, bombs, and materials of war to be hoisted by cranes to the waiting warships. I watched with amazement as primarily Japanese American dockhands manned all this activity. This was so different from mainland USA where the Japanese were tragically herded off to relocation centers far from any of the war activity.

Our planes were unloaded and taxied to the ramps along the airstrip. The fighter pilots were equipped with the FM-2 *Wildcat* fighters, the first to hit the Pacific war area. The torpedo division got a few new models of the TBM-3E and all of our torpedo bombers were equipped with rocket launchers, the first to be seen at Pearl. This sparked considerable interest from the flyers in the other squadrons.

While at Pearl Harbor I ran into several fighter pilots with whom I had gone through training. They had been assigned to some of the larger aircraft carriers and had just returned from initial raids on the Marshall Islands, Truk and some of the other Japanese strongholds. They were all very "high" because these initial strikes had been successful and our own losses had been limited. It was all

119

stimulating and exciting and we were anxious to be on our way.

Fortunately we had time to renew our skills. This included field carrier landings at the marine airfield across the island of Oahu at Kaneohe, and dive-bombing practice with live bombs on a little rock island off Maui as we flew from the deck of the Manila Bay. It was apparent that we were ready for a major attack someplace but where we did not know. We were ready to go.

TORPEDO SQUADRON VC-7
Flying from the USS Manila Bay

The Catapult Take-Off

The Cable-Arrested Landing

8

THE INVASION OF THE MARSHALL ISLANDS

Squadron VC-7 flew off the Ford Island runway in Pearl Harbor late in February 1944 to land on the Manila Bay. The aircraft carrier had already set course with a huge flotilla of ships for an undisclosed location in the Pacific for an attack against the Japanese. The fleet included landing craft, supply ships, and a vast array of warships that formed the largest naval task force ever assembled. I certainly, like many others, had no idea where the Manila Bay was going, but we all knew that we were bound for a major invasion. Late that afternoon we sighted the Manila Bay near the center of the fleet and Skipper Bartlett put us in our echelon positions for our interval landings on the carrier deck. The fighters were scheduled to land first because of their limited fuel range. All began well, but then one of the fighter pilots crashed on the flight deck, his plane exploding in a ball of fire. The crash crew quickly extinguished the flames and the plane was shoved over the deck and into the water so the rest of us could land. Fortunately the pilot of the *Wildcat* FM-2 jumped out of his crashed plane before it exploded and was not injured.

That evening the pilots reported to the Flight Ready-Room for a briefing on the mission. This was the first time we learned that we were headed for an attack and invasion of the coral fortress of Kwajalein in the Marshall Islands.

*   *   *

Let me put this operation in perspective. In 1941 the Japanese began to accomplish their plan for controlling the Pacific. First they would knock out the American defenses in the Hawaiian Islands. This would free them to immediately establish the perimeters of their new empire. This was important to Japan because she could guard her conquests and obtain room to defensively maneuver some distance away from the motherland. The outer line of this perimeter ran from the Kurile Islands to the north of Japan, across the Pacific through Wake Island, the Marshall, the Gilbert, and the Ellice Islands. Japan fortified these new bases with troops and air power. Chances for their success were reasonable. Their military machine was ready. The soldiers had been well-trained in the war with China. The tactics and weapons necessary for the type of combat expected had been tested. Japan held air and naval superiority over the United States and they knew they held a strong and defensible position. Now, for the first time in the Pacific War, the United States would move with a new dimension of strength. The February 1994 issue of Time Magazine describes the Marshall Islands engagement:

> *Admiral Nimitz threw into the attack the greatest force ever concentrated on a single military objective. The Japs were not surprised at the sight of the planes sweeping in from the horizon. For twenty-two successive days the planes had come, scattering destruction over the coral fortress. Down came the planes in screaming dives, driving the enemy deeper and deeper into their concrete pillboxes. The atoll shuddered under the impact of bomb upon bursting bomb from the carrier-based planes. The United States forces had moved into the Marshall Islands domain for the kill. The week's count has been 400 Jap planes destroyed: U.S. loss only sixty planes.*

The Marshall Islands coral atolls are scattered over eight hundred square miles of ocean. The Japanese had dotted them with air and naval bases, and Admiral Nimitz's plan was to leap-frog the territory to deep within the Marshall's two-mile-long atoll of Kwajalein. The bases that would be by-passed would be neutralized by air strikes. Before the Kwajalein landings, allied carrier planes were to eliminate Japanese air power. This happened, and three days before the landings our warships began giving Kwajalein defenses an intense bombardment.

When the assault began, it moved with precision. The Seventh Infantry Division took Kwajalein Island. However, they did encounter some opposition on the beaches and became seriously held up by clusters of Japanese soldiers hidden among the debris of the devastated island. This fierce fighting lasted for four days and by February 4th the American forces secured the island. Nearly 8,000 Japanese had died defending the little two-mile long atoll. American casualties were less than 400 dead and 1,500 wounded. This gives a background into the operation into which Squadron VC-7 was engaged.

* * *

It took a week from the time we left Pearl Harbor until we began our daily routine submarine patrols to protect the fleet. We were moving steadily closer to the Marshall Islands. When I was not flying I spent most of my time in the pilots Ready Room just below the flight deck. There we were continually briefed on the coming mission and the part our squadron would have in the attack. We were shown numerous intelligence pictures of Kwajalein Island, which would be the focus of the landing force. We memorized every feature and potential target on Kwajalein. United States intelligence teams had prepared detailed maps for us and we spent hours going over every aspect of the fortified atoll, memorizing the various features and landmarks that would guide us as we attacked from the air. The island was a little over two miles long and only several hundred yards wide, but it was drilled with tunnels, abutments, gun placements and fortifications. The problem was that the targets could not be identified because the island was covered with coconut palms. The trees completely hid the fortifications from the air. There were two steel radio towers that provided us a good focal point from which we could get perspective and orientation.

On the aerial photograph of Kwajalein that each of the pilots received, was an imposed grid. One side border of this grid showed the letters of the alphabet and the top border showed numbers. The squadron was directed to fly to a rendezvous point near the Island and circle there until directed by the Air Coordinator, who would soon call out over the radio, "I want one TBM plane from Squadron VC-7 to drop four 500 pound bombs in Quadrant K-7." The pilot in the next designated bomber in line would locate the quadrant on the map and then make the run on the hidden target, dropping the bombs as directed. It was all very business-like. Everything had a code name. Kwajalein was called Porcelain. Flight leaders from the different carriers had code names like Cornelia 99 or Magnolia 99. Because most Japanese could not pronounce "L," all of our code names had an "L" in them.

Arnold Erickson, a fellow torpedo pilot in our squadron and my best man when Joan and I were married, many years later wrote an accurate account, describing Squadron VC-7's participation in the fight for control of Kwajalein.

After much anticipation and fear, our squadron flew in formation from the carrier to the target. Our flight leader checked in with the Air Coordinator who told us to orbit at 5,000 feet in one of our three staging areas. The sky was full of planes from our attacking force, so we had to wait our turn to receive a target assignment. These target assignments were given by calling out a quadrant on the target map that every pilot had before him on the navigational chart in the cockpit. After orbiting for about twenty minutes we were directed to drop our bombs and return to the carrier. As soon as we returned to the carrier we reported to the Ready Room and were debriefed by the Intelligence Officer. The first question he asked was "How was the anti-aircraft fire?" I told him there was a little, but that I didn't think they were shooting at me. The AA fire looked like slow rising oranges in a tank of water, seemingly veering off to the right or to the left. "That's the way it looks," he said. "They were firing at you!" Had I realized that, I might have been more frightened than I was.

The Air Coordinator apparently had never had any experience with planes equipped with rockets. That was understandable because our squadron was the first ever so equipped and the code name for rockets had not yet been added to his list of available armaments. Regardless, when our skipper called in to the Air Coordinator, listing the loads we were carrying, he gave the code word for rockets. This did not register, so in his confusion he said for us to drop our bombs on a concrete block house in quadrant Q4 and then go on to a neighboring island and fire our rockets at any likely target. I dove and released my bombs as directed and then proceeded on to another little fortified atoll not scheduled for the initial landing assault. I circled the island at an altitude of about 4,000 feet, looking for a target. I chose a building at the foot of a pier, dove down releasing a salvo of eight rockets. The building burst into flames. As I pulled out of my dive, my engine went silent. I thought I would have to make a forced landing in the lagoon and I was about ready to shove the nose of the plane over into a glide pattern. Then to my amazement I saw that my airspeed registered normal and that my RPMs held steady. I still couldn't hear the engine, even though all of my instruments continued to register in the normal range. It was an uncanny feeling. As I was trying to figure out how I was able to fly in silence, a huge white-gray mushroom cloud came puffing into the sky. The edge of the cloud was about fifty feet off my starboard wing and was visible for over fifty miles. I then noticed that my plane had been blown from two thousand feet to six thousand feet, as a result of the terrific concussion from the explosion beneath me. Soon my hearing returned and the steady drone of the engine reassured me.

I had been through something, but I wasn't certain as to what had happened. I joined up with several of the planes from the squadron and we started back to the Manila Bay. My flight controls were working well, but I wondered if there was any damage to the underside of the plane that would jeopardize a successful landing. Would the wheels come down? How about the flaps and the tail hook? Naturally this all made me uneasy, but later, upon inspection of the plane, the only damage I had sustained was a jagged three-inch hole through the tail section of the plane.

During the routine debriefing in the Ready Room we found out what had actually happened. Charles Anderson had noticed high mounds of dirt near the center of the island. He fired his rockets into one of these mounds and to his surprise detonated an ammunition dump. Andy was *closer to the explosion than I was. The bottom of his plane was punctured extensively with shrapnel fragments but fortunately none had hit his flight controls.*

Arnold's account gives a good description of what went on. For me the whole operation seemed rather impersonal and unreal. For the first time I felt the concussion of my own live bombs exploding beneath me, but the Japanese were so overwhelmed by the power thrown against them that I never felt any real opposition to our attacks. For our assault forces on the ground, I found out later, the battle was very real. Undeniably, there was a tremendous sense of exhilaration to be a part of the dramatic striking force that hit the Marshall Islands. One day I counted 220 planes around me as I led a torpedo bombing section armed with four 500-pound bombs and eight aerial rockets. Having all this lethal force at my command, and feeling an important cog in the greatest force ever assembled, did stir feelings of unique value within me. But there was another side; one I dared not verbalize. I was feeling less than heroic. What chance did these little men have under this rain of bombs? They faced inevitable death, hostage to a system under which by chance they had been born. Why couldn't they just run up the white flag and then we could all go home? And then, too, I sensed a deep underlying uneasiness that time was running out. Call it premonition, I don't know.

All during the time we operated in the Marshall Islands, several of our planes were assigned the responsibility to fly search missions each day for several hundred miles from where our fleet was operating. On this particular day I was assigned to fly an individual scout and patrol mission in a relative thirty-degree vector 200 miles west-northwest of the fleet. These were always monotonous and lonely missions, but necessary because of the threat of enemy submarines to our ships. No sooner had I completed the necessary calculations for the flight on my plotting board than the abrupt order came over the ships sound system, "Pilots, man your planes." I swung up the ladder and onto the busy flight deck where my crew was waiting. A special bond grows among the men who share the strain and uncertainties of long hours together in the air. "Are you ready, George?"

"Ready, Skipper." It was the radioman, George Driesback. Jr., a blond, sharp youth from Rockford, Illinois. His father was proud of George's engagement at Attu in Alaska when the Japanese invaded this storm-lashed island. Harold Eckert, the gunner, was already in the turret freeing his two fifty-caliber machine guns. He was a quiet purposeful boy from Los Angeles who seldom talked while in the air. Harold was keen, cool, and an excellent shot. I didn't share the apprehension I felt. Old Jo-Do, my regular plane, was tied down near the fantail of the ship and we were scheduled off early in a new plane to the fleet, the TBM-3E. This was a plane I had never flown before and I knew I would miss the "old shoe" feeling of a plane that had grown to be a part of me. But that was the way it was in naval carrier warfare. Dispatch in flying a squadron off the deck is of primary concern. For this reason a navy pilot does not always get his regular plane. Again, the loudspeaker from the bridge sounded, "Pilots start your engines."

Cautiously, I taxied the bomber into position. The bright-shirted men of the deck crew, each color signified the specialized task they performed, labored in the turbulent air. One attached the catapult cable yoke to the under carriage of the plane while I set the leather headrest, made a final check of the instrument panel and built up the power to check the magnetos. The Wright 2600 rotary engine responded with a familiar and steady roar.

While this preparation was under way, the men below deck worked to build up the pressure of oil and compressed air for the catapult shot. The final check had been completed. I pushed the throttle forward to the firewall and the big bird responded, screeching and trembling within the cable yoke that held us.

"Ready George? Ready Harold?"

"Ready Captain," their response came.

I lifted my hand and moved it in a horizontal direction from left to right the signal for release. Whooosh! The *Avenger* was catapulted, accelerating to ninety knots as it left the flight deck. We were free of the carrier and in the air, but the ton of torpex depth charges and the full load of rockets and gas were forcing the laboring plane to the wave tops. Our takeoff was alarmingly sluggish. It was touch and go for several seconds as to whether we would belly into the sea, but gradually we began to climb.

The navy had the facility for taking an excellent airplane, and then with each succeeding modification, hanging on enough extra gear to cut in on its original performance. I was convinced that this was what happened to our TBM-3E.

Once these first moments of tension passed and we reached our scout and patrol altitude, I looked down again on a task force of ships that literally filled the ocean. I don't know how many there were, but there were ships in every direction as far as I could see. Five carriers moved at the center of the task force with battleships and cruisers forming the intermediate ring. Interspersed were tankers and supply ships, all supporting the landing craft used in the operation. Flying our assigned heading of 270 degrees it was not long before we flew beyond the outer circle of destroyers picketing the flotilla as a protection against the prowling submarines.

"Quite a sight don't you think Skipper?" George was always the most talkative of the crew.

The afternoon passed with routine monotony. At 1600 hours we passed over a Japanese held atoll, a spot where the sea lightened to a color of beautiful turquoise. We saw no enemy activity and flew on.

From periodic radio reports, it became apparent that a rescue mission was underway for a TBM that had crashed during the afternoon operations. I found out later that the entire crew had been killed, including the observer Raymond Clapper, the noted war correspondent, "victim of his own belief that the only way to write a valid wartime column was to participate first hand," as the Los Angeles Times later reported. Little did I realize at that moment how close I was to experiencing the mystery into which he had moved.

The setting sun was casting its trail of fire across the water as I headed back to the aircraft carrier. Then the radio came alive with chatter between airplot and some of the pilots who had made contact with an enemy submarine. I quickly plotted the location on my chart and altered my homeward course with the hope that I could make contact. By the time I arrived, I could see where the charges, dropped by the other planes, had exploded and some oil slicks on the surface of the water, but I never was certain as to the results of this contact. I was disappointed that I had not had the opportunity to drop my depth charges, for logistics and economy dictated that I save them for another mission. There was always added danger in landing on a carrier with a full load of explosives. Over five hours had passed since I had flown from the Manila Bay and it was a relief to find her in the dusk as night closed down on the fleet. I made the routine approach, flying up wind well to the starboard of the ship to a position several hundred yards ahead of the carrier. We began our 180-degree turn to the left, losing altitude—wheels down, flaps down, tail hook down, mixture rich, cowls open, propeller in low pitch and air speed reduced. I finished my turn and eased into the downwind leg, keeping the carrier abreast before making the final turn up the groove. There I would come under the direction of the Landing Signal Officer, who would direct the final phase of my landing on the carrier deck. A carrier landing is always a powered approach. The plane is held just above its stalling speed so when the final signal to cut the throttle is given, the heavy plane drops to the deck. The tail hook grabs the arresting cable, jerking the bomber to an abrupt stop.

On the downwind leg on my approach I experienced the same problems that had plagued our takeoff. Once the speed of the plane was reduced to ninety knots, normally the desired setting, there was not enough power, even with the throttle wide open, to hold the plane in the air. It was too late to jettison the explosives! Without warning the plane lurched and trembled. Like a goose hit in the wing by a volley of shot, we plummeted into the Pacific with terrifying finality. The plane smashed into the water in a death dive, hitting the sea and instantly exploding in a shattering burst of water and debris. Before the first plumes of water fell back, the rolling body of the ocean quivered and exploded four more times, as each 500-pound torpex filled depth charge blew great geysers of water into the darkening sky. Cascades of water turned me over and over. I was aware of flashes of psychedelic light, green, yellow and purple in the abysmal spectrum within which my body tossed.   The concussions hit me as lethal fists. With one last tremendous effort I tripped the release on one side of my Mae West life jacket. It inflated and supported my head. Then the storm passed and I was left bobbing in the sea in an unreal quietness. I looked around. All was gone, the flight crew, the plane and even the debris that usually floats from a crash. I was hurt and helpless, but numbness from shock and the realization that I was still alive shielded me from pain. Soon a destroyer, rolling wings of water from its bow, cut toward me. "For God's sake, there's a man alive out there! Full Reverse! Full reverse! Get a line out there." The orders blasted over the ships speakers from the bridge.

The ship veered and in an instant a life preserver, attached to the ship by a line, plopped within my reach. Instinctively, almost blindly, I locked my arms around it. Violently, I was jerked into a turbulence of water caused by the reverse action of the giant screws under the ship. The destroyer slowed rapidly. Whirlpools sucked me down under the hull. Here was yet another abyss, one that took me to another danger under the slugging blades of the ship's propellers. Would I never come to the surface again? It was an eternity, but with a power born out of desperation, I clung to the lifeline. Eventually the ship stopped dead in the water and I was pulled to the surface. Partially conscious, I again heard the shouting of orders.

"Go overboard and secure the line around him. He's still alive."

A young seaman jumped overboard and wrapped his strong arms around me. The crew on the deck pulled us out of the water and hauled us aboard. I was in a state of shock; it seemed somehow unreal.

Sometime during the night, I became aware. My loss of George Driesback and Harold Eckert was devastating . . . a pain I would carry all my years. I was in bed in an officer's cabin I tried to reconstruct the events of the crash and to determine the extent of my injuries. I remembered I had slipped out of the straps of the parachute and opened the hatch over the cockpit as the plane lowered below 500 feet on our approach to the ship. This was standard procedure.

The engine and left wing had hit the water in a nosedive. I could remember this. The shoulder harness must have held me during the initial impact of the crash. I know that my hand had been on the release lever and the initial explosion must have simultaneously pulled my hand, tripping the lever that held the safety belts and ejected me many yards from the disintegrating plane. It was apparent that I could not have survived without being some distance from the exploding torpex charges, armed when the safety wires were pulled loose by the force of the crash. This is the best explanation I could think of for my survival.

My right leg was ripped open and shrapnel was imbedded near the base of my spine. My face was gashed and I suffered contusions, lacerations and multiple blast injuries. The impact from the explosive force of the depth charges did a lot of damage to my capillaries. This caused bleeding under the skin that distorted and discolored my entire body. I was beginning to become aware of great pain that would not leave me for many months.

Sometime during that first night on the destroyer an officer entered the dimly lit room. His insignia leaves reflected dull silver above the points of his khaki collar. His dark hair showed strands of gray. His face was lined from the exposure to the sun and the wind during his long watches at sea. But, his eyes were clear and I saw in them a loneliness of command and prolonged responsibility.

"You're going to be all right," he said. His voice was deliberate and reassuring. "I got a report from the ship's doctor. I'm going to keep you right here in my bunk until we can make contact with a hospital ship. Welcome to our destroyer. I'm Abraham Lincoln, commanding officer, and you are on the USS Caldwell."

I shall never forget him. Not only because he commanded the men who, by fate, had saved my life, but because this Abraham Lincoln became my symbol of renewed life on my day of personal reprieve.

United States Forces Attack
Marshall Islands

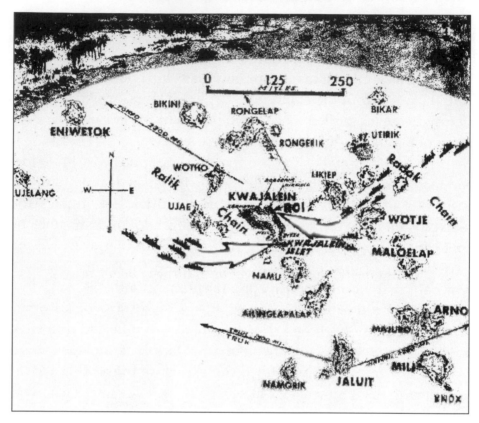

This map and the article below are taken from a 1944 newspaper describing the U.S. Naval attack on the Marshall Islands.

Most Powerful Naval Striking Force in Sea History Leads Attack

PEARL HARBOR, Feb. 1944 (UP) – United States Marine and Army troops, supported by the most powerful naval striking force in history, have battled ashore on Kwajalein atoll in the Marshall Islands and won firm beach heads near Roi and Kwajalein inlets in a successful opening of the greatest combined operation of the Pacific war, it was announced.

Clouds of planes and new secret weapons hitherto unused in war also supported the troops as they splashed across the coral reefs in their first onslaught.

134

U.S. Navy Aircraft Carrier
Squadron VC-7

Lt. Franklin W. Robinson Jr.
Leading Section of TBM *Avenger* Torpedo Bombers
February 1944

Escort Carrier USS Manila Bay

Avenger Torpedo Bombers and
Wildcat Fighters Ready for Launch

The above photo shows Navy Fight Squadron VC-7 planes on the deck of
the Aircraft Carrier Manila Bay prior to the attack on Kwajalein in
February, 1944. Squadron VC-7 was the first squadron to fly from this
little jeep aircraft carrier.

Later, with a second flight squadron, the Manila Bay was one of the heroic
little carriers which stood fast off San Bernardino Strait. Her bombing
Avengers helped turn back the Japanese fleet to save the U.S. landing forces
who were attempting to recapture the Philippines. The Manila Bay shot
down five Japanese planes and the squadron accounted for fifteen more in
the sky. In this melee, two Kamikaze planes hit the Manila Bay. One
suicide plane hit squarely on the flight deck, killing ten of the crew and
wounding eighty others.

Kwajalein

In a low-level bombing and rocket attack, Squadron VC-7, flying from the aircraft carrier Manila Bay, blew up a Japanese ammunition dump on an island in the Kwajalein Atoll in the Marshall Islands. March 1944

9

A TIME OF RECOVERY AND RE-ASSIGNMENT

After my rescue at sea, I remained on the destroyer USS Caldwell for one week. By that time the Marshall Islands were secure and under United States control. Our forces were mopping up the last areas of resistance and many of our ships, including the hospital ship USS Relief, were safely anchored within the sheltered Kwajalein Atoll. I was taken to the deck of the Caldwell, placed in a wire basket stretcher, and let down by the destroyer's hoist into a launch that had been sent to take me to the hospital ship. All the crewmen on the USS Caldwell were on deckside to witness my departure. I thanked Captain Lincoln and waved to the men as I left. It was the only way I had to show my gratitude. The launch took me to Kwajalein where I was hoisted aboard the USS Relief, a shining white hospital ship with a giant red cross painted on the side.

I write with some detail about the month I was on the USS

Relief. This was my first experience in the proximity of the results of battle. I had never before been so close to those who were experiencing the personal suffering and tragedy of war. These weeks made a lasting impression on me. Let me set the stage for the story I tell.

The hospital ship was anchored in the lagoon inside the Kwajalein Atoll. Kwajalein was the main island among the many others that made up the atoll. I can best describe the atoll as a series of tropical islands, strung like a strand of beads in a necklace around a large anchorage that protected the fleet from the open sea. There were few wounded soldiers on the ship when I came aboard. I was taken to a room that would bed about forty patients in bunks tiered four levels high, but I was the only one in the room. All that first night I lay there in pain, rocked by the explosions on Kwajalein where the soldiers of the 7th Division were still mopping up, going from bunker to bunker to blast out the remaining resistance. The initial landing had been almost unopposed, because the Japanese expected that the landings would be made from the seaward side of the island. All of their gun emplacements faced the sea. But the allied plan, because of the tragic mistake that they had made at Tarawa, changed their strategy. This time they would immobilize the Japanese defenders by throwing a prolonged and devastating bombing attack from the air by the carrier planes. While this went on for over a week, the American landing forces went through the passage between the islands and made their attack without Japanese resistance from the quiet lagoon side of the atoll. About half of the defenders of Kwajalein had been killed that first week by the bombing and shelling they had taken. However 3,000 of them still remained holed up in the rubble and the tunnels they had drilled in the coral island. Sad but true, the Japanese were always fanatical and would fight until all of them had been killed. Our soldiers moved bunker by bunker across the mutilated island, killing as they went, but in the process always taking some losses. Early the next morning, following the day I had been taken aboard, the army casualties of the 7th Division began to arrive on the hospital ship. In the annals of war, this was a minor engagement. But for me it was traumatic. For the first time I saw spilled blood and torn mutilated bodies. Now it was all around me in that crowded hospital room, the dirty bodies of the exhausted soldiers, their groans and cries for help, and the stench of battle. The doctors, nurses and corpsmen went into action. All day and all night they worked, operating, giving blood transfusions, and bandaging and casting the wounded. The screaming and the crying out for help never ceased. In the bunk above me was a handsome young lieutenant. He had been shot through the neck. A 30-caliber carbine shell, no larger than the head of a pencil, had put a clean hole through his muscular body right at the top of his spine, leaving him paralyzed from his neck down. Sobbing, he told me he was from the Big Sky country of Montana and wanted to go home. During the night he kept calling out for his mother. "Mother, Mother, help me," he would cry. Just before dawn he died. The corpsmen came in and took his lifeless body away. Emotionally, I was broken. Now the war had become so personal, so real in a way that I had never experienced. I don't think I could ever be a soldier. It seemed so much different in the air. We lost our flyers on occasion, but we had good food, clean sheets, and a shower every night. We didn't hear the terrified screams of the wounded, see the torn bodies, or smell the stench of death.

"Would it be alright if I had a bed out on the deck?" I asked the young corpsman that attended me. "I think I would do much better out on the deck in the open air."

"We're getting crowded in here," he replied. "I'll get a cot and move you out."

I was on the hospital ship USS Relief for another month. All the time I stayed on that cot. The sound of the water swishing along the side of the moving ship, the gentle tropical breeze that moved across the deck, and the watching of the sea as it slowly passed by was a solace to my mind, even though I was in constant pain.

Gradually my body turned from red and purple to sick yellow, and then eventually to its natural color. The gash on my face, which had been caused by the shrapnel, healed enough so that the bandage could be removed. My legs still would not hold me, so I could not leave my deck-side bed without being carried. It would be four months before I could take my first faltering steps and a

141

couple of years before I could move without pain. I was in for a long recovery.

Two weeks before the USS Relief reached Hawaii, the ship held funeral services for thirteen men who had died since the ship left Kwajalein. I watched the burial at sea from my bed on the deck. The chaplain read a few passages of scripture, the bugle sounded, and one by one each ramp on which a shrouded body had been placed was lifted. The corpse splashed into the sea and disappeared. How the cards of life are dealt is such a mystery. For one there is the unexplained luck of the draw, for others there seems to be an empty hand.

Sometime in early April, the USS Relief docked at the Aloha Tower in Honolulu. A crowd of greeters stood on the dock waving and cheering and a military band played appropriately as the mobile injured soldiers paraded down the gangplank. All the men debarking wore clean and pressed uniforms—a far different scene than when they had come aboard a month before in their torn, bloody, and dirty clothes. They were the lucky ones. I had a good view of all the activity from my cot on the deck.

Soon the activity ceased and the crowd dispersed. The dock was quiet again. And then from my vantage point I watched as a dozen or so flag draped coffins were lowered to the dock from the rear of the ship and placed on a train of small trailers. The coffins were pulled away and taken out of sight by a dock tractor to a shed at the far end of the dock. These were the dead who almost made it home, but in the last days of the voyage could not hang on to life. There were no bands for them. They were more of the unlucky ones. What irony there is in this chancy thing we experience as life.

Later in the afternoon, the USS Relief left Honolulu and made the short passage to Pearl Harbor. There I was taken ashore and transported by naval ambulance to the Base 8 Navy Hospital, which consisted of a number of Quonset Huts, constructed on a series of terraces on the side of a hill overlooking Pearl Harbor. This was to be my home and place of healing for the next several months.

This was a difficult time for me. The pain in my left knee continued to increase, and this was discouraging. The only sleep I got for weeks was in fitful moments of exhaustion. I was not able to write, read, or leave my bed.

Later a thoughtful nurse finally wrote a letter home. When Joan received this word, she knew for the first time where I was and that we would eventually be reunited. Her long time of waiting for news of my condition was over.

Although so much flesh had been torn from my right ankle that it was difficult to heal, the tendons were still in tact. I knew that eventually I would be able to walk. It was my left leg that was bent at a thirty-degree angle that gave me such excruciating pain. The doctor had a hard time understanding this, because there was not a mark on my leg, but regardless it continually got worse. Finally, the doctor decided to put me under anesthetic and straighten out the leg by putting a cast on it. I found out later that putting a cast on my leg was the worst thing that the doctor could have done. Gentle and prolonged therapy would have been the right treatment.

Many months later I diagnosed, on the basis of own research, that my problem was Pellegrine's Disease in the left knee joint. The reason there was so much pain in the joint was that after a severe traumatism of the medial collateral ligament, in my case caused by the violent crash and the explosions, there follows the formation of a calcified mass at the site of the ligament injury. The process of dystrophic calcification does not show up in X-rays until many weeks after the injury. But during this prolonged time, the area remains very tender and extremely painful, the medical diagnosis proclaims. This condition lasts until the ossification of the mass occurs. It takes several months for the symptoms to subside and the new bone mass remains with the patient for the rest of his life.

This was certainly true in my case, and now after more than fifty years the X-rays of my left knee are the same as they were in 1944. Orthopedic doctors later confirmed that what I have stated is true, and it became the primary basis for my established disability. I must add that through my years of regular jogging and exercise I have been able to overcome the encumbrances of the injury. I still have negative feelings about the doctor who treated me at the naval hospital at Pearl Harbor. I am sure that putting my leg in a rigid cast caused increased and prolonged pain and delayed the healing process. However, the nurses and the attendant corpsmen were caring. Too, the insights I gained during the weeks I lived with these wounded soldiers and marines, brave men who had given so much for their country, have given me a life long understanding of valor.

One special memory will remain with me forever. Several weeks after I arrived at Pearl Harbor, Admiral Chester Nimitz, Commander of the Pacific Fleet, visited the hospital ward. What an impressive man he was—tall, snow-white hair, erect and trim. With a quiet and genuine compassion, he moved through the isles of wounded men. When he got to my bed he sat down.

"How did you get hurt?" he asked.

"It was just an operational accident, Sir."

"Well, Lieutenant, you were out there doing your job, and I know it's dangerous work. The country and I thank you for being there. God bless you."

This remains as one of the very special moments of my life. I was feeling like such a failure, and hurting so much both physically and psychologically, and now in this brief moment this powerful, but humble man helped me get my life back on track. I would have done anything for him. How I wish our country had more men of the stature of Admiral Chester Nimitz. He will always be my special hero.

My right leg, too, was slow in healing. I had lost a lot of flesh around the ankle area, and this had to fill in with new flesh and then cover with skin before I could walk. It was the injuries in both of my legs that kept me from getting up on my feet. This became increasingly discouraging because the doctor told me that I could not go back to the states until I could walk. It was not until June 1944 that I could stand. I kept working, and although still in pain I began to take a few steps. A couple of weeks later I received orders to board a ship in Honolulu bound for San Francisco. I was still very weak, but nothing now was going to stop me from catching that ship home.

The first night after I left Base 8, I stayed at Hospital Point near the entrance to Pearl Harbor. The facility had been remodeled for patients in transit and officers awaiting new assignments. The walk from the front into the lobby was a short distance, but for me the longest I had taken for several months. I was very weak and tired. The next morning I took a shuttle bus into Honolulu and boarded the navy transport that would take me home. As I came aboard, I saw several marine officers standing at the far rail of the ship with their backs toward me. Even from the rear, one of the flyers looked familiar. I thought, could that possibly be John Jaqua? "John?" He turned and sure enough, there he was. What a coincidence this was. Thousands of men moved back and forth from the United States to the war zone. Here was John Jaqua, my sister Rosamond's husband, and we were returning home on the same ship.

I had not seen John since operational training at the Opa Locka Naval Air Station in Florida eighteen months before. He had been ordered to the Solomon Islands, with his best friend James Boyden, as replacement pilots for Marine Bombing Squadron VMVT 233. This squadron, flying TBM *Avengers,* lost more pilots on the push up through the Solomon Islands to Rabaul than any other marine squadron in the history of warfare. Now, returning to the States after three six-week tours of combat, were the less than a dozen of the eighty pilots who had engaged the Japanese. John's personal story is told in a subsequent chapter of this book.

I remember little of the details of the voyage home. The pain I experienced made sleep or rest almost impossible. I existed in a fog born of fatigue. On the positive side, my legs did get stronger and I could walk for longer distances, even though my left leg was in a walking cast. I do remember what for me was a dramatic entrance into San Francisco Bay. We sailed under the Golden Gate Bridge. To the starboard, on a point of the historic San Francisco Presidio, a giant American flag fluttered in the gentle breeze. The living members of VMVT 233, including Marine Captain John Jaqua, stood in silence on the bow of the ship. Every flyer's eye was on that flag as the ship passed. Not a word was exchanged between the pilots. I sensed that each man was in deep emotional thought. A home was now in reach, a loving reunion that for so many terrifying weeks had remained remote.

As soon as we docked, John and I called our wives to let them know that we were in San Francisco. I took the train that night and arrived in Los Angeles the next morning. Joan and Mother and Pop

145

were there to meet me. The sprawling arch and tiled Los Angeles station was a center for many emotional good-byes and homecomings during the years of World War II. The reunion with Joan and my parents lives as a special treasure in my life.

There were a few days before I had to check into the Long Beach Naval Hospital. Because I was now ambulatory, I could live at home. Joan was able to rent a seashore apartment near Bixby Park in Long Beach. It was a wonderful place to heal and a treasured retreat from the reality of the war that continued to rage far across the Pacific. For many sunlit hours we laid on the sand, my thoughts often drifting out across the blue peaceful waters that dissipated rhythmically on the shore. Where were the men of my old squadron now? Would I ever see any of them again?

*   *   *

It was during this time I was in Long Beach that the invasion of Europe by the allied forces happened. That the British and American armed forces would eventually carry the war into Germany was a part of the long-range strategy from the very beginning of the war in Europe. By the middle of 1944 the axis powers were on the defensive on all fronts. American forces were on the move against Japan in the Pacific. Italy was defeated and out of the war. The Allies entered Rome on June 4th. On Germany's eastern front the Russians were poised at the southeastern corner of Poland, ready for the assault on Warsaw. Our bombers were reducing Germany's cities and industries to shambles. The German U-boats in the Atlantic were being held at bay by our sea forces.

Then on June 6, 1944 the news came over the radio that the long awaited assault by our forces on the continent of Europe was underway. It was a tense and apprehensive time for us as bits and pieces of the news trickled in. We had reason to be concerned. My brother Charles was an officer on the cruiser USS Tuscaloosa. His battle station was in the main engine room where he would be sealed off from the outside world during the attack—a dangerous and frightening place to be during an exchange of gunfire with the Germans, and that there would be.

The largest amphibious assault in the history of the world was underway, preceded the night before by the largest airborne operation ever conducted. The air assault was a vital part of the larger assault from the sea. The German planes had been knocked from the sky. Now our planes were parachuting soldiers in behind the landing beachheads so that the Germans could not reinforce and supply their troops in those areas along the coast where the allied forces were landing. If the enemy controlled the access roads to these sections of the coast the landing force would be bottled up in its beachhead.

That was the tactic being used at Utah beach where the Americans were scheduled to land. We found out later that that was where my brother Charles was fighting on this historic day. Beginning before dawn, heavy, medium, and fighter-bombers worked over the beach defenses. At daybreak the warships, including the Tuscaloosa, opened the naval bombardment. The assault waves formed and the landing craft began the run for the beaches. The seas were rough. Some craft were swamped, but through it all the allied forces established their positions on shore and carried their fight directly to the Germans. It was a day that all living Americans would remember forever.

*   *   *

On the thirteenth day of July 1944, still not completely recovered from my injuries, the next chapter in my life began. I received orders from the Bureau of Naval Personnel that read as follows:

> *Upon discharge from treatment at the Naval Hospital Long Beach, California, report to the Commandant, Twelfth Naval District, for first available government transportation to the U.S.S. Suwannee (CVE 27) and upon arrival report to the Commanding Officer of that vessel for duty involving flying.*

The days that followed were, in that cliché, "bittersweet". Joan and I had two weeks before I would leave on my second tour of duty. We held no illusions this time about the weeks of separation that again loomed ahead. The reality of continued combat was grim—not an expectant adventure.

Joan and I drove north and stopped for a few days at the old Corona del Valle ranch for a visit with Dad Gould. Then we said another goodbye and went on for an overnight visit at Sequoia National Park. During the war there were few visitors. We were almost alone as we walked through the giant forest, looking up and up to the tops of the trees that laced the blue sky above. How far away the war seemed, as we strolled together under this majestic celestial canopy of tranquillity.

When we reached San Francisco, we checked into the historic St Francis Hotel off Union Square. My directions were to stay there and report each morning to the commandant's office to see if embarking orders had arrived. If the orders had not arrived, then Joan and I would have another twenty-four hours together. It was an uncertain and unnerving time for us. We never knew what day would be our last together. This daily routine went on for more than a week, but eventually it ended. Orders came to report to a ship docked across the bay at Alameda. Joan drove us over the Oakland-Bay Bridge to the naval yard in Alameda, where an old refrigerator ship was busily being loaded with supplies and readying for departure. We walked under the shed-covered dock and there in the shadow shared a quiet goodbye. Our hearts were heavy. But Joan, the loving trooper she has always been, seemed to sense that this would be only another separation. She would wait for my return, and then perhaps we could get on with our lives. I walked up the gangplank, boarded the old ship and turned for one last glance as Joan waved farewell. This surely was the saddest day of my life.

Telegram Received By
Joan Robinson
Wife of F. W. Robinson, Lt. USNR

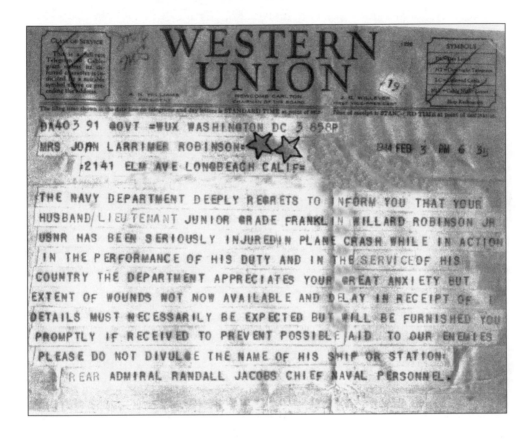

WESTERN UNION

DA403 91 GOVT =WUX WASHINGTON DC 3 858P

MRS JOAN LARRIMER ROBINSON=   DM FEB 3 PM 6 55

2141 ELM AVE LONGBEACH CALIF=

THE NAVY DEPARTMENT DEEPLY REGRETS TO INFORM YOU THAT YOUR
HUSBAND LIEUTENANT JUNIOR GRADE FRANKLIN WILLARD ROBINSON JR
USNR HAS BEEN SERIOUSLY INJURED IN PLANE CRASH WHILE IN ACTION
IN THE PERFORMANCE OF HIS DUTY AND IN THE SERVICE OF HIS
COUNTRY THE DEPARTMENT APPRECIATES YOUR GREAT ANXIETY BUT
EXTENT OF WOUNDS NOT NOW AVAILABLE AND DELAY IN RECEIPT OF
DETAILS MUST NECESSARILY BE EXPECTED BUT WILL BE FURNISHED YOU
PROMPTLY IF RECEIVED TO PREVENT POSSIBLE AID TO OUR ENEMIES
PLEASE DO NOT DIVULGE THE NAME OF HIS SHIP OR STATION=
REAR ADMIRAL RANDALL JACOBS CHIEF NAVAL PERSONNEL.

COPY OF MEDICAL TAG

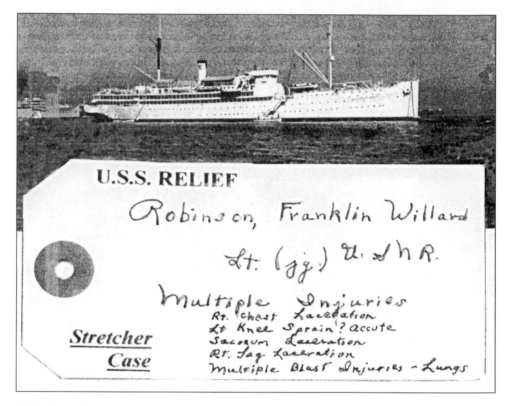

This is a picture of the hospital ship USS Relief and a copy of the tag that was on the stretcher when Lt. F. W. Robinson was transferred from the ship to Base 8 Navy Hospital in Pearl Harbor, Hawaii.

10

RETURN TO THE SOUTH PACIFIC WAR

It was late afternoon when the ship passed under the Golden Gate Bridge and headed into the open sea. Soon the continental swells lifted and dropped the heavily laden vessel in a rhythmic pattern that was disquieting to many of us who had not regained our sea legs.

For the first time I began to take inventory of the situation. I was on a refrigerator ship of some age, apparently taken over by the navy to supply their ships and bases in the far reaches of the Pacific with perishable supplies. It was a slow old boat and we would be in for a long voyage. I had no inkling where we were going during the first week at sea. Sometime during the second week, word was passed throughout the ship that we were bound for Manus in the Admiralty Islands in the Territory of New Guinea. I had never heard of the place, but was certain that it must be a long long way from the United States.

There was no one on the ship I knew, but as the days passed in quiet monotony, I made a few acquaintances. For twenty-two consecutive days we moved through a calm ocean at a speed of no more than ten knots. Neither another ship nor sight of a distant land horizon came into view. There was aloneness in this passage, an unreality when put in context with the war I knew was escalating somewhere out across the Pacific.

Then on the twenty-third day at sea, we passed a tropical island. On the port side was Guadalcanal, where on August 1942 the 1st Marine Division made the first amphibious assault of the war. The operation had been hastily planned as a needed attempt to stop the Japanese forces on their southward advance in an attempt to capture Australia and its surrounding territories. The ensuing battles, under the most difficult of situations, lasted for months in a grueling war of attrition.

Many of my friends had been involved in the Solomon Islands campaign. Bill Hayter from Long Beach, California and a member of my Sunday School class at the Grace Methodist Church, had led a marine division of *Dauntless* dive bombers on a stormy night attack against Japanese shipping that was moving against the American forces. These marine flyers were never heard from again, victims of a fierce Pacific storm that poured rain over the area with such intensity that all who flew that tragic night had no chance for a safe return.

And then my thoughts, too, were of my good friend Pat Patterson, sent to the Solomon Island campaign with the first F6F *Hellcat* fighters. Soon after, word reached us that Pat was last seen with Japanese *Zero* firing on his tail. He was never found. I recalled our days together at the University of Southern California, and then through training at Long Beach, Corpus Christi and Seattle. Later I would visit Pat's distraught mother who lived in Hollywood. She always hung on to the fantasy that someday her son would return.

My brother-in-law, John Jaqua, had flown off Guadalcanal in TBM torpedo bombers with Marine Squadron 233. It was that island off our port bow from which they had begun the push north up along the Solomon Island chain, through New Georgia and on to Bougainville. From there they launched their final attacks against

152

the fortress of Rabaul. Now the islands were quiet. The war had moved west to where our forces now were poised for the forthcoming attack to reclaim the Philippines.

Three days later we caught our first glimpse of the northeast coast of New Guinea. Now, after the better part of the month in passage, I was transferred to the United States aircraft carrier Suwanee as a replacement pilot. The carrier had seen a lot of action that included the North African landings in 1942, Runnel Island and the Gilbert Islands in 1943, and in 1944 the Marshall Islands, Palau, Marianas and Western New Guinea. Now an attack on Peleliu in the northern island territory of New Guinea was underway.

Here was the situation in the battle of Peleliu when I arrived. Most people have never heard of Peleliu, a rock bound island with several Japanese airfields in the southern Palaus island group. Air resistance had been knocked out early in the campaign, but it also became evident that this was to become one of the most costly and unnecessary land campaigns in the Pacific war. It made sense to neutralize the airfields because they were a threat to the flank of the United States forces that would move into the Philippines from Ulithi in the Caroline Islands. The battle for Peleiu began in the last days of September and dragged on until the end of November. Almost 2,000 Americans were killed in the grueling battle. Peleliu was an island of coral and limestone that had been thrust up in some prehistoric time, forming precipitous cliffs and contorted ridges. The island was full of underground rock faults and a labyrinth of caves.

The Japanese had enlarged and improved the caves, fissures, and faults, and they formed the basis of their defensive system. The Japanese efforts to defeat previous amphibious landings on other beaches had met complete failure, and the desperate banzi attacks had merely hastened the end of resistance. On Peleliu they used a different tactic. Colonel Nakagawa was in command. His aim was to delay the invaders for as long as possible. No man or weapon was ever needlessly exposed. The caves, with multiple entrances and connecting passageways, were planned to be almost unassailable. The marines would blast one cave entrance while the Japanese merely scooted to safety through another exit on the other side of the ridge. The Americans were vulnerable, for the coral surface of Peleliu had so little topsoil the men could not dig foxholes for protection. The island was gradually cleared, but the new Japanese tactics were a preview for the coming battles for Iwo Jima and Okinawa. Our planes were of little help at this stage of the battle, for all enemy air power had been knocked out prior to the actual invasion and there was nothing really left to bomb or destroy. Further bombing would have only held up our forces and put our own supplies, already landed on the beach, in jeopardy. For the short time I was on the Suwanee, I did not even get a chance to fly. The strange part of it all was that in January 1948, long after the end of the war, I received a letter from the Chief of Naval Personnel, Washington D.C. that stated:

> *By virtue of your service on the Suwanee and her attached Air Squadron you are awarded the Presidential Unit Citation for extraordinary heroism in action against enemy forces in the air, ashore and afloat. The Suwanee's valiant record of combat achievement reflects the highest credit upon her courageous officers and men.*

I never wore this ribbon on my uniform, as I did not feel qualified for this special honor.

The staging and supply area for our ships in preparation for the Philippine invasions was Seeadler Harbor in the Admiralty Islands. This had been the hideout of the famed German U-boat commander, Von Licktenburg, during World War I. The water was so clear that while passing through the inlet to the huge protected harbor, I could actually see the coral and seashells glittering on the ocean floor. It was the most beautiful and clear water I had ever seen. While we were anchored at Manus in the Admiralty Islands, the squadron doctor recommended that I have my left knee reexamined at the Naval Base Hospital #15. The Quonset hut hospital was located a couple of miles from the ship along a beautiful jungle bordered road where natives lived in their palm-thatched huts. The X-rays taken at the hospital confirmed that during the weeks at sea the process of calcification had continued from the effects of the trauma of the crash I had suffered in the

Marshall Islands campaign. The pictures confirmed that I had Pellegrini disease in the knee and that although the intense pain had subsided, the limited flexibility of the knee joint was a hindrance to effective shipboard duty.

I was at Base 15 Navy Hospital for almost a month. During this time the wounded from the complicated occupation operation at Peleliu continued to be brought in. They were the survivors of the 1st Marine Division that I learned had borne the brunt of the initial landings on Guadalcanal many months before and later the invasion of Cape Gloucester. These men had left the United States shortly after the Japanese attack on Pearl Harbor, had lost many of their comrades in the brutal jungle battles that followed, and now in the early fall of 1944 had fought from cave to cave in the rock bound island of Peleliu. To ask anyone to make such a sacrifice was to me inhuman. I felt deep compassion for these valiant marines who had given and lost so much.

I met another navy flyer in the hospital. He was Bill Barnett who had been flying PBY flying boats for many months in the New Guinea and the Solomon Islands since early in the war. He had been a member of the famous *Black Cat* squadron, flying many and varied missions, including rescuing downed flyers in enemy territory. He was exhausted and emotionally spent as a result of this prolonged assignment that had been culminated by the loss of his plane on his final mission.

Later, when Lt. William Barnett and I were transferred from the navy hospital in Manus to one back in San Diego, we were fortunate to return together.

Bill and I took off in an R4D transport one late afternoon from the Los Negros airfield in the Admiralty Islands. The plane leveled off at an altitude of about 12,000 feet. We were wearing light tropical uniforms and at this altitude, seated in the metal seats along the bulkhead, we were cold. During the night, the plane hit an intense tropical storm. The sky flashed with lightning, streaking the leading edge of the wings with fire and circulating the throbbing engines with celestial light. With each successive flash, the frightening routine was repeated. The wings of the plane actually flapped as a giant bird struggling in flight.

155

"Do you think we will make it Bill?" I asked. He was experienced in flying at night through these tropical storms.

"I hope so." He replied. "We're over the Caroline Islands and they're still held by the *Japs*."

"Well, that's reassuring. That's all I need to hear," I answered in a somewhat sarcastic way.

About midnight we landed at Kwajalein in the Marshall Islands for refueling. Even in the darkness I could tell the place had gone through a tremendous transformation since I had first seen it about seven months before. An airfield and extensive support facilities had been constructed on the atoll. Not a single palm tree had been left unscathed under the tremendous attack earlier in the year. When I had first seen the island, the soft foliage of the coconut palms covered it. Now it was a military base devoid of beauty. Not a palm tree was in sight. Apparently, too, the debris of war had been buried under an endless cement slab of the runways.

Shortly after midnight we took off again on the second leg of the flight that would take us to Johnston Island, another little lonely atoll slightly higher than the ocean itself. In the early dawn the plane made its descent over the sea flooded coral reefs, habited by vast flocks of sea birds. We landed on the remote Johnston Island airstrip for another refueling stop. Soon we were in the air again, bound for Hawaii and landed near Honolulu on the afternoon of October 8th, 1944.

Four days later, Bill Barnett and I were on the aircraft carrier USS Ranger, bound for San Diego and home. It was a fast passage and for the first time at sea we enjoyed the luxury of our own officer's cabin.

"Bill," I said. "I know our orders state that we are to report to the San Diego Naval Hospital. That's such a busy place now and I know from experience that we could go on up to the Long Beach Naval Hospital. That would be a much better place for us."

"Sounds good to me," he responded. "Let's go."

The Ranger docked on the channel at the north side of the North Island Naval Air Station. A large contingent of friends and relatives stood on the dock, greeting the returning seamen as they debarked from the ship. Bill and I did not tarry. We both went to the closest phones and called our wives.

"Joan, we've just landed in San Diego. Why don't you drive down as far as Santa Ana and we will meet you at the train station? We should be there by 5:00".

"Wonderful," she responded. "I'll be there."

Bill had said farewell to his wife almost two years before on the dock in San Francisco, as he left for Australia and the war. Dorothy returned to Billings, Montana to wait out the lonely months, hoping that he would survive and someday return. They had been married only a month before this separation.

"I got her on the phone," Bill said. She is going to come on the train to Los Angeles."

We boarded the ferry and crossed the channel from Coronado to San Diego. From there it was a short distance to the train station. We were soon on our way to reunions that only those who have been separated in times of war can truly relate. Never again would I be ordered to combat duty.

11

THE LAST MONTHS OF WORLD WAR II

On the 25th day of October 1944, I reported to the Long Beach Naval Hospital for continued treatment of my crash injuries. I was under medical supervision from November until January 1945. During the time that I was in Long Beach, far across the Pacific the greatest naval battle in the history of the world took place. It was the Battle of Leyte Gulf. I had missed this historic engagement on the high seas for recontrol of the Philippine Islands.

Now, over fifty years later, I still wonder about my feelings in not being a part of this important action. Fate always took me close to these great conflicts, and then at the last moment pulled me away. My mother was clearer, "God has a reason", she said. "You are being saved for something special." My escapes from death did seem to confirm this, but there was a frustration, too, that I have never completely resolved. I am human enough to have wanted to be a legitimate war hero, but realistic enough to give thanks that I wasn't going to be a dead hero. I still wonder how my life would have turned out had I been on either the Manila Bay or the Suwannee during the violent and crucial battle of the eastern Philippines. The dreaded Kamikazi planes in their suicide dives critically hit both these carriers that had been my home for a period of time that same year.

The Manila Bay was one of the heroic little carriers that stood fast off San Bernardino Strait and turned back a large Japanese battle fleet to save the U. S. landing forces as they embarked to regain the Philippines from the Japanese. During this engagement two Kamikaze planes crashed with their bombs on the flight deck. In the melee ten were killed and eighty were wounded. The ship's crew shot down five Japanese planes and the pilots had fifteen more kills in the sky.

The Suwannee, the carrier I had just left a few weeks before, was twice hit and severely damaged by these Japanese suicide planes during the battle for Leyte Gulf on October 23rd. Although many of the crewmembers were left dead and wounded, the Suwannee continued to aggressively take the fight to the enemy. Her guns and the pilots who were in the air, against tremendous odds, ended the battle with the complete rout of the Japanese ships. These two little carriers, from which I flew, had a major role in the defeat of the Japanese forces in the final months of the Pacific war.

*   *   *

Simultaneously, during the summer and fall of 1944, the American forces carried out their assault on Saipan in the Mariana Islands. The Japanese had controlled this island for many years and would defend it as if it were their homeland. On June 14, 1944 the 2nd and 4th Marine Divisions began the action. It soon became apparent that fighting was going to be severe and prolonged. As Japan sent a large surface fleet to support their beleaguered defenders, Admiral Spruance deployed his stronger naval force against the enemy and gave Japan a resounding defeat. That day the Japanese lost 300 planes. The Americans lost thirty. It was the most one-sided carrier air battle of the war, forever to be referred to in history as the Great Marianas Turkey Shoot. But it had been a costly campaign on the ground. More than 3,400 Americans had been killed and 13,000 wounded. Over 24,000 Japanese gave their lives in the defense of Saipan. This capture of Japanese territory was significant, because for the first time U.S. long range bombers could now hit the mainland of Japan. It was from the Mariana Islands the following summer that the Enola Gay, a B-29 long-range bomber, took off for the atomic bomb drop on Hiroshima.

Meanwhile, in Europe, the allied forces continued their advance from the beaches at Normandy up through France and into Belgium to the German border. It was then that Hitler decided that the German army would end the year 1944, a year of unbroken reversals for him, with a dramatic offensive in the west. On December 16th three German armies began assaulting the American lines on a seventy-mile front into Belgium. This campaign would become known in history as the Battle of the Bulge.

I was still in the Long Beach Naval Hospital, and we followed these dramatic events as Christmas 1944 approached. By December 19th, the shape of the German penetration was clear. General Eisenhower and his commanders conferred to plan countermeasures. On the 23rd the weather cleared. Cargo planes dropped ammunition and supplies around Bastogne where the major forces faced each other. Fighter and bomber planes began working over the German columns crowding the roads, and the heavy U.S. bombers began striking back at supply routes and the rear staging areas. December 26th brought the crest of the German advance. What a tense Christmas this was for our country, for so many of our soldiers and airmen were involved in this bloody and perilous fight. The long casualty lists that appeared in the paper each day brought a stark reality and a deep grieving in our nation. Too, we knew that what had happened to our forces in Germany was only the forerunner of what would happen when the United States invaded Japan. It had been a long war of continual carnage. In the Battle of the Bulge the Germans had penetrated the allied lines for a depth of sixty miles. Casualties on both sides were high,

7,000 for the allies and more than 100,000 for the Germans. The Western Allied Offensive into Germany had been delayed, for it took most of January to regain the territory lost and resume the advance to the Rhine River. The American forces did not achieve that crossing into Germany until March 23, 1945. By that time the Russian offensive in the east steamrolled toward Berlin. The reserves with which the Germans might have stopped the Russians had been destroyed in the Battle of the Bulge.

*   *   *

In January 1945, I was released from the Long Beach Naval Hospital and received orders to report to the Auxiliary Naval Air Station in Holtville, California. This was the base where in the summer of 1943 our squadron, VC-7, had trained in specialized night attack bombing. The airfield was located in the lower Imperial Valley between El Centro and Yuma, Arizona, bordering the fascinating sand dunes that constantly shift in the wind. The dunes extend over a large portion of this vast desert area. My orders read:

> *25 January 1945*
> *Report for assignment*
> *Assistant Operations Officer,*
> *Naval Auxiliary Air Station.*
> *Holtville, California.*
> *For duties that include administration*
> *and experimental test flying.*

This was good news! Joan and I would be together for an assured period of time. We left Long Beach in our 1939 Ford coupe and began the 220-mile drive through the San Gorgonio Pass, by Palm Springs, and along the west side of the Salton Sea. It was a familiar journey that we had made just a little over nine months before when our squadron, VC-31, had been transferred from Seattle to El Centro. But a lifetime had passed during those preceding months. Now we were beginning a new chapter—a new adventure together. Before dark we arrived at the wind-swept forlorn little hamlet of Holtville, California. We were under no delusion. Life would be difficult here on the desert, but we were thankful, even in the midst of the uncertainties we faced. Housing was a major problem. Nothing was available for us. The first week we lived in a little shack motel on the highway to Yuma. I am sure our room served as a stop for the "Okies" when a few years before these desperate farmers and their families, in their old jalopies, left the Oklahoma Dust Bowl and stormed the agricultural areas of California.

Eventually, I was able to rent a little old house in El Centro, some sixteen miles west of the base. We were lucky and thrilled to find a place we could call home. Immediately, Joan went to work cleaning, painting, and arranging the few belongings we had to make the place livable. She was such a trooper! No woman should ever have to endure the uprooting, the emotional traumas, and the uncertainties she dealt with during the months that had followed our marriage in Seattle scarcely two years before. Now Joan was carrying our first child. Gail would be born the following November.

There was no air conditioning in those days. In El Centro, during the summer, the temperatures regularly reach 110 degrees or above. I remember a scorching 122 degrees in our flight ready-room at the base. I always wore gloves when I climbed into the cockpit of a plane during that summer heat. Without protection the metal would burn a pilot's hands. I remember Joan sitting in the yard of our El Centro house, holding a hose over her head and letting the tepid water flow down over her protruding body in a valiant attempt to get a little cooler. It was a terrible time to be pregnant.

My assignment at the base was varied and interesting. Squadrons preparing to leave for the war came for short periods to intensively train before departing on their assigned aircraft carrier. The Holtville Naval Station was primarily a night training base where the pilots could hone those specialized attack skills. It was dangerous flying, especially the low level attacks on Salton Sea targets, and we did lose several flyers while I was at Holtville. One night two different planes hit the water and disintegrated. Both pilots were killed, victims we presumed of vertigo, training and

163

flying without lights in formation, as would be required in night combat. Both pilots had been married for a short time and it was our duty to notify the new widows.

The base was open for flight twenty-four hours a day. An operations officer had to be on duty throughout this time, so I rotated on the night shift. The night work was preferable, except for the fact that Joan was home alone. Also, it was too hot to sleep during the day.

Besides being in charge of the flight operations when I was on duty, I had the challenging responsibility as the test pilot for the air station. Whenever a plane was damaged and then fixed in our base shop, it became my responsibility to take the plane on a test flight. My job was to validate the plane as ready for operational service with the squadrons. This was a challenging assignment. For the first time in my naval career I now flew the current fighter and bomber planes that were taking the air from the United States aircraft carriers on the strikes against Japan. There were older models of combat planes that were also tested at the base. While in Holtville I flew the TBM *Avenger*, the SBD *Dauntless*, the FM2 *Wildcat*, the SB2C *Helldiver*, the F6F *Hellcat*, and the F4U *Corsair*. For me, it was a tremendous opportunity to fly this array of world-class navy bomber and fighter planes. There was exhilaration in wringing out the war birds in the clear desert skies above the Imperial Valley.

Another interesting assignment, as an operations officer for the base, was to investigate the circumstances of plane crashes when they occurred. On one occasion a pilot lost control of his fighter plane, for some reason, and bailed out at about 8,000 feet. The plane went into a step dive and plunged into the rocky earth in the north escarpments of the Chocolate Mountains fifty miles northeast of the base. We had an operational Piper Cub assigned for rescue and search missions. So, I took off and eventually sighted a black scar in the rocks that I suspected was the crash sight. I was able to land the little plane in a restricted opening in the rock and cactus strewn terrain. It was a short walk across a gully to the spot I had seen from the air. I had found the right location. There in the bottom of a ten-foot hole of blasted rock was the pulverized aircraft engine. There was not a piece of the plane left that I could not have picked up in my hands. The force of the crash disintegrated the plane. Fortunately, the pilot had bailed out of the plane and survived the crash. Not all of our pilots were so fortunate.

Two of our fighter planes collided in the air. One of the damaged planes returned to base, but the other one was so badly damaged that the pilot had to bail out. This happened over the vast sand dune area just northeast of Holtville. It was approaching summer and the heat was intense. We had no way, at that time, to get rescue equipment into the area. The injured pilot could not reach the water we dropped near him. He died of thirst in the blowing sand. In this day and age he would have been rescued by helicopter. Had the war lasted another six months I would have been sent to the East Coast to ferry a new helicopter back to the Holtville Naval Air Station to be used in just such rescue missions. That had been the recommendation of our Commanding Officer after this tragic event.

*   *   *

At the end of February 1945, news came that our forces were on the attack at Iwo Jima. For the Japanese, the defense of Iwo Jima was again the defense of their homeland. The Americans wanted Iwo as an advance air base for the support of the B-29's flying out of the Marianas on their bombing and fire raids to the heart of Japan. Not only would the Iwo base make it possible to provide fighter escort to Japan for the Superforts, but also an emergency landing field on the island would save many crippled planes and pilots from a possible fatal forced landing in the sea.

The fight for this little eight square mile island became most difficult. We began to receive troubling news concerning the campaign. Iwo Jima is composed of black volcanic ash, rough ridges, gorges, and steaming fissures in rocks that are still being forced up from the sea. In their labyrinth of tunnels and caves the Japanese soldiers fought to the last man. Before the island was secured, 28,000 Japanese soldiers and American marines died. My brother Chuck, Engineering Officer on the heavy cruiser Tuscaloosa was there. His ship kept blasting the Japanese batteries and doing what they could to support the valiant marines. Chuck had made the long passage from Europe to participate in this action.

By the first of March half of the island was in American hands. Tanks, flame-throwers, rockets, demolitions, and the fire of supporting war ships gradually overcame Mount Suribachi; the highest point on the island, bristling with emplaced weapons and riddled with caves and passageways. Finally, a patrol of forty men, ordered to seize the crest, worked their way up the face of the mountain. On the summit they raised the flag. A photographer was there to record the historic moment. This is now probably the most famous picture of World War II. The scene was immortalized in a giant bronze statue near Arlington Cemetery and Washington D.C. As the mopping up on Iwo Jima began, we received news that our forces had invaded Okinawa. This was April 1, 1945.

*   *   *

During the later part of April, Joan and I had an opportunity for a short leave, so we drove home to Long Beach to spend a long weekend with Joan's folks. These were special times for us. Good families are always important, but in wartime these loving contacts exhumed special warmth and pathos. On April 24th we said goodbye and began the drive back to El Centro. On our way we stopped to visit my mother who was living in Desert Hot Springs.

Mother spent extended periods in the desert during the years that her boys were in military service. It was her way of coping, a kind of escape from the realities of the world, as she experienced them. She had rented a small cement block cabin on the outskirts of Desert Hot Springs, across the valley from Palm Springs and the towering escarpment of Mt. San Jacinto. My mother wrote:

> *I lived in a one-room cabin for two months and have no doubt that it was, as old-timers said, the windiest spring they had ever seen. The streets were unpaved. The wind would pick up sand and gravel and throw it against the windows, setting up such a clatter that I could imagine myself a thousand miles from habitation.*

166

But the wind did not blow every day. There were times when it was breathlessly still. The sun was mild and warm and the tiny flowers opened, carpeting the desert, white, pink and yellow.

I would face Mt. San Jacinto, a sheer monument capped with snow. Through the pass into the Los Angeles basin long trains moved day after day carrying materials for war, and overhead airplane motors throbbed, muted by the distance. The war was in full swing with all of its destruction and killing. But day-by-day it all grew more and more impersonal to me. When I came to the desert, I was weary with the world. Now I was a captive of the wind, the sand and the rock. I was finding a peace.

Joan and I arrived at Mother's humble cabin. She had cookies and prepared a cup of tea. Our time with her was tender . . . as rare morning dew, clinging to a desert flower.

Shortly, we were on our way again. Little did we realize then that this was to be another historic day. I remember it clearly. As we drove along the highway on the western side of the Salton Sea, the startling news came over our car radio that Franklin Roosevelt, President of the United States, had died suddenly in Warm Springs, Georgia. He had started his unprecedented fourth term as president, and was the recognized leader of the free world. He was a man of great charisma to most Americans, and he established policies during the great depression that would forever change the course of our nation. Two months before he had met with Churchill and Stalin at Yalta for the last of their Big Three conferences where plans had been made for the final phases of the war. Since that time his health had been failing, but his death did come as a shock. Harry S. Truman, taking up the task of guiding the nation, pledged his continued support of Roosevelt's war and peace policies. Joan and I arrived back at our little El Centro home that evening.

April was a beautiful month in the Imperial Valley. By this time I had become familiar with my job. I especially enjoyed taking the planes high in the air, where it was safe to spin, roll, snap and loop with abandon. There was such exhilaration in commanding a high-powered modern fighter plane through aerobatics. The FM-2 *Wildcat* fighter is the only plane I ever flew that could do continuous loops and still gain altitude. One day I took this little plane into an

167

inverted spin. We were at about 10,000 feet. Centrifugal force tried to pull my hands and feet away from the controls. It was violent through a 4,000-foot spin toward the earth. I reversed all my controls, a standard procedure for recovery, and the wonderful little plane responded. It was ready to go to war.

Good news came to me on May 1st, 1945. I had been appointed to the rank of Lieutenant (Sr. grade) USNR with the continued designation: Naval Aviator. This not only meant a little more pay, but no longer would I be considered a junior officer. I pinned the double silver bars on the tips of my collar with pride.

*   *   *

By the end of April, 1945 the Western Allies reached the Elbe and the Russians drew closer to Berlin. Hitler still refused to capitulate to end the suffering and death of the German people. He had taken refuge in a concrete bunker deep underground, but his followers had deserted him. Germany surrendered on April 29, 1945. A million Germans laid down their arms. The war with Germany was over. Hitler killed himself the next day. America celebrated with joy. But that joy was tempered. Americans still faced the reality of the desperate days that lay ahead before the unconditional surrender of Japan could ever become a reality.

While all of this was going on in April of 1945, another major development was taking place. It was the most tightly guarded secret of the war. Allied scientists had built an atomic bomb! When Truman became President, the bomb was ready. Truman and his advisors felt that by dropping the bomb on Japan the sudden shock, emphasizing the futility of continued resistance, would cause the Japanese to surrender. On July 26th a joint ultimatum, known as the Potsdam Declaration, issued by Truman of the United States, Churchill of England, and Chiang Kai-shek of China, warned Japan of the uselessness of continued resistance. The Declaration ended with the warning that Japan's alternative to surrender was "prompt and utter destruction." The Japanese chose to ignore the Potsdam Declaration and the stage was set for the drop of the atom bomb.

Of course we didn't know anything about this development at

that time. As far as the military personnel knew the preparations for the culminating attack on Japan itself was underway, which it was. In the Marianas, General Spaatz, Commanding General of the U.S. Army Strategic Air Forces, had received orders to deliver the bomb as soon as weather would permit visual location of the target area. The target was Hiroshima, Japan's eighth largest city, a military port and the headquarters of sizable army forces, and the home of war industries. The Enola Gay, a B-29, operating out of the Marianas, carried the atom bomb. It was dropped on August 6, 1945. It exploded with the force of twenty thousand tons of TNT.

Despite the death and destruction that was wrought, the Japanese would not surrender, even after the United States sent another ultimatum warning them of the ruin they faced. Three days later the second bomb was dropped on Nagasaki. The Emperor called an Imperial Conference and directed the government to accept the allied terms. Word of surrender reached Washington on the afternoon of August 14th. We heard the electrifying news that same afternoon.

Here were my circumstances at the time of this historical surrender. A navy medical board had sent orders that I was due for a routine medical check up. I went to report to the San Diego Naval Hospital. It would not be necessary for me to stay in the hospital, so Joan and I rented a motel cabin in the little town of Alpine some thirty miles east of San Diego. On this historic day, later known in history as VJ Day, we heard horns blowing and the town's sirens screaming.

"What's all that?" Joan asked.

"I don't know. Maybe the war is over," I said, almost in jest. But we soon found out that Japan had surrendered and the war really was over. It was a time of great celebration that lasted well into the night. The San Diego area was a major staging point for naval and marine personnel that had been slated to join those already on the approaching islands to Japan for the final great assault of the war. Now they would not be needed. World War II was over!

*   *   *

As I sit here today and write of this event, over fifty years have passed. I am disturbed that some of today's so-called historians are trying to alter the historical facts as we experienced them in the summer of 1945. "Historical revisionists", as they are called, take the position that the atom bombs should never have been dropped; that the United States was in error. You never hear them say, that as tragic as the consequences of those explosions were, thousands of American and Japanese lives were eventually saved. The carnage from an Allied invasion of Japan is incomprehensible. From that horrendous disaster, we all had been spared.

*   *   *

Getting out of the navy took a lot longer for me than getting in. My final release did not come until the 30th of November, 1945. I had to go through a series of medical reviews that included orders to the San Diego Naval Hospital and eventually transfer to the Long Beach Naval Hospital. Fortunately, I was not confined to the hospitals, and on most days only had to make the 9:00 A.M. musters. We lived for a number of weeks at my parent's home in Long Beach and I actually made the drive each day to San Diego, where I was required to stand for muster. Fortunately, I was soon transferred to the Long Beach Naval Hospital. I was there when our first child, a beautiful little girl we named Gail, was born in that same facility. Gail's arrival made our life complete. Joan and I were ready to get on with our lives; the care of a family that eventually included two more children, Franklin W. III, always called "Tri" and another wonderful little girl, Dana Hope.

Shortly after, we rented a new little house in Avalon Village a short distance north of Wilmington. From there I drove each morning to the University of Southern California campus where I had enrolled in classes that would qualify me for a War Emergency Teaching Credential. Actually, I was not officially released from the hospital until January 1946. A month later on February 27, 1946 I appeared before the Navy Review Board and was granted my request to be placed on inactive status in the United States Naval

Reserve. We were free at last, or so I thought, to get on with my life as a good husband and loving father to my little girl.

By the end of 1946 I had completed a home that we built at 5925 Troost Avenue in North Hollywood, and I had a challenging job as a teacher at Canoga Park High School. I continued working on my degrees and administrative credentials at U.S.C. I also kept up my flying skills by joining a reserve bombing squadron at the Los Alamitos Naval Air Station. It was a busy and demanding schedule.

"It's just too much," Joan said one day. "I think you need to quit that flying business and concentrate on your studies at USC. Your future is there, not in flying," she said.

I knew she was right, and although I loved the flying and the continued association with fellow navy pilots, there had been some frustration. Either because of bad weather, or the lack of an available plane to fly, I was only getting into the air about once each month. I was realistic enough to know that this was not enough flight time to maintain the skill needed to be a responsible pilot in these high-powered military planes. So, in February 1949 I drove once again from our home in North Hollywood to the Los Alamitos Naval Air Station for what I knew would be my last flight as a U.S. Naval Aviator.

The day was brilliant and an old TBM Grumman *Avenger* was waiting on the ramp ready to be mounted. I checked out a parachute and was cleared by operations for the flight. As the engine fired, I became flooded with nostalgia. Here I sat in the familiar cockpit, touching again the controls, hearing the unique drone of the 2600-horse power Wright rotary engine, feeling the elevators and the rudder respond to the stick in my hand as I made the final checks before taking to the air. This needed to be a special flight. As I rolled down the runway, heading into the prevailing westerly wind, the ground flashed by as the bomber picked up speed. Then the old familiar plane lifted me with authority into the clear sky. I would fly to the desert I knew so well. Soon I was flying through the Banning pass, marked on the north by Mt. San Gorgonio, and on the south by the shear wall of rock that towered upward to the snow capped summit of Mt. San Jacinto. Off to the northeast, lying there on the desert floor at the base of the Little San Bernardino Mountains was the little community of Desert Hot Springs.

Even at my altitude of 5,000 feet I could locate the house my parents had built in Cholla Gardens. Down I came at over two hundred miles an hour for what would be a final symbolic salute. There in the yard stood Pop. He raised his hand as the plane roared by. In a memorable way I had finished my last flight as a United States Navy Pilot.

*   *   *

Several days later I received a communication from the Secretary of the Navy:

In accordance with your request and by the direction of the President, your resignation from the U.S. Naval Reserve is hereby accepted under honorable conditions.

Navy Planes Flown by Lt. F.W. Robinson
1944 – 1945

SB2C Navy Dive Bomber (1945)

F4F *Wildcat* **Navy Fighter (1944-1945)**

Navy Planes flown by Lt. F.W. Robinson
1945 – 1946

Douglas SBD *Dauntless* Navy Dive Bomber (1945-1946)

Gumman *Hellcat* F6 Fighter (1945)

12

CHARLES W. ROBINSON, LIEUTENANT, USNR

In 1941 my brother Chuck Robinson graduated from the University of California at Berkeley with a degree in Economics. Ships had always held a fascination for him and I remember his desire to go to sea. He had volunteered for Navy Officer Training School, had been accepted and was to report to the Naval Academy in Annapolis, Maryland. He came to our home in Long Beach, California and asked me to take him to Terminal Island. He had gotten a job on an old ship that was docked there. It was operating as a tramp freighter picking up cargo as it moved north up the Pacific Coast for eventual return to the ports on the East Coast. This job would provide him with free passage to his date with the U.S. Navy.

I remember going aboard the ship with him. Right away I came to the conclusion that he was in for an unusual adventure. The ship was dirty, old and unkept and the crew looked very rough to me. I told him goodbye with some trepidation and wished him well. On December 6, 1941, as his ship approached Panama, a submarine passed by flying the Japanese flag. The following day, the infamous December 7th, just before reaching the Pacific entrance to the Panama Canal Chuck, by circumstance, heard a news broadcast on a little battery radio he had purchased. It was electrifying news. "Planes from the Empire of Japan have bombed Pearl Harbor!"

Chuck went immediately to the captain of the ship with the news.

"Are you sure? I haven't heard anything about that," the captain responded. By the time they reached Panama the news had been confirmed.

Fortunately it was a protected passage as the tramp steamer made its way through the canal. But the German submarines were waiting in the Caribbean Sea and all along the Atlantic coast. These submarines attacked half of all the allied ships in the area during that first week of the war. A storm hit the area just as Chuck's ship passed through. The waves were so intense that it perilously shifted the load of lumber on the deck, causing the ship to list at twenty degrees. Chuck always believed that this near disaster saved them from a torpedo attack. "Any submarine that had us in their sights would be certain we couldn't have made it to port," he said. "I do think that saved us".

When Chuck arrived at Baltimore, he immediately reported to the Naval Academy at Annapolis, Maryland. Upon completion of this training he was commissioned as an Ensign, USNR, with qualifications in steam engineering. The navy recognized his unusual talents and he was selected to stay on at the Naval Academy as a member of the teaching staff, an assignment he held for several months. Then in 1943, upon his request he received orders to report to the heavy cruiser USS Tuscaloosa as the engineering officer.

Our family had always been aware of his participation in World War II. But it was not until 1997 that I asked him to write of his experience. The involvement of the cruiser Tuscaloosa in the historic invasion of Europe on D-Day, June 6, 1944 was important. Chuck tells of the perilous moments when his ship approached Utah Beach at Normandy to knock out the German gun emplacements in the cliffs above the beach.

Behind Utah Beach was a wide lagoon, passable only by a few causeways. If the enemy controlled the causeways, the landing force would be bottled up at the beachhead. A successful landing at Utah beach and control of the limited accesses to the area was the key to the control of the entire Cotentin Peninsula and Cherbourg. Following is the personal account by Chuck Robinson of that memorable day when the allied forces stormed the shores of Europe in the greatest invasion in the history of the world.

*   *   *

Early morning on June 6, 1944, ships of the allied navies began a do or die attack on the beaches of Normandy, France, aimed at destroying Hitler's war machine. I was on one of those ships, the cruiser USS Tuscaloosa, which had been moving slowly about two miles off shore since midnight, anticipating this moment. The forty-eight hours following the initial attack left me with indelible impressions difficult to share with anyone who has not lived through a major battle. I don't mean to imply that I was in any way a hero in this battle, as I was locked in the engine room with little personal freedom.

To put this into better perspective, I will give a bit of background on how I ended up with a front row seat at one of the greatest battles in world history.

In June 1941 I received a notice from the U.S. Government that I had drawn a low number in the military draft lottery of that year. Thus, with no desire to become a military hero, but rather to avoid having my future carved out for me by some Washington bureaucrat, I volunteered for navy officer training at Annapolis to commence in December that year. After an intense training program to convert an economist into an engineer, I graduated and remained at Annapolis for several months to teach steam engineering. Eventually, I requested sea duty and soon received orders to report to the cruiser, USS Tuscaloosa. This warship became my home for nearly three years. The first two years were spent on the Murmansk Run where we protected the allied convoys as they negotiated the German submarine infested waters from north of England to the northern coast of Russia. During these perilous times we had several encounters with enemy surface ships and aircraft off the North Cape of Norway and Spitzbergen.

Eventually the Tuscaloosa was ordered to Belfast Lough in Northern Ireland. There we were advised that an important military official would conduct the Saturday morning inspection of our crew of which my division was last.

During this inspection, I was suddenly confronted with the imposing presence of General Eisenhower who, we learned later, was on board to give us a briefing on the Normandy landing. In these inspections it was my task to salute and say, "Good morning Admiral, M-Division ready for inspection." However, in this case I was so shocked at Eisenhower's unannounced arrival that I couldn't think of the word "General." This created a most embarrassing situation for me. I'll never forget Eisenhower's reaction. Sensing my dilemma he put his arm around my shoulders and said, "Lieutenant, I'm very much looking forward to inspecting your division." This not only saved me from embarrassment in front of my crew but also made me a life-long supporter of that great military and political leader.

After the inspection, General Ike came on the ship's address system and shared with us plans for the Normandy landing. He stated that our ground and air forces were going in and they wanted the U.S. Navy alongside. He forewarned us that this would be a perilous mission as his staff had projected a loss of forty percent of the attacking ships.

Two days later we headed south for Normandy but the

weather prediction was bad and as we rounded Plymouth, England, we were ordered to turn back for twelve hours and come to this same position twenty-four hours later. In this way we adjusted to the one day delay in the original schedule for the landing and took up our position on midnight of June 5th, remaining about two miles off Utah Beach for some six hours before the landing.

My battle station was in the main engine room where we were sealed off from the outside world for more than twenty-four hours after the battle commenced. We soon became the special target of a large German shore battery firing from the bluffs above Utah Beach. We responded by firing our eight-inch guns on their fortifications above the beach. Captain Waller began evasive tactics that somehow protected the ship although shells continued to explode in the water on all sides. Each sounded like a direct hit to those of us located in the engine room.

This cat and mouse game required abrupt changes in the vessel's speed and direction, which forced on us in the engine room to rapidly adjust our steam turbine controls. This was probably healthy in that we didn't have time to contemplate a shell penetrating the hull and exploding in our high temperature steam environment. That would have been fatal. In spite of the obvious risk to our men, there was little opportunity for the kind of personal heroism exhibited by our many soldiers storming the beach.

As engineers, we were generally the last to know what was going on outside the engine room. I quote from an August 1944 Readers Digest article written by war correspondent, Ira Wolfert, who did see what was happening. Here is that account.

Close to us was the U.S. cruiser Tuscaloosa. A German battery had challenged her, and she and an American destroyer had taken up the challenge. The Germans were using a very fine smokeless powder that made it impossible to spot their gun sites unless one happened to be looking right there when the muzzle flash gave them away. They also had some kind of bellows arrangement that puffed out a billow of gun smoke from a position safely removed from the actual battery. This was to throw off the spotters. But their best protection was the casements of earth-and-concrete twelve feet thick.

The affair between the battery and the warships had the color of a duel to it. When the Germans threw down the gauntlet you could see the gauntlet splash in the water. It was a rangefinding shell. Then the shells started walking toward our warship, in a straight line. If you followed them on back you would eventually get to the battery. This was what our warship commanders were trying to do. It was a race between skills. If the Germans landed on the ship before our gunners could plot the line of their shells, then they would win. If our gunners could calculate more rapidly, then we would win.

Captain Waller, in command of the Tuscaloosa, held his $15,000,000 warship steady, setting it up as bait to keep the Germans shooting while his gunners worked out their calculations.

There was a destroyer that held with our cruiser. The splashes kept coming closer. Our ships did not move. The splashes started at 500 yards. Now, I thought, the warships would move. But they remained silent and motionless. The next salvo was 200 yards off. The next one would do it, the next one would get them, I was thinking. The next salvo blotted out the sides of the vessels in a whip of white water, throwing a cascade across the deck of the Tuscaloosa.

Now in this final second the race was at its climax. The Germans knew our ships would move. They had to guess which way they had to race to correct range and deflection for the next salvo. Our ships had to guess what the Germans would think, and do the opposite.

The destroyer had one little last trick up its sleeve. And that tipped the whole duel our way. Its black gang down below mixed rich on fuel and a gust of black smoke poured out the stacks. The ship had turned into the wind, so that the smoke was carried backward. The Germans could not tell whether it was the wind doing that or the destroyer's forward speed. They decided that it was forward speed and swung their guns, and straddled perfectly the position the destroyer would have occupied had it gone forward. But the destroyer had reversed engines and gone backward.

Now the game was up for the Huns. The warships swung around in their new positions and brought their guns to bear, their shells scoring direct hits. The Germans now lay silently and hopelessly in their earth.

Wolfert was accurate in his report of our initial engagement with the German heavy artillery guns, and it did satisfy his victory-hungry readership. However, rather than destroying the guns, the battery came to life in about ten minutes and we were heavily engaged for another twenty-four hours. We took over 100 near misses but miraculously, no direct hits. It must have been extremely frustrating to the German gun crew who had selected the

Tuscaloosa for destruction, as any one of the large shells would have disabled or sunk our ship with a direct hit. Our subsequent attack on the heavily fortified harbor of Cherbourg a few days later secured Normandy for the allied forces.

*   *   *

We participated in the landing in Southern France in September of that year, and in the later battles in the Pacific at Iwo Jima and Okinawa where we faced continuing Kamikaze attacks. The Japanese were desperate. They kept throwing these suicide bomb laden planes against us. The United States Naval Fleet was attacked by hundreds of these Kamikazi human flying bombs. For ninety straight days the men of the Tuscaloosa were called to general quarters to repel these attacks that the Japanese were basing their hopes on to repel the invasion forces. Before Okinawa was secured, thirty-six American ships were sunk and nearly 400 damaged. More than 700 fleet aircraft were lost, 4,800 sailors were wounded and 4,900 were either killed or missing. Okinawa was one of the costliest naval battles on record, but again the Tuscaloosa was miraculously lucky because, although we did have many near misses, we never did receive a direct hit or sustain any serious damage.

The Tuscaloosa, a heavy cruiser by virtue of its eight-inch caliber guns, was very lucky. It was the only ship in its class that was not sunk during World War II. What amazing and memorable adventures we had on that old cruiser! But the invasion of Normandy, when our forces stormed the beaches of Europe in the greatest invasion in the history of the world, remains as the impression of my life. The impact of this experience is still with me. I have faced continued crises in life, but somehow I know that these challenges can all work for good if I will just maintain a positive attitude.

*   *   *

At the end of World War II, Charles Robinson completed his

USS Tuscaloosa

Masters Degree in Business Administration at Stanford University in California. Several years later he became president of the Marcona Corporation that developed a large iron ore producing operation in Peru. To transport the iron ore, he founded the San Juan Carrier Corporation, the largest dry cargo shipping company in the world. These massive ships took their cargoes through the Panama Canal and on to the great smelters on the East Coast, across the Pacific to Japan or around South America to Europe.

He resigned from these companies during the President Ford administration to become Deputy Secretary of State under Dr. Henry Kissinger. Later he was Senior Vice-President of Blythe Eastman Dillion & Company, an international banking firm with offices on the Avenue of the Americas in New York City. He now heads his own companies as president of the Energy Transition Corporation and Robinson Investments Inc. of Santa Fe, New Mexico and Dyna Yacht Inc. of San Diego, California. His beautiful home is located on a hill overlooking Santa Fe, New Mexico. Charles Robinson is also a member of the Board of Directors of the Nike Corporation. He is a living testimony that hard work, basic intelligence, and vision for life does have its special rewards.

13

JOHN E. JAQUA, MAJOR, USMCR

This is the story of my sister's husband, John Jaqua, and his heroic involvement in the longest and the most costly aerial campaign in the entire Pacific War. There were numerous other great air to air battles, such as at Midway and the Mariana "Turkey Shoot," but none that lasted continuously over an eighteen-month period. From August 1942 until January 1944 this desperate fight to stem the advancement of the Japanese south from the fortress of

Rabaul, through the Soloman Islands to Guadalcanal, raged. In this prolonged action more planes and airmen were lost than in any other action in the battle against the Japanese. As the battle intensified over those months, Captain Jaqua was thrust into the conflict, flying the Grumman *Avenger* torpedo and bombing plane on numerous missions from Guadalcanal to Rabaul from June 1943 until the area was secured by allied forces in January 1944.

In 1995 I visited John Jaqua at his magnificent ranch on the McKenzie River just east of Eugene, Oregon. I asked him to tell me about the experience he had in World War II, and I recorded his memories on tape. I have written this story as he told it, but first let me put it into historical perspective. It is only as one understands those perilous days, will there be an appreciation for the dramatic fight that had to take place to stop the terrifying advance of the Japanese war machine.

The war with Japan began in December 1941. In the attack on Pearl Harbor the Japanese had in one devastating blow destroyed the American forces ability to immediately respond. Fortunately, a few of the United States aircraft carriers had been at sea during the attack on Pearl Harbor. The Japanese continued on their plan of advancement southwestward until stopped at the battle of the Coral Sea the first week in May, 1942. The Battle of the Coral Sea was the first naval battle in history in which the two opposing forces did not sight or fire their guns at each other. Carrier planes were the offensive weapons. Although both sides claimed victory, the Japanese inflicted a higher loss than they sustained, for the Yorktown was damaged and the Lexington had to be scuttled. On the other hand, the Americans had stopped the advance on Australia, and had inflicted so much damage and plane loss on the Japanese carriers that they were unable to participate in the Battle of Midway a month later. This was critically important, because the defeat of Japan at Midway was an important turning point in the war.

The line of advancement had been stopped. But behind that line in the south Pacific, the Japanese held the Solomon's. Up and down this 500-mile chain of islands, anchored by Guadalcanal on the south, thousands of soldiers, many airfields and hundreds of planes were put in place to protect their gains. The Japanese fortress of Rabaul was the supply base for their operation. Rabaul is located 900 miles northwest of Guadalcanal on the north end of New Britain Island on the Bismark Archipelago. Massive volcanic mountains drilled with tunnels and bristling with guns protected the major harbor, supply base and the five airfields from which they launched their attacks. This 800-mile stretch of islands would become the great battleground in the coming eighteen months in the fight to control the South Pacific.

Following the Battle of the Coral Sea, allied commanders, realizing that the Japanese were fortifying the Solomon Islands, ordered an offensive to seize the newly established Japanese airfield on the northern shore of Guadalcanal. It was important that Japan not be allowed to regain the initiative for their further expansion. On August 7, 1942, marine-landing forces went ashore on the northern coast of Guadalcanal and on the nearby islands of Florida and Tulagi. A fight took place on Tulagi before the marines seized the control of the hills dominating the anchorage between Tulagi and Florida. There was almost no opposition on Guadalcanal. By the evening of August 7, the U.S. Marines had driven the surprised Japanese from the airfield and had established a defensive perimeter against the expected Japanese counterattack. This came soon, but in a manner that caught the American naval escorting fleet completely by surprise. Undetected by the Americans, a Japanese naval squadron slipped past Savo Island during the night of August 8-9. It sank four allied cruisers in a few minutes and escaped unharmed.

The defeat at the Battle of Savo Island, combined with the intensive Japanese aerial attack from Rabaul, left the United States forces with only one reasonable option. That was to withdraw their naval covering forces and supply transports from the waters near Guadalcanal. The U.S. Marines suddenly found themselves isolated in the small perimeter they had established around newly named Henderson Field.

Japanese planes now began a series of bombing and strafing attacks that would continue for many weeks to come. At the time, Japanese warships and transports began rushing southeastward through the Soloman Islands from Rabaul, carrying reinforcements to Guadalcanal. As their strengths built up, veteran Japanese jungle fighters began to harass the marine defense perimeter. During the following weeks the Japanese continued to rush soldiers to Guadalcanal by single ship and by convoy. The American Navy, as well as army, marine, and navy aircraft struck back to try to prevent the arrival of these reinforcements. But night after night, Japanese vessels steamed through "the Slot", an inside passage between the islands of New Georgia and Santa Isabel, to land more troops and bombard the marine positions around Henderson Field.

In two weeks during the late summer of 1942, the *"Tokyo Express"*, as it was dubbed, in spite of all the opposition landed 6,000 more troops on Guadalcanal. The marines fought tenaciously and night after night they threw the attackers back into the jungle. It became a sinkhole for the Japanese.

By the beginning of 1943 the Japanese, realizing that their defensive perimeter had been breached, began to move vast stores of supplies, ships, planes, ammunition and soldiers into Rabaul. They were building up their forces for a do or die engagement for the Solomon Islands!

The opposing forces were in place as the summer of 1943 began, and the United States began their offensive north. It was into this situation that John Jaqua, as a new member of the reorganized Marine Bomber Squadron 232, flew in to Henderson Field at Guadalcanal and began a series of engagements that would not end until Rabaul would be neutralized and the Solomon Islands secured. Here is his account of those desperate and heroic months.

*   *   *

I was a Junior at Pomona College when the Japanese bombed Pearl Harbor. We were all pretty well shaken up by the news and a lot of the guys on campus started volunteering to go into the service. My good friend, Jim Boyden and I decided to try to qualify for the navy flight program. It seemed like the best deal to us. Well, to make a long story short, we were accepted, and ordered to report for Elimination Training at the Long Beach Naval Air Station.

I was engaged to Rosamond Robinson, another student at Pomona College, and she was from Long Beach. Jim Boyden and I needed a place to live while we went through this flight training, as they had no housing for us on the base. "Robin" said she thought we could stay with her parents. We were not the first to stay with the Robinson's during the war. Their oldest son and his fraternity brother had stayed with them when they had gone through this same training program a short time before.

We left Long Beach when we finished our final flight check in the old N2N yellow bi-plane trainer and eventually reported to the giant naval air training base in Corpus Christi, Texas. When I finished primary and basic training, I was assigned to advanced training in Squadron 13 at the main base. The navy instituted this specialized torpedo flight training after the Battle of Midway, because so many torpedo planes had been shot down that they needed a new batch of pilots.

I graduated from Corpus Christi in the fall of 1942 with a 2nd Lieutenant commission in the U.S. Marines, and my "Wings of Gold." Jim and I had orders for operational training at the Opa Locka Naval Air Station out of Miami, Florida. There we were trained in field carrier landings, formation and night flying, and attack techniques. We trained there for a little over a month and had the opportunity to fly a number of different planes, most of which had been operational with the fleet. When I finished, I received orders to report to the El Toro Marine Air Station in southern California. I trained both there and at the North Island Naval Air Station. During this time Robin and I got married. The navy took over the historic and beautiful Coronado Hotel, and it was wonderful for us to have a short stay there while I qualified on the Saratoga as a "carrier pilot." This famous old ship had taken a *Jap* torpedo out in the South Pacific and was now being used for training.

My new orders came through. I was to report to Marine Squadron 232 to fly TBM Grumman *Avengers*. Squadron 232 had started out as a dive bombing squadron, but had lost so many pilots in their first tour in the Solomon Islands, that when the depleted squadron was reorganized it was commissioned as a bomber/torpedo squadron, equipped with the new TBF planes. Colonel Mangrum, who had been the head of the air strike forces in the early days of the Guadalcanal operation, was our Skipper. He had flown there with Marion Carl, a leading Marine Ace.

We left late in the spring of 1943 for New Caledonia and Espiritu Santo where we put the final touches on our training before going into combat in the Soloman Islands. We had a lot of new pilots in Squadron 232. Even our skipper Major Smith was fairly new to the Grumman *Avenger*. Three of us, Jim Boyden, Hank Melby, and myself had the most time in the TBM's. Squadron 233 was ready to go, except they were still short of a few experienced pilots, so the three of us went to 233 as replacements. They gave us a few days to work with our new squadron.

Overly aggressive fighter pilots unable to control their thirst for revenge and adventure overran the place. The result was a wild atmosphere and a lot of flamboyant personalities. One of the most flamboyant was Major Boyington. Boyington's squadron was VMF-122. They had just gotten the new F4U *Corsair* fighters, and were scheduled to leave for Guadalcanal. I met Gregory Boyington on a rainy tropical night, June 7, 1943. We had a big party going on in a barracks near the airfield, downing liquor that had been provided by an R4D transport returning from Sydney with a load of pilots fresh from a week of boisterous drinking in Australia. Greg had been drinking in the officers club before he got there, but he was not through with the evening's activities. Anyway, Boyington thought he was a pretty good wrestler, being an intercollegiate wrestling champion in his day. After a few more drinks he challenged our whole squadron to a free-for-all-wrestling match. None of us wanted to get involved in something like that. I didn't pay too much attention to him because I knew he was drunk. Boyington just kept after this kid Gorman who was one of the DC-3 pilots. I think he was from Idaho. Gorman didn't really want to fight but "Pappy", as he was called by the kids in his squadron, just kept pressing him, so the two of them went into a back room. In a couple of minutes Gorman came back out. "I just broke Boyington's leg," he said, in a matter of fact way. That finished the fight in a hurry, and we could all get on with the party.

Now Boyington in his book, Baa Baa Black Sheep, gives a different version of this incident. He said, "It was a free-for-all. Somebody tackled me from the side in the darkness with a shoestring tackle. My anklebone had snapped audibly like a twig, and the following day found me with my leg in a cast up to the knee."

I take the story Gorman told, because Boyington was too drunk to remember what happened anyway. I understand "Pappy" Boyington was sent to a hospital in Auckland, New Zealand to recover. Regardless, he was back in the fall to lead his Black Sheep squadron, and was assigned to fly cover for us on those massive attacks on Rabaul. I never thought too much of him. He was too much of a maverick, and instead of flying close cover for us like he was supposed to do, he would take off with his kids and mix it up with the *Zero's*. That would leave us vulnerable to other attacking Japanese planes. I was always glad that Gorman whipped him when he challenged our bombing squadron. Actually, I later saw Boyington shot down just after he made his twenty-sixth kill to set the new record. I'll tell about this incident later on in the story, because it didn't happen until January, 1944.

Two days later on June 9, 1943, our squadron left Espirtu Santo for Guadalcanal. This would begin our first of three six-week combat tours. I had been a marine aviator for a year and a half, but I had never launched a torpedo, made a bombing dive, or been fired at in combat. This was all going to change in a hurry now.

We flew our *Avengers* from Turtle Bay in Santos to Henderson Field, a distance of about 450 miles. As we approached Guadalcanal, ground controllers warned us that "condition red" was in effect. An enemy airstrike had been picked up by our coast watchers far up in the Solomon chain of islands, and were now being monitored by our radar. The Japanese planes were still quite a distance away, so we would have time to land and disperse our TBM's. The fighter planes at Henderson had taken off and intercepted the *Japs* to the north and dispersed them before they reached us. Our landing instructions were to approach Henderson Field from around Cape Esperance, the northwest tip of the Island. As I passed over Cape Esperance and turned in over Lengo

Channel, I saw the ominous conical bulk of Savo Island. It was here that so many of the American, Australian, and Japanese ships were sunk during the vicious fighting that had taken place the year before. Since those sinkings the area had been known as Ironbottom Sound.

We landed on the main runway and were met by guide jeeps that escorted us to the revetments where we parked our planes. These protected areas were dispersed throughout the stands of palm trees in an attempt to keep our planes from being damaged by the nuisance night attacks that had continued over the months. After turning our planes over to the waiting ground crews, we pulled our meager belongings out of the bomb bay and followed our guides to the Quonset hut that was to be our home. We slept on canvas cots protected by mosquito nets. We were shown our large bomb shelters as well as the locations of numerous foxhole-type one-man shelters that dotted the squadron area.

Guadalcanal is not a tropical paradise. Located less than ten degrees south of the Equator, its climate is wet and hot, with an average temperature well into the eighties. The combination of heat, humidity, and a dense interior rain forest causes rain to fall each day. Rainfall over all of the islands in the Solomons is greater than the rainfall over the ocean around them. The island, like all the major islands in the Solomons is volcanic, although there are a lot of coral reefs and small shallow islands around. Guadalcanal is about seventy-five miles long and has mountains as high as 8,000 feet, high enough to give you trouble in bad weather and at night.

When I was on Guadalcanal, we were bombed at night some. They never were able to get through our defenses for a major bombing attack, but these nuisance raids were disconcerting. At midnight the Japanese would send over a single bomber, usually a twin engine *Betty*, and intentionally unsynchronize the engines. This would make a distinctive racket and we all knew what was coming. A single 250-kg bomb would drop at odd intervals to either pit the runway or damage a plane, or one of the field's facilities. We never knew where it would explode, so we all had to heed the wailing sirens, stir from our exhausted sleep, and hide in our foxholes. This night enemy flyer was dubbed "Washing Machine

190

Charlie" and his visits got really tiring.

Meals were served in a central Quonset hut accommodating several squadrons that were operating off the main runway. There was no refrigeration available for food, so we never saw fresh vegetables, unprocessed meat, or anything like that. Everything we ate was canned or dehydrated. The first breakfast I had at Henderson Field was powdered eggs, pancakes, chipped beef on toast, and lousy coffee that I never liked anyway. Eventually, this gave a lot of us trouble with our stomachs. Between the heat and humidity, lack of sleep, bad food and recurrent dysentery, nearly all of us eventually lost weight and suffered from obvious loss of energy. It was a terrible way to fight a war.

We didn't have too much trouble getting fuel for our planes. By this time they had established fuel storage facilities on the near island of Tulagi. They set up a plan to barge in during the nights the fuel that we needed. Getting enough fuel to operate had been a real problem before we arrived. Actually, Major Joe Foss, the famous Marine Ace, had taken off from Henderson Field one time with just enough gas to make a couple of passes around the field. On each pass he shot down an attacking *Zero*. That was quite a feat.

We were in place and ready to go for the massive assault on the island of New Georgia about 120 miles north of Guadalcanal. Let me put this in perspective. The allies, after many months of preparation were now ready to launch their campaign up the Solomon Islands to Rabaul. On June 30, 1943 we began the first of these bitter battles, the aim of which was to obtain airfields to cover a later advance on Bougainville. On the north end of New Georgia was the sizable and well-defended Japanese air base at Munda Point. The Americans decided not to assault Munda directly, but to land at several points and fight an overland battle to the airstrip. The amphibious landings went well, but the Japanese wanted to hold New Georgia as a key outpost protecting Bougainville, and they responded to the invasion with a lot of hard fighting. The Japanese ships came down the Slot during the night and the navy fought them with several destroyers and cruisers of Halsey's Third Fleet. The *Japs* were good night fighters and had better torpedoes than we did. As a result losses on both sides were high. Meanwhile, on shore the soldiers found the going a lot tougher than they had thought it would be because of the jungle, craggy hills, streams, stinking swamps, and the stiff defense by the enemy. The advance was slow and illness was high, but by the end of the first week in August the air base was in American hands.

It was about this pending campaign that we were briefed shortly after we arrived at Guadalcanal. It was there that we learned the exact time and places of the New Georgia invasions. We had to learn times and places, for there were to be a half-dozen landings and assaults throughout the morning of June 30, 1943. The big initial show, the one to which we were assigned, was at Rendova, an island near Munda Field. The aerial part of the assault was to be massive, the largest continuous blow to be administered thus far in one day by allied air units in the Pacific. Our job was to support the landings on New Georgia and Rendova and protect them in any way we could. This meant flying on up to Bougainville on occasion for some bombing runs against those support installations. I don't remember all the fighter squadrons that flew fighter cover for us, but one of them was Marine Squadron VMF-121. They did a great job in keeping the *Zero's* off our tails, and the hits we took were mostly from ground fire.

Our first missions were to protect the beachheads on Rendova and Munda. We carried four 500-pound bombs that we would drop after a dive on the enemy installations. If we were supporting a landing operation, we would report over the target to the Air Control Officer and he would give us our instructions for the dive-bombing run. It was all pretty routine, because we had good fighter cover and the enemy had not yet rebuilt up their plane inventory after all their losses a couple of months earlier. Rendova is a smaller island, south of Munda and off the west coast of New Georgia. The first inkling I had that Japanese fighter planes were challenging our landings was when I heard our fighters open up on the radio. About fifty *Zeros* dove through the cloud cover up near Munda Point and engaged VMF-121. There was a lot of talk and chatter going on over the air and I knew a lot of action was taking place. Later I found out that the marine pilots had knocked down over sixty enemy planes, but in the melee we did lose four pilots and their planes. These losses don't seem like much, but over the course of the weeks that followed these numbers added up. Although the Japanese failed to repulse the Rendova landings on the first day, the battles over the beaches continued for the next two weeks. The Japanese suffered crippling losses in airplanes and aircrews, and they only scored hits on four of our ships. This was a fine testimonial to our fighter pilots and our radar controllers.

We did participate in some longer missions on up into Bougainville. On these flights we flew in a tight-staggered formation for greater protection. This way an enemy fighter could not penetrate our formation and our turret gunners with their fifty caliber shells could put up a protective cone of fire. This, with the protection of the fighters above us, gave a good cover. On July 16th we pulled off a big attack on the Kahili airfield at the north end of Bougainville. We rendezvoused over Munda. We had seventy-eight bombers, thirty five of which were TBM,s, and we were protected by ll4 fighters. It was the most impressive friendly formation I had seen up to that time. The approach was uneventful. It was a beautiful morning, with a clear sky above us. Visibility was unlimited. The volcano that looms over Kahili was drawing closer, and I was looking down at the Japanese shipping in the Shortlands anchorage. Suddenly, my earphones crackled with the news that many Japanese fighters were scrambling off the nearby airstrip at Ballale. Some of us made our bombing dives on the airfield while others hit the shipping in the bay. There was some ground fire, but the *Zero's* never got to us; they were too busy with our fighters. We were able to do quite a bit of damage to the base and the fighters accounted for about fifty enemy planes reportedly shot down during the attack. I'm not sure about our losses, but they were minimal.

During the New Georgia campaign the PT boats were very active, knocking off barges, landing scouting parties and troops, and engaging shipping. On the night of August 1st, John F. Kennedy, future President of the United States, had his boat cut in half during the night by a Japanese destroyer in Blackett Straits. Of course, he was just another navy officer then, but his heroism in seeing that his crew survived became a major story in the years ahead when he ran for political office.

At Munda the obliterated Japanese air base was being reconstructed by the Sea-Bees as soon as the *Japs* were pushed off. When I thought of the thousands of tons of bombs dropped on that gutted place, I wondered how anyone had survived. But human life is hard to knock out, even when the terrain is pounded to a pulp. In the case of the Japanese they seemed to have the ability to just fade away in the jungle, some of them to hide there until after the war was over. The cost of life and material had been high, but the Seabees performed a miracle. In a few short weeks they had enlarged and lengthened the runways, and built the facilities that would enable us to operate many miles closer to Bougainville and Rabaul. Our squadron, VMVT-233, was the first to land planes at the new airbase, and from this field we would launch our future attacks. But soon we would be entitled to our first leave in Australia.

After six weeks in combat, the pilots were pretty well worn down. I always felt sorry for the ground forces that were not given relief from the horrible duty they had in the Solomon's. But the truth was that they weren't flying those high-powered planes where your reflexes and skills had to be maintained. Some may have felt that we were pampered, but that was the way it was. We left our planes in Gudalcanal and all climbed into a DC-3 for the flight back south to Espiritu Santo. This was the staging and final training center for our thrust north to Rabaul. Although we hadn't taken the losses we would later on, we did need some new planes and additional pilots to fill out the squadron. It was a busy time for us as we pulled the reorganized squadron together and made our preparations for our second combat tour. At the end of this time, and we had really looked forward to it, we took off again in a military transport for our week in Sydney, Australia that they said was "for rest and relaxation." That was hardly an appropriate term for what went on. The first thing most of us did was to take our uniforms to the cleaners to have the mildew and the jungle what ever taken out. Clean uniforms and a good press job made a lot of difference in the way we looked. It was a real treat to get a good fresh meal again. I had a new appreciation for fresh eggs, milk, orange juice, and good Australian beef, none of which we could get back on the islands. Once we got all of this squared away it was set that we would all meet at the Hotel Australia. That was the place of action for the American pilots and a lot of partying went on there during the war. Sometimes we would get a large table at one of the nightclubs. The Princes and Romanos were two very popular nightspots. We left "down-under" more tired than rested for our long flight back to Santos, but we always looked forward to these respites from the reality of our lives.

When Bombing Squadron 233 returned to the Solomon's early in the fall of 1943 we operated out of Munda, on New Georgia Island northwest of Guadalcanal. Munda had been transformed into the major airfield for the push on north. By now the navy *Hellcat* fighters and the *Corsairs* were also flying out of Munda, and they gave us good protection from the almost daily raids the *Japs* attempted with their flights from Bougainville. When the TBM's were sent on our raids up into Bougainville, the fighters gave us good protection from the *Zero's*, but they couldn't do too much to protect us from the ground fire that was always thrown at us when we made our final low level diving attacks. That's when we took most of the hits on our planes, and it started getting a lot harder because we never had a day of rest. It was just one attack after another.

In August, 1943, the Third Amphibious Force had begun landings of soldiers and marines on the island of Vella Lavella, fifty miles north of Munda and a little over a hundred miles south of Empress Augusta Bay on Bougainville. This was an important development because our fighters would eventually fly out of there to give us greater protection on our missions to later support the landings on Bougainville. My brother, Will Jaqua, was the Supply Officer for the 58th Seabees and this was the unit that was given the assignment to go into Vella Lavella and construct the airfields for our fighting squadrons. It was a good deal for me, because once they raked out a clearing for me to land, I just dropped in on my way back from a raid on Bougainville. Actually, I was the very first American plane to land on the island. Will was darn surprised and couldn't do enough for me. It was a great reunion to meet way out there. Before I took off, he had the men load me down with a lot of fresh food supplies that we had no access to on our base. You can imagine, I was a very popular person when I got back to my squadron on Munda. After that I took every excuse I could find to land at Vella Lavella on my way back from Bougainville to Munda. Will was always there to load me up with these precious supplies. These meetings were the few happy times I remember during the entire time I was overseas.

A couple of times we were sent on a bombing mission to Rabaul about 400 miles to the northwest. Of course the fighters couldn't give us cover on these long flights, because they didn't have the range that we did. This meant almost a thousand mile round-trip flight in daylight, because we did have to put on some extra miles during the actual attack, and all of this without fighter protection. Fortunately, we had pretty good intelligence information, so we were not sent on these long missions at times when there were a lot of enemy planes at Rabaul. See, the Japanese had to shift their resources around quite a bit to repel the carrier attacks that had started against them in the Marshall Islands and in northern New Guinea. The main staging area for Rabaul was Truk, and when they needed planes and experienced carrier pilots to fight the Americans in other places, Rabaul would be left without the air replacements they needed. This, once in a while, would give us a little window of opportunity to hit this major staging base at Rabaul. Rabaul was extremely well protected by ground anti-aircraft artillery that defended the good harbor and five airfields that surrounded it. This entire major base was in a very concentrated area surrounded by towering volcanoes that were drilled with tunnels and fortified anti-aircraft batteries that were ready to repel any who attempted an attack. I don't ever remember making a raid on Rabaul when we didn't take some losses.

The invasion of Bougainville was planned for the first of November. But before this could be done the Japanese defenses on the island had to be neutralized. This kept us very busy during that last two weeks in October 1943. We flew every day, regardless of the weather. We had more aircraft available than ever before, and there were the added ground facilities to keep our planes running.

Munda was a busy place. The navy had brought in the new F6F fighters and there were still some of the old SBD divebombers in operation. The marines, flying their fast *Corsair* fighters, also gave us close support. The navy ground crews worked side by side with the marine ground crews and the *CASU* maintenance units worked side by side with both of them to keep as many planes as possible in the air. It was a real joint effort.

The high command had decided that they were through with the costly and slow attacks on island after island on the way to Rabaul. Now they would just establish a beachhead and secure it for an airfield and supply base for the next leapfrog hop on up the island chain. Thousands of Japanese soldiers were either by-passed on the islands that were not attacked, or isolated behind the perimeters of the beachheads the allies would establish. This saved thousands of American lives and hastened our advance against the Japanese. Of course the Japanese tried to replenish their isolated troops, but this became increasingly difficult as we gained air superiority.

One of the unique missions they gave our squadron was to lay demolition mines in the ocean to blow up the Japanese ships as they would try to sail through the island passages during the night, in an attempt to either supply or rescue their beleaguered soldiers. One of the passages that the Japanese used was through a narrow opening at the northern end of Bougainville and Buka Island. We dropped the mines in this passage, and although I never knew just how much damage they did, they must have been effective, because later on in the war we were ordered to lay more mines at the entrance to the harbor at Rabaul.

My TBM *Avenger* was hit several times during those months in combat, but strangely not in our major attacks when I most expected to get hit. When I was hit it was more in a haphazard manner and when I least expected it. The worst hit I took during the entire war was in a little routine flight out of Munda. We only tried to hold the little area around the airbase, and a lot of the Japanese were still on the island. I was asked to take an army engineer up around the northern end of New Georgia to find a route for Colonel Liversedge's raiders to attack the Japanese who were holed up in the jungle up there. I didn't think they had any anti-aircraft batteries in the area. Three of us were to take off together for a simple reconnaissance flight to scout out a possible route for their attack. My plane started up OK, but it was running so rough that I told this Army guy to get out and go with Hank Melby in one of the other TBM's. In the meantime I just jumped into one of the other planes that was ready to go, and soon caught up with the rest of the formation. As we cruised in over the jungle I took this unexpected hit right through the plane in back of the cockpit. It tore out all of the gun turret and the main canopy where this engineer would have been sitting. Also, about half the tail was shot off, and one wing took a major hit, but somehow I still had enough control to make it back to Munda and land. Those TBM's were pretty rugged and on occasion took a lot of punishment and still got us home. Anyway, the humorous part of the whole episode was that when we landed and taxied in and parked, this army fellow climbed out of Melby's plane and got a look at my *Avenger*. When he saw the big hole in the place where he would have been sitting, he just flopped on the ground. He went out cold, and we all had a good laugh out of that.

The actual landing on Bougainville came on the morning of November 1, 1943. It took the Japanese at somewhat of a surprise, because they were expecting the attack to take place farther south on the island. The allied plan to take larger jumps and bypass some of the Japanese strongholds was now well under way. The landing at Empress Agusta Bay way up in the middle of Bougainville, bypassing the bases around Kahili was in accordance with this concept. By the end of the month the Americans had cleared the area around the bay. They established a defensive perimeter around their gains and constructed a base and airfields. The Japanese stronghold at Rabaul was now only 235 miles away. The isolated Japanese forces to the south of us were now helpless without their naval and air support. This was no small thing because we had just jumped over an estimated 30,000 soldiers and hundreds of Japanese seamen in the southern part of Bougainville. During the weeks that followed the landing at Empress Augusta Bay, the Americal Division and the 37th Infantry Division fought numerous small actions to expand and fortify our perimeter. Again Japanese air and naval operation was lively. The Japanese had come off second best in the Battle of Empress Augusta Bay on November 2nd, but Admiral Koga responded by sending a force of seven heavy cruisers from to Truk to Rabaul. The cruiser force posed a serious threat to the landings and Halsey sent Vice Admiral Spruance and the newly formed Fifth Fleet to attack them on November 5th. Koga's heavy forces sustained enough damage to cause him to pull back to Truk. Of more consequence, Koga had reluctantly committed his carrier planes to Rabaul's defense, and by November 20th, when the Americans landed in the Gilbert Islands, he had lost so many carrier planes that he was almost powerless to defend the Tarawa action.

We lost a few pilots and crew during the campaign for Bougainville, but not as many as we would on our third tour of duty. One of our worst losses was when our skipper, Major O'Neil, was shot down on our very first tour. It just came as a great shock. He was such an excellent pilot and I just felt that if anyone were invincible it was O'Neil. He was such a great leader and a cool head. We would have flown anywhere with him. We were all feeling pretty low. By that time we had lost eight pilots and their crews. That meant twenty-four out of our squadron were gone, and the big push on Rabaul hadn't even started.

Here is an interesting story about another pilot that we lost. We had taken off from Munda for another raid on Bougainville. It was a routine attack on one of the *Jap* positions. Actually it only looked like a little native village to me, but I guess that our intelligence sources had it figured out right, because it turned out to be a stronghold. Anyway, this kid Pylant, from Georgia, got knocked down by antiaircraft fire. We weren't sure exactly what happened because we were all busy making our own runs. However, he didn't join up when we were finished and we never saw him again. Our skipper at the time was Major Coln, and he wrote Pylant's mother a letter of condolence. She answered a few weeks later and he shared the letter with us. In the letter she said that she had a dream that convinced her that her son had bailed out of his plane and walked away from the area unharmed. In the letter she had enclosed a map detailing the area and the path her son had taken. The map looked in perfect detail to me of the actual area of the attack. It didn't work out, because we never heard from Pylant again, but who knows. He might have later been captured and died in some way. I was always so amazed about this because she had everything diagramed on the map just the way it was. Every little beach, inlet, and rock island was there. How can you figure something like this?

Just before our second combat tour was over, we moved to the new hastily constructed air base on Bougainville. The marines and the army had set up a perimeter around the airstrip, and were well dug in to protect us from the thousands of Japanese soldiers that were still on the island. Bougainville is one of the larger islands in the chain, about 110 miles from one end to the other.

Two full army divisions, under the command of General Hodge, protected the whole perimeter. They were the Americal Division and the 37th Division. So, we had all of these military personnel to secure that little area. They had an infantry guy stationed at about every foot around that protective line, so we felt quite safe from any penetration by the enemy. But there was an amazing thing about all this to me. They had organized a group of Fiji natives who had been trained to infiltrate enemy lines and bring back reports to the American commanders. It made General Hodge mad at our defenders, because these natives would sneak out at night undetected through our own lines, make their sorties into the Japanese strongholds, and then return through our lines in total darkness without ever being detected. One time these natives actually went in to a Japanese encampment and stole the shoes of the Japanese soldiers while they were sleeping. It was totally amazing the way they operated, and the information they brought back was tremendously helpful to the allied forces.

Once we were established on Bougainville, we started attacking the ships coming down the straits from Rabaul pretty regularly. The *Japs* continued to suffer great losses. We could make these daytime raids, because we were getting great fighter cover. The fighters that covered us were mostly F4U *Corsairs* flown by marine pilots, and they were just raising hell with the *Jap Zero's*. I tell you, you just wouldn't believe what happened unless you were there and saw it. Sometimes our fighters would shoot down as many as 300 planes in a single mission and we would lose less than ten. Our fighter pilots just gave us one hell of a cover.

See, what was happening was that the *Japs* were staging all these planes down from Truk to Rabaul. They knew that holding Rabaul was their last chance at stopping our advance, so they committed everything to holding on. The hundreds of planes that just kept coming at us seemed inexhaustible. But it eventually did weaken them. They could keep producing planes, but they didn't have the skilled pilots to replace all they were losing.

It had been a rough six weeks and we were ready to get out. We hated thinking about ever coming back to the Solomon's, but of course we didn't have anything to say about that. Anyway, for now we would get the respite we needed.

By late fall of 1943 Marine Bombing Squadron 233 was back at the base on Bougainville with a new and reorganized bunch of pilots, ready for the final push to annihilate Rabaul. Rabaul had a great harbor full of warships, five airfields choked with planes, scores of coast defense guns, hundreds of antiaircraft guns, and 100,000 soldiers. Underground it had quarters and supply dumps so vast that the garrison never went hungry. Rabaul continued to be the big staging area for their prolonged and increasingly futile attempt to defend their forces trapped throughout the Solomon Islands. The five well-protected airfields at Rabaul were still operative as 1943 was coming to an end. It was our job to join other units in seeing that they were knocked out for good. The problem was that to get to them we had to come down between some high mountains, and of course they would open up with all their guns to keep us from getting in. Besides the airfields, this was our only approach to hitting any of the ships that were active in the harbor. Actually, we had to fly in lower than a lot of the batteries that would throw their ack-ack at us. Then, in order to get out after our bombing dives we just flew out at low level through the entrance channel. We did a pretty good job at getting to the airfields and then hitting the ships that were in the harbor. One time we got four ships in one raid. We never did use torpedoes, because we found them to be faulty. Our best results came from the 500-pound bombs. We came down in pretty steep dives, considering the *Avengers* were designed as torpedo bombers and didn't have dive-flaps on them. Just as we pulled out of our dive at low altitude, we would release our bombs and skip them into the side of the ship at the waterline.

Those first runs on Rabaul still stand out in my mind. There was so much fighting going on in those raids. It wasn't unusual to have 200 of our fighters engaged in attacking the *Zero's* right over our heads as we came in. What made it so spectacular was that I could see debris and parts of planes coming down like pine seeds all around me. Our high cover was F4U's. These *Corsairs* were faster than the *Zero's*, so they could make their runs and then zoom right back up to altitude and come in again for another run. There wasn't any of this dog-fighting in the old sense where they just stayed together and mixed it up. The speed of their planes plus their added fire power with their 50-caliber guns did give the marines an advantage that they didn't have when in the early days of the war they flew the F4F's. I was glad for their advantage, and by this time we did have better pilots than the Japanese.

They did such a good job in protecting us that the enemy planes were not our major concern. Most of our losses came as a result of the ground fire that was thrown at us during an attack. I could see the tracers coming on occasion and was able to dodge the bullets pretty well until that final run when I had to hold steady on the target. That's when I got it.

As the Japanese continued to lose planes and pilots, their replacement pilots were not as well trained as their predecessors had been. As their pilot experience and ability declined, Japanese losses continued to mount. Their losses were staggering. By the end of 1943, Japan had lost about 3000 planes and pilots in their failing struggle to hold on to the Solomon Islands.

Although Rabaul was dying, our attacks continued through Christmas and on into February 1944. It was before dawn on January 3, 1944 on Bougainville. We got baked beans for breakfast at the edge of the airstrip the Seabees had built after the marines had taken a small chunk of land on the beach. As I ate my breakfast before taking to the air, I glanced over at the row after row of crosses. It was too far away to read their names, but I didn't have to.

I knew that each cross marked the final resting place of some Marine who had gone as far as he could in this mortal world.

Soon we were in the air again making that run to Rabaul. A few hazy clouds were hanging around as they usually did, and they lightened as the day began. I spotted a few enemy planes coming up through the scattered clouds, but our fighter cover was soon on them. Once this contact with the enemy was made there was a lot of chatter on the radio. Our planes were having difficulty in making a coordinated attack because of the clouds. Some were still at altitude and others had dived toward the water to tangle with the *Zero's* that were there. There was quite a fight that developed around me. One of the F4U's caught fire and I could tell that it was going in. Just at the last moment, the pilot bailed out. His chute popped open just before the pilot hit the water. It was so fast, just boom, boom and the flyer was in the water. I found out later that it was Major Gregory Boyington, skipper of the famous Baa Baa Black Sheep squadron. We didn't know then whether he eventually died or was captured. On that last flight he was credited with his 26th plane, so he got the record he wanted so much. It seemed like such a coincidence that I was the one who saw him go down. After the war, I found out that he drifted to an island, was captured by the Japanese, and was held in a prison camp until the end of the war.

The worst duty we had in all that Rabaul campaign was when the high command got the idea that we should lay mines at the entrance to the harbor, so that the ships could not go in or out to re-supply the base. This was a night operation for us, and to lay the mines in an effective pattern we had to fly down the channel in a single file at 200 feet altitude and at a 200-knot airspeed. All the searchlights would be on us, and they soon could establish our course and direction. We presented a perfect target for them, because we were lighted and they fired right down on us. It was bad enough for the first planes in the line, but for those that followed it was just like knocking over those ducks in a shooting gallery that came down the line one after another. The anti-aircraft fire was very heavy. We just got blasted from every direction. We had to fly through an alley of fire. See, the harbor was right between these volcanoes that were so heavily fortified.

February 14, 1944 was the last mission the squadron flew. What a way to spend Valentines Day! It was a useless attack because we had just been up to Rabaul and the base as a staging area had been destroyed and all the ships that hadn't been sunk were gone. But, some high command sent up the orders to Bougainville for another night mine laying operation, so of course we had to go. That was the last time I ever saw my close friend, Jim Boyden. I really never knew what happened, but he was with us when we started that last run down the channel. The searchlights were so blinding you couldn't keep track of anyone. As usual, we took a lot of fire and I don't know how anyone made it through, so I'm certain that he got hit. To lose my best friend on the last mission we flew, after three tours in combat was devastating. On top of that, in my opinion, it was a totally useless attack. That is a terrible experience that I will never forget.

You know, they told us that our squadron lost more planes and men than any other marine flight squadron in the war. We had thirty-two pilots in the squadron. I think that there were eight of those original flyers that made it through the three combat tours. But of course we had a lot of replacements, too, and we lost a high percentage of them in those last days. Now, my best estimate would be that we lost forty pilots and about a hundred crewmen. Regardless, there were only about ten pilots out of the whole group that returned to San Francisco in the late spring of 1944.

*   *   *

After I returned to the States, I still suffered from stomach trouble and was hospitalized for a while with an ulcer condition. Eventually, the doctors got the ulcer under control and I was released with orders to join Admiral Hill's staff. This was a difficult but amazing assignment. The marines, of course, had made a series of strategic landing assaults on the Pacific islands as the United States forces had moved back on the offensive against the Japanese war machine. These amphibious offensives started with Guadalcanal and Tulagi in the Solomon Islands in August 1942. Then the marines attacked island-by-island all across the western

Pacific to the Mariannas in June 1944 and Iwo Jima in February 1945. The final assault, before the actual invasion of Japan, would be on Okinawa. In all of these previous battles the marine commanders had learned the importance of a system that would effectively coordinate the armaments from ships and air power, which would support the infantry in their attacks against enemy fortifications that restricted their advance. It was an intricate relationship that demanded continual improvement. Admiral Hill and his staff, of which I was now a part, were assigned to this project. I was an Air Support Officer working directly under Commander Robb.

Our first assignment was to set coordinates where the marine divisions would be landing in the south near Naha, the Capital of Okinawa. We developed a grid that was placed over the map of a given area. Each little square had a grid number and a letter of the alphabet. In this way the Air Support Officer could work with the field commanders, calling appropriate armament into a specific grid area, such as A3 or D2, and so on, where the ground forces were meeting enemy resistance. We would have different types of planes on call for different situations— fighters to strafe, dive-bombers, and air-to-ground rocket fire. It would be our job to get all of this firepower directed at just the right targets in front of our assault forces, so that they could continue their advance.

Admiral Hill's flagship left Coronado and proceeded to Hawaii where we participated in an extensive dress rehearsal for the eventual assault on Okinawa. We arrived off the southeast coast of Okinawa the last week of March 1945 and joined the forces that were battering the potential invasion areas with bombs and heavy artillery fire. It was intense! April 1 was D-day for Okinawa.

Let me put the overall invasion of this island, just 350 miles from the mainland of Japan, in perspective. The invasion of Okinawa was the largest Pacific operation in all of World War II in the Pacific. Our large naval forces, both planes from our aircraft carriers and heavy armaments from our ships, had leveled the capital city of Naha at the southern end of the island. The Japanese forces expected an initial landing in this area. Two corps of Lieutenant General Simon B. Buckner's Tenth Army began landing on the beaches farther north, which had also been softened up by bombardment from our ships and planes. Buckner's forces met light opposition and secured the area before noon. This was important as they immediately seized the airfields. One corps moved north and in three weeks secured the northern two-thirds of the island.

The 24th Corps turned south and faced an entirely different situation. They met the formidable Japanese forces as they reached the rough terrain along Kakazu Ridge. American troops took heavy casualties. The Japanese hit the 96th Division with a counterattack. This was not the usual banzai suicide charge, but a coordinated and well-planned assault. Our forces held, but they could make little headway against the tunneled fortifications that laced the entire rocky ridge.

The Sixth Marine Division had landed on the Oroku Peninsula and eventually eliminated that pocket of enemy resistance, while the other three marine divisions cleared the southern extremity of the Island.

The last major obstacle the marines faced was behind Naha, the Capital city of Okinawa.. This was the rugged rocky cave-combed ancient burial site behind Shuri Castle. The Japanese had taken over this sacred area from the Okinawa people as their last line of defense. A regiment of the Second Marine Division was brought in to flush out the Japanese defenders holed up in the tunneled ridge behind Shuri Castle. This was one of the areas where I was sent to work with the marine commanders on the problems of air-to-ground coordination, as our forces moved to clear the enemy from their honeycombed fortifications. The marines needed close and accurate support from our aerial bombing and rocket fire.

Fifty-five years later, the memory of my assignment on the front lines of these engagements is vivid. On April 4, 1945, I left my quarters on Admiral Hill's flagship, boarded a landing craft and came ashore on the secured beaches near the destroyed capital city of Naha. I had never seen such destruction. The only thing still standing in the entire city was the twisted steel skeleton frame of a destroyed elevator shaft. The Okinawa people were wandering the outlying country roads. They had left their homes because of the bombing and sought refuge in the mountain burial caves back of the

Shuri Castle, only to be driven out of these historic catacombs by the Japanese who wanted the area for their defensive line. You know, there never was any great love between the Japanese and the Okinawans. The Japanese had treated them badly. It was a pitiful sight to see these innocent people wandering in the search of protection and security. I met with the Regiment and Company commanders to work out some of the coordination problems that always develop in an operation of this kind.

I made several more of these trips before Okinawa was secured on June 14. My most vivid memories are of the cave-to-cave assaults on the Japanese at Shuri. We called in plane after plane to release their rocket fire. It was the first time, too, that I had seen flamethrowers used in combat. Marine attackers moved right into the face of the caves and fired the caverns with napalm. It was terrible to see a Japanese soldier running from a cave, his whole body on fire, only to collapse and die on the rocks. Proximity to such violence was a new and unnerving experience for me.

During June the Sixth Marine Division eliminated one pocket of Japanese resistance on Oroku peninsula, while the other three divisions cleared the southern extremity of the island. For the final effort, a regiment of the Second Marine Division was brought in, and while visiting its forward observation post on June 18, Army General Simon B. Buckner was killed. The jeep in which he was riding took a direct hit from an artillery shell. I shouldn't say this, because I really don't know. But what I do know is that there was a lot of conjecture, from the marine officers with whom I worked, that friendly artillery killed Buckner. Anyway, soon after on June 21, 1945 the battles ended and Okinawa was secured.

Okinawa was the most costly battle of the Pacific war. Army and marine losses, added to the naval losses, put American casualties at more than 49,000. Of this number, 12,500 were killed. Japanese losses were more than 100,000 killed. The material losses were the greatest of the war. Wave after wave of Kamikaze suicide planes continued to hit our ships. On April 6th alone, over 700 of these planes attacked our ships. Before Okinawa was secured, thirty-six American ships were sunk and nearly 400 damaged. More than 700 of our planes were lost and 4900 of our seamen killed. We were directing a lot of our fighter protection cover by radar from our command ship, but there were just too many planes attacking to stop them all. I tell you, those destroyers that were out there on the picket lines took a tremendous beating.

Okinawa was the last battle before Japan would be invaded. Okinawa fell and still the Japanese did not surrender! The bloody mess would have to go on. Thus our staff began working on the plans for an invasion of Kyushu, the main island of Japan. The attack and invasion by the United States forces was scheduled for November 1, 1945. We were all weary, but there seemed to be no end in sight. We were ordered back to Hawaii to train the forces that would invade Japan.

In early fall we sailed to the Philippines, our final staging area for the assault on Japan. Two weeks before the scheduled landings on Japan we received the startling news; atomic bombs had forced the surrender of Japan! World War II was finally over. Shortly, I received flight orders to Hawaii and from there I boarded an aircraft carrier bound for San Francisco. Near the end of my service, I was promoted to the grade of Major, USMCR.

*   *   *

This ends the personal World War II story as told by John Jaqua. It is important to add that Major Jaqua returned home as a highly decorated war hero. He was awarded medals that included: the World War II Campaign Medal, the Pacific Campaign Medal, the Asiatic Pacific Campaign Medal, seven Air Medals, the Battle Campaign Medal with five stars, and the coveted Distinguished Flying Cross Medal, "for undue bravery in pressing his attacks against the enemy through intense enemy fire".

Following World War II, John Jaqua returned to Pomona College in Claremont, California to complete his B.A. degree. The year, 1946, proved to be a busy one for him. His first son James Boyden, named after his friend who was killed on their last mission over Rabaul, had been born in 1945. In 1946 his daughter, Anne, arrived followed by two sons, Jon and Stephen. Besides his studies, John Jaqua was involved in athletics, and was elected captain of the

Pomona football team.

Following graduation, the Jaqua family moved to Oregon where John entered the University of Oregon Law School. This was a move that had been encouraged by his uncle, David Evans, head of a prestigious law firm in Eugene. The unexpected death of David Evans was a great shock. It precipitated a heavy responsibility upon John Jaqua when he immediately, upon graduation, moved into a leadership position in his deceased uncle's law firm.

Later John served as President of the Oregon Bar Association, and has been for many years a member of the Board of Directors of the Nike Corporation, the well-known athletic equipment company. But John's real love has been the development, over the past fifty years, of his beautiful farm that fronts a three-mile stretch of the McKenzie River near Eugene, Oregon. This is where their four children were raised. The farming and cattle operations continue, and it is also the center for numerous community social and athletic activities. This showplace, the McKenzie Oaks Farm, is still the home of John and Robin Jaqua and the base for their philanthropic activities.

There has been great reward in recording this previously untold story of my brother-in-law, Major John Jaqua, USMCR, and the heroic contribution he made to the defeat of the Military Empire of Japan.

Marine Squadron VB-233
Attacks Shipping in Rabaul Harbor

"Our only approach to attacking the ships in Rabaul Harbor was to fly down between the high mountains that guarded the entrance. These cliffs were fortified with antiaircraft batteries that opened up on us at point-blank range. I don't remember making a raid in which we did not take losses. Our best results came when we pulled out of our dives low over the water, then skipping our 500-pound bombs directly into the waterline of the Japanese ships. One time we got four ships in one attack."

John Jaqua, Captain USMC, 1943

Marine Flight Squadron VB-233 Advances

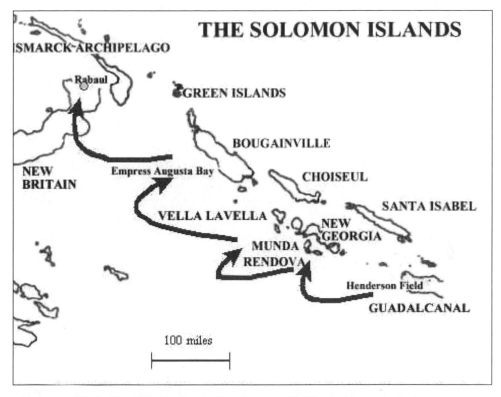

THE SOLOMON ISLANDS

- **June 9, 1943. VB-233 lands at Henderson Field on Guadalcanal**
- **August, 1943. VB-233 begins attacks on the island of Vella Lavella**
- **September, 1943. VB-233 begins attacks on Munda and New Georgia**
- **October, 1943. VB-233 begins attacks on Bougainville; establishes a forward base at Empress August Bay**
- **November 1943 through February 1944. VB-233 itensifies attacks on Rabaul until the harbor and the airfields are neutralized**

TBM Grumman *Avenger*
Primary Marine Corps Bomber in the
Solomon Islands Campaign Against Rabaul

"My new orders came through. I was to report to Marine Squadron 232 to fly Grumman *Avengers*. The squadron had started out as a dive bomber squadron, but had lost so many pilots in their first tour in the Solomon Islands that when the depleted squadron was reorganized it was commissioned, Marine Bombing Squadron 233. The Grumman *Avenger* was the plane I flew during the entire time I was in combat."

John Jaqua, Captain, USMCR

Marine Flyers
in the Solomon Islands
1943 – 1944

From left to right: John Jaqua, Jim Boyden and Hank Melby

Assault on Okinawa

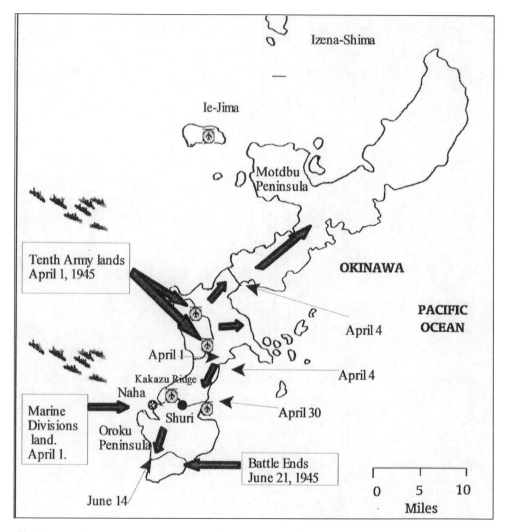

Sixth and Second Marine Divisions land simultaneously with the Tenth
Army. Major John Jaqua is assigned as Land Support Officer to coordinate
landing support for Oroku Peninsula and Shuri offensive.

14

WILLIAM BARNETT, LIEUTENANT, USNR

I met Bill Barnett in September, 1944 when we were in the Navy Hospital at Manus in the Admiralty Island north of New Guinea. I was immediately attracted to this young flyer who was recuperating from the prolonged months he had been flying in the war zone as a PBY *Catalina* flying boat pilot. I had heard of the renowned *Black Widow* Squadron. They were called *Black Widows* because they flew their black painted planes many times at night on reconnaissance and rescue missions far into enemy territory.

In the deadly twenty months that Lt. Barnett flew in VP-101, the *Black Widow* Squadron, he took Australian Commandos and dropped them off in the jungles behind enemy lines, scouted, flew enemy harassing missions, and rescued downed American flyers in enemy territory. His flight logbook shows 117 missions flown from Port Moresby in New Guinea to Rabaul, north of the Solomon Islands. His squadron earned the admiration of every flyer, soldier, seaman, and marine in all that vast territory over which they flew.

His job kept him in the air for as long as thirteen hours at a time. Night after night he was there in the air, flying blind, relying solely on the plane's antiquated instruments and hoping that, from time to time, there would be a break in the weather that would give sight of an enemy submarine, barge, or warship to report. Pilots in these slow lumbering planes were the advanced eyes for the American forces. These *Black Widows* that flew in the South Pacific during World War II will never be forgotten.

*   *   *

As I have related, Bill Barnett and I met for the first time in the hospital in the Admiralty Islands in September 1944, where he had been admitted from combat fatigue and I for residual crash injuries. We returned together to the United States in October 1944 and were admitted into the Long Beach Naval Hospital. Following our release from the hospital and our return to active duty, we lost track of one another for over fifty years. During those years I often wondered if Bill had returned to his beloved Montana following the war. I had no inkling as to what had happened to him. In 1995 I initiated a computer search and found that there was a Bill and Dorothy Barnett living in a remote little place called Roscoe, Montana just north of Yellowstone National Park. I picked up the telephone and called. What wonderful news it was to find that my old friend and his wife Dot were alive and well. Through letters, telephone calls, and a short visit with Bill Barnett in Boise, Idaho in 1997, I now have the needed information. Within the historical context of that desperate time, I tell the story in his own words. Here is that heroic account.

I was raised and went to school in Billings, Montana. I have always loved that Big Sky Country and I now live only a few miles from where I grew up as a child. I went to college at the University of Montana. This gave me the needed college credit that would later qualify me for enlistment in the United States Navy for flight training.

When the war started in Europe, the United States Government started the Civilian Pilot Training program to build a pool of prospective military flyers. It sounded great to me, so when I had the opportunity I enrolled in the program offered through the Rocky Mountain College in Billings, Montana and qualified for a Limited Commercial Pilot's license. On graduation, a full navy commander from the Sand Point Naval Air Station in Seattle was there to recruit future pilots for the navy. He was very persuasive and I was convinced, so I signed up.

Shortly after the attack on Pearl Harbor, I went to the Corpus Christi Naval Air Station in Texas. I graduated there in September 1942 with a commission as Ensign, USNR, and my Wings of Gold. My advanced training was in seaplanes.

Dot and I were married on the last day of my leave. I had orders to report to Norfolk, Virginia for operational training in Martin Mariner and PBM amphibians. From there I went to the Naval Air Station at Banana River in Florida. That is known as Cape Canaveral today, where the space vehicles are launched. That is where I got the specialized training I needed to fly the PBY *Catalina* flying boats, the aircraft I would fly throughout the South Pacific war in the campaign against the Japanese.

Dot went with me to San Francisco, where I would leave for my assignment to Fleet Air Wing-10, Squadron VP-101, operating somewhere north of Australia. At that time I did not have a clear idea what was going on with the war in that far off place. I was aware that the Japanese were advancing on Australia, but that is about all I knew. I had no idea what my situation would be. Amidst all of this uncertainty, and not knowing whether we would ever see each other again, Dot and I said good-bye. My new bride stood there on the dock in San Francisco waving as the ship eased away. It was Christmas Day, 1942.

The ship on which I sailed was the Alexander Ramsey, an unescorted Liberty Ship, bound for Sydney, Australia. We sailed for twenty-one days without seeing land, zigzagging our way across the Pacific Ocean, hoping that we would not encounter an enemy submarine. One day the Skipper informed us that the ship in front of us and the ship behind us had been torpedoed by *Jap* subs. We had not shared the sea alone.

Eventually, our ship arrived safely in Sydney, Australia. For several days I tried to arrange transportation to Perth, a city far away on the southwest coast of Australia. I was to meet my new squadron there. There were no airlines flying across that country in those days, so I had to be a little creative and rustle up my own transportation. You might say I hitchhiked across the country by plane and an open coach railway, eventually arriving at Perth where I made contact with Navy Patrol Squadron, VP-101. That was January 28th, 1943.

It was not long before I learned the history of this patrol unit. The *Japs* whipped squadron VP-101 out of the Philippines when they took over the islands. Three Chief Petty Officers, with a few enlisted men for crew, managed to escape with three PBY-1's and make it down through the Java Straits to Australia. These three planes and the men who flew them were the start of the revised squadron. These three valiant men were promoted immediately to U.S. Navy Warrant Officers. Gradually, the squadron became re-established with new pilots and planes. I was getting in on the ground floor, you might say, with the new VP-101 Squadron.

Here was the situation. The Japanese had moved into New Guinea in March 1942 when they took Lae and Salamaua and began using them as advanced bases. Their next goal had been Port Moresby on the southeast coast, from which Japanese planes could dominate the heavily populated and industrialized Brisbane-Melbourne sector of Australia. In bombing attacks the enemy had destroyed the allied airfields at Darwin on the northern coast of Australia. The United States then brought in seaplane tenders to Perth on the western coast of Australia. From there, VP-101 could run patrols up through the Java Straits and protect shipping coming across the Indian Ocean. Amphibious assaults on Australia having failed, in July the Japanese landed a force on the northern side of the Papuan peninsula in the Buna-Gona area of New Guinea. From there they had begun an amazing advance of their ground troops in an attempt to capture Port Moresby. I say amazing, because of the terrain over which they came. New Guinea is geographically extreme, a vast water-soaked jungle bisected by a jagged mountain range. The Owen Stanley Mountains are among the most rugged in the world, and tower in places to 13,000 feet. Their slopes, sometimes almost vertical, are covered by a dense tropical rain forest. Sometimes it rained as much as ten inches in one day. Why the *Japs* would even attempt to negotiate these steep jungle infested trails in their effort to capture Port Moresby is beyond my understanding. Anyway, they had gotten about a hundred miles on their advance by the summer of 1942 before they were stopped. By 1943 the Japanese had retreated to their strongly held pockets around Buna, Gona, and further northeast around Salamaua, all located on the far north coast of New Guinea.

In the fall of 1943, I arrived at Port Moresby with VP-101 and our lumbering PBY flying boats. I flew a number of different kinds of PBY missions while I was in Port Moresby. They included anti-sub patrols, protection of convoys, search and rescue missions, scouting, and in some cases we were sent out to harass the *Jap* ships that came down under the cover of darkness to reinforce their beleaguered forces. We didn't have attack capabilities, really, but in the night, enemy ships could not identify our planes. A dropped bomb or a few shots from our 50 caliber guns could keep them pretty nervous.

One of our most hazardous assignments while at Port Moresby was when we dropped Australian commandos in distant jungle areas near the Japanese strongholds on the north New Guinea coast. The flight I want to tell about took place on November 16, 1943. This is how it happened.

In 1943 the Japanese, realizing that their defensive perimeters were threatened by the American successes on Guadalcanal and in Papua, began to strengthen Rabaul. Much of the allied success was due to the Australian Commandos who operated throughout the war far behind the enemy lines. The only way that these Australians could get into position was to be flown in by our PBY's. They also needed to be supplied. We respected the Aussie soldiers for what they did in the war. As the campaign was launched to neutralize Rabaul, the activity of these commandos increased.

On November 16th we received orders that Lt. (JG) Barnes and I were to take a load of soldiers into the Sepik River area and drop them off in the jungle behind the enemy lines. This meant a flight of almost a thousand miles roundtrip. We had to fly up over the Owen Stanley Mountains, then on to the drop area, unload the commandos and start the flight back to our base by noon. This was necessary because the clouds always built up in the afternoon over the mountains, making the return flight most difficult. We took off from Port Moresby before daylight, heavily loaded with commandos and the foods and supplies to support them. Just as I lifted the plane off the water, the starboard propeller RPM tachometer dropped clear off confirming that the engine had lost power. I had no idea just how high I was off the water, but I guessed about forty feet. I cut the throttles and yanked the yoke clear back to my belly. That's all I could do.

Those moments seemed like a lifetime, but the tail dropped and we full-stalled back into the sea. If we had been a few feet higher when the engine cut out, we would have nose-dived into the water and that would have been curtains for all of us. A loaded PBY, airborne on take-off that loses an engine cannot sustain flight. The torque from the other engine rolls the plane over for a dive into the water. By dropping two sea anchors I was able to, with some semblance of a straight course, taxi the plane back to the tie-up buoy with the one engine that was still running. It was a close call and delayed our flight to the next day. Then two PBY's, including my own, made the predawn takeoffs without a problem and made the slow climb to 11,000 feet without incident. That altitude was our service ceiling and for safety precaution we did put on our oxygen masks. It was a beautiful clear morning. The lush jungle grew over the precipitous slopes of the Owen Stanley Range, with some of their jagged peaks towering a thousand feet higher than we could fly.

Late that morning I located the Sepik River, one of the larger rivers in New Guinea. It cut the dense jungle with enough breadth to land our long-winged seaplanes. The landing had to be up current on the muddy river, regardless of the wind direction. I watched as the other PBY made the landing. There was always apprehension in landing in these remote and unfamiliar places. I felt great responsibility for the brave men I carried. The pilot appeared to make a good landing, but soon it became apparent that the plane was in trouble. The hull was taking water fast. While he still had control, he gunned the engines and forced the big plane onto a sandy beach along the river. When I got to him I discovered that he had hit a submerged log that had penetrated the bow of the hull and pierced the plane up to under the cockpit.

Fortunately, I had been able to make a good landing on the river and beach our plane alongside the damaged craft. There, I unloaded the commandos and their supplies. The problem now was to figure out what in the world we could do about the damaged PBY. It looked like a hopeless situation to me, but we had to make some decision.

Fortunately, the Aussies had set up their command camp only a few hundred yards away, near a tribe of pygmies. I had heard about them all my life, and it was fascinating to see these little people. Not one of them was over four feet high. They hated the *Japs* with a passion, and welcomed the Australians as their saviors. All the little men carried bamboo spears, and were naked except for a little sheath that covered the penis. We laughed. I guess that was to protect the vital part from the blood-sucking leeches that were so prevalent. The women were very shy and hid out along the edge of the jungle. They appeared to be completely naked. In the short time that I was there, I was able to trade some candy and a knife for beautiful spears. They were about five feet long with sharp poison tips. Little bamboo sheaths protected these lethal tips.

The crew of the damaged plane decided to stay with the commandos. I was to return to Port Moresby for saws to cut the log loose from the impaled plane, and the materials they would need for a temporary patch job on the ruptured hull. That was the only logical decision to be made. My problem was that it was well past noon, because of the delay, and the towering clouds had built up over the mountains. I had two alternatives for the flight back to the base. Either I could fly through the clouds and over the mountains on instruments, knowing that some of the peaks were higher than the plane could fly, or I could chance flying over enemy territory without fighter protection. I decided on the high mountain flight. It was a long and tense trip back over the Owen Stanley Mountains, but once on the other side we broke out of the clouds for the quick descent down to our home base.

Another plane was assigned to take a rescue crew back to the Sepik River the next day. They were able to repair the plane, and eventually the plane and all the crews made it safely back to Port Moresby.

When the famous *Black Cat* squadron left the Solomon Island campaign in early 1944 we replaced them and carried on with the work they had done so effectively. As the fight had intensified, more and more American pilots needed to be rescued. Search and rescue was a lot of my job. By the summer of 1944, the Americans controlled the sky all up through the Solomon's. The allied tactic of bypassing and isolating large Japanese forces was now so successful in eastern New Guinea and in the Solomon's that it became unnecessary to make a costly land attack on the Japanese fortress of Rabaul.

There were large pockets of Japanese soldiers still left on Bougainville and Rabaul. They had tunnels dug into the cliffs high above St. George's Straits and the Duke of York Island. From these protected and concealed positions they could still fire upon the allied shipping that used these strategic passageways. The *Japs* had their artillery on railroad tracks in the tunnels. They would pull out the guns and fire a few rounds and then retreat back into their tunnels. This created a major problem for our ships as they came through the narrow passage in range of the fortified promontories. Fleet Air Wing 17 got orders to knock out these enemy positions, using marine bombers and fighter planes. These squadrons began to attack the fortresses, but not without some losses Many were shot down or damaged before they could return to their bases. That's where VP-101 came in.

As the battle lines had moved on up through the Solomon Islands, the seaplane tenders moved with us. These ships tended our planes and gave us a mobile base. I stayed aboard the sea plane tender, USS Heron, when they moved us clear up to Green Islands for rescue operations around Rabaul. We had several anchorages in these islands that put us within fifty to 100 miles of the rescue operations. Our squadron was now under the command of Lt. Commander Bedell and our code name was Dumbo. I flew 23 missions that summer and our crew rescued three pilots. My flight log shows the following entries:

June 8, 1944. Two F4U fighters hit by gunfire and crashed off Cape Liguan. No survivors.

June 17, 1944. Pilot Flight Officer R.W. Walker, ditched a F4U Fighter.

July 9, 1944. Lt. Taylor US Marine Corp. (Received a broken nose in the crash)

September 6, 1944. 2ed Lt. L.L. Parker, Marine Squadron VMF-212, rescued.

I want to tell you the story of the rescue of Lt. L.L. Parker. That was to be my last flight in a PBY in action during World War II. It was fitting that it would be in my old plane *What The Hell*. I was feeling pretty well strung out by that time anyway. It had been two years since I had left my new bride on the dock in San Francisco. There had been no let up in the tension I had been under for months. I had lost a lot of weight, and I longed to be back in the trees, the meadows, the familiar mountains and the clear steams of my home in Montana. Many times I felt that I would never make it home again. War does something to the brain. Weariness was upon me. That was September 6, 1944.

I received word that there was a downed pilot off Rabaul. We had three officers assigned to the rescue mission Lt.(jg) Smith, Lt.(jg) Roth, myself, and an enlisted crew of eight. When we arrived in the general area where the rescue was to be made, I became very concerned because the waves were running eight to ten feet high. I estimated the wind at twenty-five to thirty knots. That made it difficult to land a plane. Our fighter escort had lost sight of the downed pilot who had been reported to be in his life raft. Eventually I did see him bobbing in the rough water, but I didn't want to expose our crew to this kind of danger to save one man. That was a terrible position to find myself in. I made a few more passes to determine how best to approach a workable rescue, and in doing this lost sight of the pilot. What frustration!

By the time I located him again, the waves seemed to have calmed a bit and we made the decision to land. It was a good stall landing and I expected to plump down like we should in a rough sea. But, just before we hit the water in a tail down position, a big wave hit that tail section. This dropped the bow of the plane right into the next wave. The water hit us with such force that some rivets flew out of a section of the flying boat's hull. At first I thought the engines would stop, because such a wall of water had hit them. To my dismay and relief the engines regained some RPM's and I was able to maneuver the big bird into position. While I taxied around looking for the pilot I had lost sight of again, our great crew took sharpened lead pencils and forced the points into the holes where the rivets had popped out. That seemed to stop the leaks in the hull. It took us about thirty minutes to find the pilot and get him aboard. We found out later that his name was 2nd Lt. L.L. Parker, a marine pilot attached to squadron VMF-212. He had gotten so sea sick bouncing around the rough sea in his raft, that by the time we got him he didn't much care whether he lived or died. He was in bad shape.

I realized about this time that the rough landing had damaged the port outrigger float and that it had started to take in water, causing a drag to the port side. This was serious because the waves were still high. After several failed tries to take off I ordered the crew to throw overboard everything loose, including the Norton Bombsite. I started to jettison the fuel. We were only about fifteen minutes from our base, and we would not need the extra fuel. We tried again, but still couldn't get off the water.

We all realized that we were in a very dangerous situation.

224

Here we were, stranded in the water a mile from the Japanese batteries. We had been spotted, and shooting at us began with their small arms fire. The option of beaching our damaged plane in this situation was out of the question. I thought of one other course of action that might save us, but it was a dangerous one. Because the left port float was gradually being flooded with water, I might be able to bring the plane back into balance by applying extra weight to the starboard wing. "Tie a life line from the top hatch out to the end of the starboard wing," I ordered. Two of the crewman crawled out on the tossing wing. This added weight began to bring the wings back into some semblance of balance. In a very calculated and risky endeavor, I forced the throttles open and attempted a take-off with two men holding on for their lives at end of the starboard wing. The plane labored along in the choppy water. We just couldn't get up enough speed to get the giant hull up on its' step and free of the water. There would be no more flying for old *What The Hell*.

The port wing began to take on more water. This put the craft in a thirty-degree list, and I knew the plane would soon sink. Time had come for us to abandon ship. Hurriedly, we inflated two nine-man life rafts. It would be important that the crew not get separated in the rough seas, so we decided to tie the rafts together. The long rope kept us tied, but thirty feet apart, so that when one of the rafts was lifted by a wave the other raft would not be dumped. We got into the rafts none too soon. One wing of the PBY was now straight up in the air and the other wing was buried under the water. It was sad to see the plane, which had been so much a part of our lives and seen us through so many perilous times now lying there dead in the water. In a short time we would sink old *What The Hell* with our own guns, sending her to the bottom to join the hundreds of other warplanes that had been lost in the brutal fight to destroy Rabaul.

In the evacuation of the plane we took along two parachutes and two seaplane sea anchors. These anchors for the planes were canvas bags with a hole in one end, similar to a windsock, with a tether rope attached to the larger end of the sleeve. We also had a little water, a ration of Spam, and our life jackets. We were armed with three Colt 45 automatic pistols and some ammunition. The

Japs could see us from the beach and they continued to fire at us. Two things helped us from taking a hit. The sea was still so rough that it made our bobbing rafts hard to hit. Then some of our fighter planes located us and kept us covered by strafing the gun placements on the shore. This was about one o'clock in the afternoon.

One of our biggest problems was Lt. Parker, the pilot we had rescued. He was so sick that he had little comprehension of just what was going on. He had no intention of getting back on a raft again in those rough seas. Several of the crew had to manhandle him to get him on a raft. He was in bad shape.

The wind was still blowing us toward the enemy beach. Fortunately the tide began to change and by putting our parachutes in the water, we held our distance from the shore. By this time the wind abated somewhat and the warm afternoon sun helped. We were much more comfortable in our rafts. One of the pilots had left a big ditty bag in the plane when we were transferred from New Guinea to the Solomons. Unknown to me, he hadn't tossed the bag overboard when everything else went. Guess What! The bag held his cherished collection of good liqueurs. So, while we sat there in the rafts waiting to be rescued we had a few sips—a little lifesaver you might say.

The parachute and sea anchors were still holding us off the beach O.K. The marine fighter pilots came back and kept on strafing the Japanese gun positions. Actually they were now providing protection for another PBY from our squadron that had come to pick us up. We had only been in the water for a little over an hour. What a glorious site to see that big plane make its landing approach. The hull touched the water and settled without a problem. When the plane reached us we scrambled aboard. All of us were in a hurry to get out of there while the Japanse gunners were still pinned down.

The takeoff was one that I shall always remember. The crewmen were seated backward on the bottom of the plane. All of a sudden the wind picked up again. Lt. Commander Steve Bedell, our Executive Officer asked me to man the co-pilots seat. As he poured the power to the engines, the plane began to move. Soon we

226

were hitting the wave tops and with every hit our teeth would jar. What a beating the plane was taking, but eventually we broke free. It was a glorious feeling to be in the air again. From my cockpit seat I had a wonderful view as we made a pass over *What The Hell*, still wallowing there on her side. We sent a blast of 50-caliber machine gun rounds through her body and I watched as she sank and disappeared.

After we arrived back at our base, I made my official report to Commander Bedell on what had happened on that memorable day. He said:

"You have had enough. You are on your way to the hospital in Manus in the morning, and then home!"

Lt. William Barnett at the Controls

PBY *Catalina* Patrol Plane

Squadron VP-101

Perth, West Australia, 1943

PBY *Catalina* Patrol Plane
BlackWidow Squadron, VP-101

PBY, *What The Hell,* flown by Lt. William Barnett, USNR
New Guinea and Solomon Islands
1943 – 1944
This picture was taken at Port Moresby, New Guinea

15

ALBERT K. EARNEST, CAPTAIN, USN

I first met Bert Earnest at the Sand Point Naval Air Station in Seattle, Washington in February 1943. We had both been assigned to active duty involving combat flying in the newly commissioned Composite Squadron VC-31. I flew with Bert Earnest for the next fourteen months, first in Squadron VC-31 and then in Squadron VC-7. In February 1944 the squadron was attached to the CVE carrier, Manila Bay, and we flew together during portions of this combat tour. Naturally we talked periodically about his previous experience in the Battle of Midway. Although his war record has been highly publicized over the years, some of the facets of his decorated career have never been heard in the personal ways that are shared between friends. It has been my privilege to perhaps give some added perspective to his story. Before I do, let me put this account in the historic circumstances that led to the Battle of Midway.

Bert Earnest can best be described as a tall, dark-haired, good looking man, who is a literalist, soft spoken and sharp in the cockpit. His hometown was Richmond, Virginia and he had graduated from the Virginia Military Institute. Bert had always wanted to fly, and upon graduation from VMI in 1938 he took the Army Air Corps examination, but he was disqualified because of a vision problem and figured that was the end of it. However, Bert had a friend who took the navy preflight medical and discovered exercises which brought his vision up to requirements. Taking his friend's suggestion, Bert was able to make this improvement also, and passed the physical for navy flight training, earning his Wings of Gold on November 21, 1941, two weeks before the Japanese attack on Pearl Harbor. Three months later he reported to Commander John Waldron's Torpedo 8 Squadron in Norfolk, Virginia.

He qualified as a carrier pilot in the old Douglas *Devastator* (TBD-1). Bert said, "The *Devastator* was easy to fly around the boat, but too slow and vulnerable in combat." All of his combat would come in the new Grumman *Avenger*. The TBF/TBM was a much more formidable airplane. "It was a nice flying bird, but you worked like hell due to the heavy control pressures," he added. Bert was destined to take the TBF *Avenger* into combat for the first time at the Battle of Midway. This would mark the first time during World War II that Japanese air power would experience defeat.

Here was the situation in the Pacific during the last week of May 1942. Admiral Nimitz, Commander of the Pacific Fleet, knew through decrypted messages from Tokyo that the Japanese were going to attack Midway Island. They were sending a force of 162 warships and auxiliaries, including four large carriers, three light cruisers and nine battleships. Against this armada Nimitz could pit only seventy-six ships, no battleships, and only three carriers, the Hornet, Enterprise, and Yorktown. Admiral Nagumo, who commanded the Pearl Harbor raid, was in charge of the Japanese carriers.

Shortly after dawn on June 4th a U.S. search plane spotted the Japanese carriers 240 miles northeast of Midway. While the three American carriers set an interception course, the unsuspecting Japanese began attacking Midway. Having completed their strike, Nagumo's planes came back to land on the Japanese aircraft carriers. That was just when the first American torpedo bombers came in low for their attack. This drew the Japanese *Zeros*, which were flying air combat patrol at altitude over their fleet, to dive down and attack the torpedo bombers. The *Zeros'* attack on the torpedo planes was devastating. The first three U.S. squadrons scored no hits and their losses were disastrous. Only six of forty-one torpedo planes returned to the American carriers. But the sacrifice made by the low flying torpedo flyers had not been in vain. Had not the Japanese planes dived down from altitude, the dive-bombers, who arrived a few minutes later overhead would not have been free to make their successful attack. Additionally, when the dive-bombers made their attack they found the Japanese carriers loaded with their refueling planes. The United States Navy bombers caught the Japanese off guard and in the process sank three of Nagumo's carriers. Only the Hiryu remained, and in a desperate effort to recover the initiative, Nagumo ordered his planes to attack the Yorktown. The Japanese planes damaged the U.S. carrier, which was later abandoned and sunk, but not before the planes from the Yorktown sank the Hiryu.

Admiral Yamamoto assembled his decimated fleet and withdrew. He had lost four carriers, 250 planes, and more than 2,000 men. He had also lost the initiative in the Pacific War, and although there would be a lot of fighting ahead, this was the turning point for the United States in the war with Japan.

*   *   *

I now write of Bert Earnest's participation in this historic battle. The story did not come to me from this quiet man in one sitting. Rather it is the cumulative bits and pieces he shared with me during more than a year that we spent together. Also there have been several articles that have been written about his experience, one that Bert Earnest wrote for the U.S. Navy Foundation Magazine. These accounts have helped as I now tell the story in his words. I have verified the facts and have placed them in their historical context. This is his story.

*   *   *

I am Bert Earnest. I finished my flight training in November 1941, at Miami (Opa Locka) Florida, and received my navy wings and commission as an Ensign. This was just a few days before the attack on Pearl Harbor by Japan. I was scheduled to go to sea on the aircraft carrier Hornet with Torpedo 8 Squadron. Just before the squadron left on the Hornet with their TBD Douglas *Devastator* torpedo bombers, my orders were changed when the squadron was split. I was left behind with Lt. Harold "Swede" Larson, our new commanding officer, and several other pilots, to wait for the first delivery of some new torpedo bombers built by the Grumman Aircraft Company. Few knew at that time about the TBF-1 *Avenger*, a plane that would eventually play a major role in the defeat of Japan.

With a little training in the new plane behind us, we flew from Norfolk to the North Island Naval Air Station across the bay from San Diego and eventually on to Alameda, California where our planes were loaded on a ship bound for Pearl Harbor. The plan was that we would be there in time to fly aboard the Hornet, once again joining up with Commander Waldron and the rest of our friends in Torpedo 8. It didn't work out that way. We arrived in Hawaii on the 28th of May, just a day too late. The Hornet had already sailed with Torpedo 8 and their TBD's for the secret showdown at Midway.

Our skipper, Swede Larson, figured that he could get at least six of us ready to go the next morning for the flight to Midway. The service men worked all night to install the belly tanks in our planes,

234

so we could make the long flight to Midway. Almost all of us volunteered to make the flight, but we only had six planes ready. I was chosen as one of the six to go. It was a 1,200-mile flight out over the water without navigational aids, and because the mission was so secret we could not use any radio communication. I was relieved when two VP-24 patrol plane navigators volunteered to fly with us. Using their Norden Bomb Sights to give us our drift calculations, we had a much better chance of finding that little sand island in the far Pacific. Tragically, both of these brave men were lost when they volunteered to fly with the squadron during the Battle of Midway.

Since we had never trained as a squadron, I had not been assigned a regular crew. I was happy to be teamed with Radioman Third Class, Harry H. Ferrier as my radioman and tunnel gunner, and Seaman First Class, Jay D. Manning, as my turret gunner. Both were fine young men whom I had known around the detachment. They were about eighteen years old. I was 24, the old man of the group. On June 1st, 1942 the six planes under the command of our Executive Officer, Langdon K. Fieberling, took off from Ford Island at Pearl Harbor for Midway. Eight hours later our detached segment of Torpedo Squadron 8 arrived in our new Grumman TBF's at the little sand island of Midway. The *Avengers* we flew would be the first to enter the battle against Japan.

The crews on Midway took off the auxiliary gas tanks and armed the planes with the one-ton torpedoes. There was a lot of tension and activity on Midway. Those of us in Torpedo 8 (detached), as we were officially designated, settled back as best we could to await the violent fight that we all knew would come. On June 3rd the report came. The Japanese fleet had been spotted heading for Midway. We didn't get a lot of sleep that night because we knew that the next morning we would be flying out to engage the invading force.

An hour before dawn we were in our planes waiting for the order to take off. About 6:00 A.M. a marine officer climbed up on the skipper's wing, and I knew he was getting an up-date of some kind. A moment later another marine came over to my plane and shouted up to me, "Enemy forces at 320 degrees, 150 miles." We immediately started our engines, taxied out to the runway and took off. The six of us flew outbound, climbing up through the scattered clouds to about 4,000 feet. I got sight of a flight of Japanese planes headed for Midway, but they apparently were loaded for the attack and didn't bother us. Manning, the turret gunner, told me that he could see firing and explosions on Midway.

It was a little over a hundred and sixty mile flight to where the Japanese ships were reported to be. I was concerned because we did not have any fighter protection. What fighter planes there were at Midway were assigned to protect the island. Also, we never did make any attempt to join up with the dive-bombers as was originally planned. Why, I have never known. Perhaps the plan was changed at the last moment because the TBF's were faster than the dive-bombers. It might have been better had a coordinated attack developed, but this didn't happen and we just pressed ahead on our 320-degree course. In about an hour I spotted a large force ahead of us with at least two aircraft carriers. Almost instantly Manning called out, "Attack! Enemy fighters!" Then I heard his turret gun begin to fire. The *Zeros* were all around us. There must have been twenty to thirty of them on our tail, so many they were getting in each other's way. The air was filled with tracers and I could hear the plane taking hits. Pretty soon our turret gun fell silent. Ferrier took a look up the tunnel to the turret to see why, and saw Manning hanging limp in his safety harness. Ferrier tried to fire his .30 caliber, but our hydraulic system had been shot out and the tail-wheel dropped down blocking his fire. A bullet grazed his wrist, then he received a stunning blow to his head and lost consciousness.

I dove down to about 200 feet and headed for the nearest carrier. As scared as I was I couldn't help but be amazed at the maneuverability of the *Zeros* as they swarmed around us. Bullets were clanging off the armor plate behind me and a cannon shell tore into the wing of the plane. Shrapnel penetrated the canopy and hit me in the neck. Though blood splattered around the cockpit, I don't remember feeling a thing. When I was still some distance from the carrier, the plane started down. I had lost elevator control when the cable was severed. It was obvious that I would soon hit the water. I still had rudder and aileron control so I eased the plane in the direction of a Japanese destroyer or light cruiser and launched my torpedo. I have no idea what happened to it, as I was much too busy as I was about to hit the water. Instinctively, I rolled the elevator tab back, and the aircraft responded. A couple of the *Zeros* continued to pepper my plane with their machine-gun bullets as I made my retreat, but we were still flying. One thing this did was to hold off the fire from the ships. The Japanese gunners did not want to chance hitting their own planes.

After what seemed like hours, but probably was only about five minutes, the *Zeros* left. Either they were running out of fuel or ammunition, or they were called off to intercept the dive-bombers that were beginning their attack. By that time I was so tired it was a major struggle to keep awake. The flight to get back to Midway in some ways was more difficult and nerve wracking than the attack itself. I drove myself to keep my mind clear. My compass had been shot out and none of my instruments were operative. I couldn't close the bomb bay doors or lower the flaps. I could still raise and lower the nose of the plane by using the trim tab, and although this was makeshift, I could adjust our altitude in this way. Also, I could estimate the general direction of Midway by the position of the sun, but Midway is such a small little island to find in that vast ocean. Fortunately, my estimate was close enough and in about an hour I spotted black smoke billowing up from the island as a result of the morning attack. Suddenly, I heard Ferrier on the intercom, "Are you O.K. Skipper? He had regained consciousness and realized he was still alive, although he had lost a lot of blood. "Manning is dead." Ferrier climbed up into the middle seat behind me as we flew on.

On approaching Midway, I attempted to lower the wheels on the plane with the emergency release lever, but only the left wheel dropped down. Although they tried to wave me off, I came right in to the bomb-pocked runway. Considering that I had no flaps and only one wheel down, the landing was quite smooth until the starboard wing lost its lift and dropped to the runway. We spun around coming to a halt quite conveniently just off the edge of the runway.

The crash wagon came speeding out and the men took the

dead gunner and Ferrier from the plane. I looked over the damaged plane with some of the maintenance crew stationed on Midway. We counted 147 shell holes in the plane and none of us could figure out how the *Avenger* had kept flying. This was one of the first six TBF's to be flown into battle and the only one to make it back. All the others had been shot down, killing the fifteen men that manned them. Fate, in a positive way, had been with Ferrier and me on that disastrous day. How I wish I could have brought Jay Manning back alive. He was buried at sea in the lagoon between Eastern and Sand Islands. Ferrier and I had the sad duty of inventorying and packing our shipmate's personal belongings for their long passage home to his loved ones.

Except for my part in the Battle of Midway, I was completely in the dark as to what really happened. I didn't know that the Hornet and the rest of Torpedo 8 were even in the attack. Later that day after my return to Midway, old friends from dive-bombing Squadron 8, off the Hornet, landed on Midway to refuel, but they didn't have too much information at that time. It was a day or two later before word came that all of my old flying buddies in Torpedo 8 had been wiped out. That was shocking news. I didn't hear until later that Ensign George Gay had been shot down, along with all the others in the squadron, but was later rescued by a PBY patrol seaplane. So, Gay and I were Squadron VT-8's only surviving pilots. My radioman, Harry Ferrier, was the sole surviving air-crewman. It had been a terrible day for the torpedo planes. Out of the forty-seven that had attacked the Japanese ships during that memorable twelve minutes, the Enterprise lost ten out of fourteen planes, the Hornet fifteen out of fifteen planes, and the Yorktown ten out of twelve planes. And you add the five out of six of the TBF's that our division lost, that's a total of forty out of the forty-seven planes shot down. Not a single one of these planes was credited with a verified torpedo hit, but the historic conclusion is that the sacrifice of these men made the American victory at the Battle of Midway possible. Naturally, I have spent time over the years reviewing the reports and evaluations upon which this statement is based. This is how it happened.

As the torpedo planes came in to launch their torpedoes at the Japanese carriers, the ships maneuvered violently in evasive action. This made it impossible to launch their planes that had come in to refuel. The U.S. torpedo bombers had found the Japanese fleet before the dive-bombers and the fighters arrived overhead. When the Japanese fighters, that had been sent to altitude to intercept the American planes, saw only the low-flying torpedo bombers, they all dove down to engage them. This cleared the sky for the dive-bombers who arrived at altitude when all the other planes were down right over the water. Unopposed, the SBD Dauntless bombers went into their vertical dives, releasing their bombs to explode on the hapless Japanese carriers loaded with planes ready to take to the air.

By nightfall on June 4th, the four Japanese carriers had been sunk. The loss of these fast Japanese aircraft carriers with all their planes was a disastrous blow. They had lost the initiative in the war. The next day United States forces followed up by sinking a few more Japanese stragglers and damaged ships including a Japanese cruiser. If there were a solace in losing all of my friends, it was the knowledge that their sacrifice made the difference between defeat and victory in the greatest carrier battle in the history of the world.

I returned to Pearl Harbor on June 9th in a marine R4D transport plane. After three days leave at the Royal Hawaiian Hotel, I joined the reorganized Torpedo 8 under the command of Swede Larsen. Following the battles of the Coral Sea and Midway, the U.S. Navy's carrier air group was further limited. The new Torpedo 8 was assigned to the Saratoga Air Group, and we were sent to cover the Guadalcanal landings in early August. On the 24th of August, during the battle of the Eastern Solomon's, we engaged the Japanese carrier Ryujo in a coordinated bomber and torpedo attack. I got credit, with three other torpedo pilots, for sinking this capital ship.

A week later the Saratoga got hit by a torpedo from a Japanese submarine, which put her out of commission for several months. We were able to get our planes off the carrier and I went with Torpedo 8 to the Cactus Air Force at Henderson Field on Guadalcanal. The marines held the airfield but the Japanese controlled the rest of the island. Our living conditions were horrible and we didn't get much sleep for we got bombed every night. We made several attacks on Japanese shipping and kept them from reinforcing their beleaguered troops on Guadalcanal. However, on October 13th, we received a particularly heavy bombardment during the night that left most of our *Avengers* destroyed or badly damaged. I had made six torpedo missions, the most any U.S pilot had accomplished at this stage of the war. I doubt that anyone would ever survive more attacks than that. The last combat flight I made off Guadalcanal was on October 13, 1942. I returned to the States and was ordered to the newly commissioned Composite Squadron 31 stationed at the Sand Point Naval Air Station in Seattle, Washington. That was in February 1943.

*   *   *

This ends Bert Earnest's personal account. But it is not the end of the story, for the Pacific War with Japan still had a long way to go. Bert had several more months of combat flying ahead of him as a member of the Torpedo Division of Squadron VC-7, flying from the aircraft carrier Manila Bay. He flew the TBM *Avenger* in the support of several landing operations on the Pacific atolls and islands, as the United States began the long march westward toward Japan.

Bert Ernest said, "My biggest thrills involved a series of hairy landings on the aircraft carrier Manila Bay. This little aircraft carrier was so slow that it couldn't make over thirteen knots. This gave little margin for error in making a carrier landing. In those no wind conditions in the tropics that meant that you were hitting that small fifty foot allotted space on the rolling deck at over eighty miles an hour. This, nearly as much as the battles of Midway and Guadalcanal, remains as a vivid and tense memory. I made over 200 cable-arrested landings on the Manila Bay."

Albert K Earnest remained in the navy for the rest of his professional life, holding a number of flight test and command positions in his distinguished career. During this time he received many awards including three Navy Crosses, an Air Medal, the Purple Heart, Navy and Presidential Unit Citations, and several battle stars. He was also inaugurated into the Navy Aircraft Pilot Hall of Fame. After the war the damaged plane he flew at Midway was shipped to Pearl Harbor and then to San Diego where it was unfortunately junked. Two TBM-3 planes with his name on the cockpits are now on permanent display. One of these *Avengers* is at the Pensacola Naval Air Station Museum in Florida and the other is at the Admiral Nimitz World War II Museum in Fredericksberg, Texas.

Bert Earnest retired with the rank of Captain and now resides in Virginia Beach, Virginia. The last time I saw Bert was at the VC-7 Squadron reunion in Monterey, California in 1986. Since that time we have corresponded. He wrote that Ensign George Gay, the only other Torpedo 8 pilot to survive the crucial Battle of Midway, had died of a heart attack and that in accordance with Gay's request, his ashes had been distributed at sea over the area where his squadron mates had perished. Bert Earnest, alone, remains—a valiant flyer that I proudly call my friend and a fellow torpedo plane pilot for the United States Navy.

The *Avengers* of Torpedo 8
Attack Japanese Carriers at Midway

"The *Zeros* were all around us. There must have been twenty to thirty of them on our tail. The air was filled with tracers and I could hear the shells tearing into my plane."

Ensign Albert K. Earnest

16

LEONARD MUSKIN, LIEUTENANT, USNR

I first met Leonard Muskin in Corpus Christi, Texas in June of 1942. He was a tall and muscular cadet who had been an All-American tackle on the University of Nebraska football team that played Stanford in the Rose Bowl of 1941.

We trained together in the first torpedo squadron ever formed, at the Corpus Christi Naval Air Station in Texas. I remember him again at the Opa Locka Naval Air Station in Miami, Florida. We were in the same section when we practiced simulated field carrier landings prior to our actual qualifications on an aircraft carrier. But it was not until we both reported for active duty involving flying in the newly commissioned Escort Scouting Squadron 31 at the Sand Point Naval Air Station in Seattle, Washington that we became friends. He attended our wedding when Joan and I were married there on March 4, 1943. We flew together for fourteen months, first in training with the squadron, and then during our first combat tour in Squadron VC-7 on the Escort Carrier Manila Bay.

Following his tour on the Manila Bay, he chose to remain in the Pacific and was assigned to a torpedo squadron on the Essex, a large combat carrier. While on the Essex he experienced an amazing naval career that included his successful torpedo attack on the Japanese battleship Musashi during the historic Battle of Leyte Gulf in the Philippines. This torpedo hit on the largest battleship ever built contributed significantly to its sinking. The Battle for Leyte Gulf, involving several key battles in 1944, eliminated Japanese naval power and marked the end of the battleship as a major naval weapon.

It was over fifty years later when Joan and I went to Leonard Muskin's office on Wilshire Boulevard in Beverly Hills, California, that he agreed to tell us this story. It is a story that needs to be recorded, for it is both unique and historical. First, it took place in the greatest naval battle in the history of the world. Second, it is a story about the sinking of the largest battleship in the history of the world. There was great excitement when the mysterious battleships, the Yamato and the Musachi, first appeared. Few Americans had even seen them before this battle, much less attacked them. They mounted a larger main battery than any of the U.S. battleships and were a third larger in size. The two leviathans of the sea were built for world conquest, displacing 63,000 tons, or half again the weight of our heaviest battleships. The main battery consisted of nine guns, each with a bore of more that eighteen inches. No navy in the world could match this firepower. The barrel of one of these guns alone weighed 180 tons. To fly directly into a barrage from these guns and launch a torpedo with success defies imagination. But this is what Leonard and his crew did. I take pride in insisting that this firsthand account be recorded for posterity. Here is the story he tells.

*   *   *

Well, I'm glad you came today. I'll never forget that tour on the Manila Bay. It was just one of those little jeep carriers that had to do all the dirty work and never did get the credit it deserved. You remember, our assignment was to support the landings on those islands on the way to Japan—bombing, strafing, firing rockets, and anti-sub patrols. That's about all we got to do. In many ways it was a lot tougher than flying off those big attack carriers. You didn't really get the glamour that you got when you flew off the larger carriers. That was just the way it was and it was just the luck of the draw as to what carrier assignment you got.

So we were on the Manila Bay for about five months, and then one day the Skipper got us all in the Ready Room and said:

> I've got great news for all of you. We're going back to Pearl Harbor and then back to the United States. That will complete our first tour of duty. When you've completed two tours of duty, then you will get to choose where you want to instruct. You won't have to go back again to combat overseas.

Everyone cheered because we were all ready for shore leave. But I began to think, "I don't want to go through all this again. I'd rather stay out, finish my second tour and once and for all get this whole experience behind me." There was another reason I thought this way. This might give me a chance to get on one of the big attack carriers and that is what I really wanted to do. For these reasons I went to the Skipper and asked him if I could be transferred to another squadron and go back into combat. He looked amazed and said, "Are you really sure you want to do this?"

"Yes, I'm sure," I said.

And so he made a request to headquarters at Pearl Harbor for my transfer. From my standpoint, my decision was based on logic and common sense, but others saw it as irrational. Some saw it as heroic. It wasn't either one. The discussion of my request took place while the squadron was at the Barking Sands Naval Air Station on the Island of Kauai. We had flown our planes to this island just before the Manila Bay went into the shipyard at Pearl Harbor for some minor repairs. The island of Kauai is a little over a hundred miles northeast of Oahu.

Soon orders came directing me to report to an office of some Admiral at Pearl Harbor. They gave me a fighter plane at Barking Sands and I took off for Ford Island at Pearl. It was the first time I had flown a navy fighter plane and I was feeling pretty independent and free, so I did some aerobatics on the way. We couldn't do this in a torpedo bomber.

When I landed at Pearl Harbor, I reported to the Admiral, as directed. The Admiral treated me as some kind of hero. "Just tell me the carrier you want to go on," he said. "Here are the carriers that are available and here is a book that will give you the name of every pilot, crewman, and mechanic on each carrier. If you see anyone who was in your squadron while you were in training, or any familiar person you would like to be with, just say so and I'll send you there."

Each carrier listed between 3,500 and 4,000 people and I saw right away this would be an impossible task for me to select from these lists. In frustration, I responded, "Just send me to a carrier that is in the class of the Essex."

"You want the Essex?"

"Yes, that's just fine."

"O.K. I'll get you on it. When do you want to leave?"

"As soon as possible. I don't have anything to do around here."

Before I knew it, I was on a flight back to Kwajalein where I was to join the torpedo squadron that was assigned to the aircraft carrier, USS Essex. The COMPAC Headquarters had wired the Essex that I was coming, so they expected me. I hadn't seen that little island atoll in the Marshalls since we had bombed it early that year in March 1944. It was very dark when I arrived, but in the morning I saw the island and I was surprised at all the changes that had taken place. We had bombed it pretty bad. Now all the rubble had been cleared away and the entire island was a runway lined with buildings. I don't remember seeing any of those palm trees that once covered the island. The war had taken its toll on this once beautiful place. Now the atoll was barren.

Soon, I was taken to the Essex, which was anchored in the lagoon. They gave me quarters, and that sort of thing, but I didn't meet anyone that I knew. The next morning, after the Essex got underway, the skipper said he wanted me to go on a little patrol and search with the torpedo bombers. It didn't seem necessary to me to fly a patrol because we were a long way from any enemy base or ship. I soon found out that what they really wanted to do was to find out how good a pilot I was. I found out later that they had the provincial idea that pilots off the small carriers were not as sharp as the so-called big boys. I thought to myself, "My God are they wrong! I can prove it." There doesn't begin to be the leeway for error on a small rolling deck that exists on the larger carriers.

Anyway, when I went up to the flight deck to get my assigned plane, I saw all the torpedo pilots gathered there to watch me. It made me kind of mad, so I just turned to them and said, "What arresting wire do you want me to catch when I hit the deck? How about the number one or two wire?" I know it sounded a little cocky, but you know we had to catch one of the first three wires on the Manila Bay or we would crash the cable barrier. You had a much larger landing area on these big carriers. To make a long story short I went around the flight pattern, got my cut and hooked the first wire. That shut them up and I didn't have any more trouble.

We left the Marshalls and started looking for the Japanese fleet. We found some of their ships around the Philippines and on up toward Formosa. I'm going to skip over some of this now, because I know you primarily want to hear about the Battle of Leyte Gulf. But I will say I got a lot of good flying in and participated in attacks that sunk quite a few Japanese ships. This stirred up the Japanese naval forces because this was the first time in the war that they had been challenged by our carrier forces so close to their home shores. Admiral Bull Halsey commanded our task force and he was always pretty aggressive. He did everything he could to get the major ships of the Japanese fleet to come out of Tokyo. They were somewhat reluctant because they had already lost most of their experienced pilots and they knew we had produced a lot more of these new carriers than they had available. When they did send some ships out, they were decoys. They sent their major force, undetected, south through the China Sea. Then they sneaked from there through the Philippine Islands straights for a rear surprise attack on our amphibious forces that had begun their landings on Leyte. They almost fooled us. Their stealthy movements nearly resulted in an allied disaster. That's when we got the emergency call that our forces were in trouble, so we turned south in a hurry and sped to their assistance. This set us up for the Battle of Leyte Gulf, the largest naval battle in the history of the world. I tell you all this so you will understand the circumstances of my participation in this historic event.

On the way down we got some more details on the situation. The small carriers were there at Leyte supporting the landing operation when all the Japanese battleships, cruisers and destroyers started coming in on their southern flank. The only force between the landing ships and the enemy were these little jeep carriers including our old carrier the Manila Bay. The Manila Bay was the key to keeping the Japanese at bay, giving time for us to arrive. This little escort carrier performed gallantly off San Bernardino Strait and turned back the big Japanese battle fleet to save the landing forces in Lingayen Gulf. Pilots from the Manila Bay shot down fifteen planes and the gunnery crew on the ship accounted for five more. Two Kamikaze planes hit her, one squarely on her flight deck wounding eighty of her crew. However the Manila Bay was back in action the next day.

Of course, when we got the word about all that was going on south of us, the Essex, along with the rest of the task force, reversed course and sped all out to the rescue. Admiral Halsey gave the orders, "Don't worry about keeping formation. Just get down there and help as fast as you can!"

First we made contact with several of the Japanese carriers and we just destroyed them. They didn't have a lot of air cover as far as I could see. Four of these carriers were destroyed in quick order. Now the rest of the Japanese fleet was left without any air cover at all, but regardless their ships just continued to come at us. It was no longer a battle between opposing carriers at a distance like most of our operations. Now it was capital ship against capital ship, slugging it out within sight of land, the deadliest sea fight of all time. When our forces saw the Musachi there was great excitement. This, along with the Yamato, was the new mystery battleship that we had heard about, the largest by far in the world.

When we got orders to launch our attack, you can imagine the emotions we felt. I took off in my TBM Grumman torpedo bomber and joined up on the wing of our skipper. I was loaded with a two thousand-pound torpedo. We flew just a short distance before we found the Musachi. She was running from us so we came right up on her stern. This was no position to launch an attack and I just prayed she would make a turn. There were other planes launching an attack from the other side and the Musachi went into evasive maneuvers. Would you believe it, she began a turn that brought her broadside to me. When I saw that I just turned under our skipper, who for some reason continued on ahead without changing his course. There, now just in front of me, was the full side of this giant ship. I tell you it was huge.

The Musachi looked like a floating island and I knew there was no way I could miss her. However, she was throwing up a lot of fire, bringing all of her guns to bear on me. The AA was intense! All the aircraft batteries and the big eighteen-inch cannons were shooting at me. It was just a curtain of fire; unbelievable! I made my approach at 300 knots, but of course I would have to slow way down to 200 knots to make a successful launch. I actually felt like I was standing still. Let me tell you, this can scare a fellow to death. I could hardly see the ship by this time because of the fire and the smoke, but I knew that I had the perfect bow shot on her if I could just keep flying. This was my chance of a lifetime; a shot at the largest battleship in the world and that was what I had dreamed of. I couldn't veer or dodge anymore because it was time to launch the torpedo. A successful run is possible only if the torpedo is dropped from a plane that is not slipping, sliding or turning—a perfectly steady platform at the precise moment of launch. The guns were bearing in and the shells appeared to be bursting all over the nose of the airplane. At the last minute some of the other planes came in so the ship had to spread its fire. I got off a good launch and with the release of the torpedo, the plane took a jump, as it always does when you lose a ton of weight. I closed the bomb bay and then pulled up the wing flaps that I had lowered to reduce the plane's speed enough to get a good launch. Now I was real low and I needed to get out of there. When I flew across the Musachi I could see the Japanese running around the deck. But right over the ship was the best place to be, because by that time they were firing at all the other planes that were coming in to attack.

I'm making all this sound very dramatic, but the truth is that the chance of getting out of an attack like this alive—well as you know that's pretty slim. We all knew it when we volunteered to be naval torpedo pilots. I thought every attack we made was tough, but this was by far the toughest. This was the most anti-aircraft fire I had ever experienced. As soon as I flew across the ship and began to get away, I had the sensation that my flaps were still down and the bomb bay was open. I looked down at the ocean and I felt I was almost standing still, but it was an illusion because in reality I was getting out of there under full power. There was a sense of unreality about it all. When I calmed down, I realized I was indicating an air speed of 230 knots. That's about as fast as you can fly right over the water in that old plane. I know now that it was only because I was so anxious to get out of there that it all seemed so slow.

I kept making evasive maneuvers as we made our retreat and this continued to give my gunner and the radioman a scare. "Mr. Muskin are you hit? Are you hit?" They were really panicked because they knew that if I couldn't fly the plane they would be killed. Those poor guys had a terrible job and I give them a lot of credit. They are the bravest of all. I assured them that I was OK and just getting the hell out of there.

I could see that the battle was going on all around. The sky was just black with smoke from the anti-aircraft fire and the burning ships. Our Third Fleet planes and ships continued hitting the Japanese task force all that day. On the way out I saw one of their ships roll over after being hit by a number of bombs and torpedoes.

Finally, I got twelve or fifteen miles away from where the main battle was taking place. Our squadron had been directed to rendezvous in this area. Only about ten of our planes were there and there should have been about a hundred. That didn't surprise me because the fighting had been so intense. A lot more survivors did eventually come out of it, but we did lose a lot of people. The losses were more than worth it, for we really did annihilate the Japanese fleet as an effective fighting force and the successful allied invasion of the Philippines was assured. The Japanese naval force never did recover, and the few ships that did escape were later picked off. October 24, 1944 had been quite a day. At dusk, having taken sixteen bomb hits and ten torpedoes, the stricken battleship Musachi sank with about half of her crew of two thousand. In all phases, the battle of Leyte Gulf cost the Imperial Navy four carriers, three battleships, six heavy cruisers, four light cruisers, nine destroyers, and 387 aircraft. The U.S. Navy lost the light carrier Princeton, two escort carriers, and three destroyers. Later I found out that that the Battle of Leyte Gulf had been the largest naval engagement in history and ended in a resounding victory for the United States forces.

When I got back to the Essex and the surviving pilots were debriefed, I got credit for the initial hit on the Musachi. That was quite an honor and I was later decorated with the Navy Cross for the successful attack. Most of us got awards that included the Navy Cross, the Distinguished Flying Cross, or the Silver Star. So, that's my story on the sinking of the Musachi. Over fifty years after those few dramatic moments, that event is still very clear in my memory. You just don't forget an experience like that.

*   *   *

Leonard went on, and the story he told me was fascinating.

*   *   *

How about your son, Tri? I remember him when he was only a year old. You mentioned that he had a spiritual experience that eventually led him into the ministry. Well, I had a religious

251

experience once and I still wonder about it. It was such a mystery and maybe you will be able to explain it.

It happened on the last combat mission I flew. I was still on the Essex when a submarine crew radioed that they had spotted a cruiser, and three or four destroyers, and some cruiser escorts heading back to Japan as fast as they could. Apparently, they were remnants of the Japanese fleet that had escaped the Philippines. We were ordered to make the attack and my name was on the list to lead the torpedo planes. This was unusual for me, as I always had flown wing on the commander.

It was about noon when we took off from the Essex. I told my crew, "You better hope we don't have another attack like the one on the Musachi, because our luck might run out. I'd hate to get killed on our last mission." Everyone felt the same way. We had one good thing going for us this time though. We would be dive-bombing. Dive-bombing with four 500-pound bombs is a lot better than making one of those terrible torpedo launches.

We had a good cloud cover, so I took the formation through the overcast. The pilots didn't stay close enough to maintain visual contact. When I came through the cloud covering and looked around, no one had followed me. The other planes were still in the clouds. Right then I knew this was going to be one of those botched up flights where nothing turns out right. We had made many devastating attacks, but this one was terrible. Our fighter planes didn't clear the decks of the enemy ships with their low-level strafing, the dive-bombers missed, and I began the attack alone. I never did see the torpedo bombers. About half way down, the Japanese ships started firing on me. I finally cut my bombs loose and hoped one of them would make a hit on the cruiser I had selected as my target.

As I pulled out of my dive, I made a turn to see where the bombs hit. I never did see an explosion, because right then anti-aircraft fire hit my wing. There was a hissing sound as a big shell blew a hole in my wing. For some unexplained reason the shell did not explode, but that was enough for me. So, I just turned again and got out of there as fast as I could. I had my plotting board and pulled it out to figure the course back to the Essex. I could only estimate where I thought I was, because in an attack and an escape you don't really know your exact course and speed. I took the heading home that I thought was right, but knew I'd better check it with my radio YEZB heading. The carrier sends out in radio code a letter of the alphabet for each fifteen-degree quadrant from its position. When you hear the signal, you just fly the reciprocal of that heading as it shows on the chart. That will take you back to the hub, which is the location of your carrier. These radio beams do not bend with the horizon but are transmitted out on a straight line. So if you are flying at a distance, you need altitude to receive the signal. I climbed but never did get the reassuring signal. It was obvious that my radio wasn't working, as I couldn't pick up anything.

It was three o'clock in the afternoon and I had a long way to go to get back to the carrier. The sea was stormy too, and I wasn't eager for a forced landing in the water, or to return with a damaged plane in the darkness to a moving carrier deck. I flew for quite a while, realizing that I was in an increasingly serious and marginal situation. I was apprehensive and less sure of my position with each passing mile. What a way to end my last combat mission— lost, scared, and with little chance for rescue and survival.

Then, out of nowhere came an SB2C dive-bomber. The pilot was flying by himself and joined up on my wing. Usually when you get a join up, the pilot gives you a look or a high sign, but this pilot never looked at me. He just stared straight ahead and then made a gradual turn to his starboard. He seemed so certain of his direction that I just went with him. Never once did he give me so much as a glance. It was a cinch that one of us was wrong. He was definitely taking a different heading than mine, but he seemed so certain. I was in no position to question.

I didn't recognize the squadron number on the tail of his plane. This was unusual, so I jotted the number down on my navigation pad. It was getting a bit darker by this time, and the pilot still hadn't looked at me or given any sign of acknowledgement that I was even there. I was so puzzled. It was strange and weird, sort of like one of those stories you see on television about the supernatural.

Just at dark we came upon the U.S. fleet and there was the

Essex on the exact course we had been flying. As I pulled away, I raised my hand in salute to the pilot who had saved my life, but he gave me no answer. He just turned around and flew off into the darkness. The Essex made her turn into the wind and took me aboard.

After I landed, Commander McCambell, the leading ace fighter pilot, called me in for a debriefing. "It wasn't one of our better attacks," I said. "But I do want to thank the SB2C dive-bomber pilot who guided me back to our fleet. Without him I would be landing in the rough dark sea about now, and that would have been the end for sure."

I gave McCambell the number and the lettering on the tail of the dive-bomber as I had recorded it. "Well, I'll find out for you," he said. He made a few inquiries. "Yours was the only plane that landed. None of the other carriers had a plane with that identification number. And there was no other carrier group within 2000 miles of our position. You must have imagined it or something."

To this day I cannot explain what happened. How I wish I could recall the number of that SB2C. I would still be seeking the answer. I do know that the pilot, whoever he was, saved the crew and me from a watery grave in the far Pacific.

*   *   *

"What do you think? Could it have been an angel?" Leonard asked.

"Well, it was certainly your angel," my wife Joan responded.

"I have always given thanks for a guardian spirit." Leonard wistfully responded.

*   *   *

Lt. Leonard Muskin received a second Navy Cross for "pressing his bombing attack against a Japanese cruiser through heavy and intensive fire without support, bringing his plane, damaged by enemy anti-aircraft fire, back to the aircraft carrier Essex under the most difficult of flying conditions."

He returned to Pearl Harbor on the Essex, and then was sent back to the States where he finished the war as a navy flight instructor. After the war, Leonard moved to Beverly Hills, California and entered the home construction business. He was very successful and acquired a fortune during the post-war boom. Since that time, he has invested extensively in large Los Angeles business properties and still maintains a distinctive office on Wilshire Boulevard.

Leonard enjoys life with Lucy, his loyal wife for over fifty years, in their beautiful Beverly Hills home overlooking the greater Los Angeles area. It has been my privilege to tell the story of this valiant flyer who deserves the good life he has earned.

Sinking of the Musachi

At the Battle of Leyte Gulf

October 24, 1944

"I was loaded with a two-thousand pound torpedo. We flew right up on the Musachi. Would you believe it, she made a turn that brought her broadside to me. The Musachi looked like a floating island and I knew there was no way I could miss her. However, she was throwing up a lot of fire, bringing all her guns to bear on me. The AA fire was intense. I had to fly through a curtain of fire, but this was my chance of a lifetime: a torpedo launch at the largest battleship in the world."

Leonard Muskin, Lieutenant, USNR

SB2C Dive Bomber at Dusk

"Then out of nowhere came an SB2C dive bomber. The pilot stared straight ahead and then made a gradual turn to his starboard. He seemed so certain of his direction that I just flew on his wing."

Lt. Leonard Muskin, 1944

For He will give an angel charge over you to accompany, guide and preserve you in your way.

Psalm 91:11

USS Essex at Night

"Just at dark we came upon the Essex. As I pulled away, I raised my hand in salute to the pilot who had saved my life, but he gave no answer. He just turned around and flew off into the darkness."

Lt. Leonard Muskin, 1944

17

ARNOLD ERICKSON, LT. COMMANDER, USN

I first met Arnold Erickson at the Sand Point Naval Air Station on Lake Washington in February 1943. When Squadron VC-31 was commissioned, we were two of the thirty-six pilots that had been ordered to the new squadron. We were assigned to fly the Grumman TBF *Avenger* torpedo planes and soon became good friends.

Three weeks after meeting, I asked him to be my best man when Joan and I were married. He agreed and was with me when I went to the Union Station in Seattle to meet Joan as she arrived after a three-day train ride from Los Angeles. I flew with Arnold Erickson for longer than a year, first in Squadron VC-31, and later in VC-7 when we flew from the aircraft carrier Manila Bay early in 1944.

Following his tour on the Manila Bay, Arnold Erickson decided he would rather have a new and challenging assignment as a carrier Landing Signal Officer. He might have been marching to a different drummer than the rest of the pilots. I often thought of him as a delightful maverick. Anyway, our commanding officer consented and Erick was assigned for Landing Signal Officer (LSO) training at the Barbers Point Naval Aid Station in Hawaii. LSO's were the officers who stood on the fantail of the aircraft carrier and with their bright signal paddles guided the landing planes back to the deck. Erick, who by nature was sensitive and seemed to question why he had to be in the business of killing, now chose the high pressure and demanding job of an LSO officer. This still remains an enigma to me. But that is what he did. Ironically, Arnold Erickson was to experience more actual combat and would be closer to tragedy than anyone else in our original squadron. Here is his story.

*   *   *

I was assigned to the large combat aircraft carrier USS Franklin. The size of the ship took my breath away, especially when I compared it to the Manila Bay. This was a real attack carrier. I could sense that a cruise on this ship was going to consist of more than anti-sub patrols and the direct support for our landing forces on Japanese held territory. We had five squadrons and over two thousand men aboard.

As soon as we were at sea, they briefed us on the mission. We were part of a huge diversionary attack on Okinawa. The Franklin's planes were to bomb Naha, the capital. To accomplish this, our carrier would have to maneuver so close to the Japanese territory that their land-based bombers could come out and attack us. Naval intelligence told us that the Japanese had five thousand bombers ready for such an attack. As this was the typhoon season, our task force moved in behind a typhoon as the storm moved toward Japan. The planes were cabled securely on the carrier deck. Canvas covers were put over the engines to protect them from the seawater that would splash over the flight deck. As we moved in behind the storm, the seas did become extremely rough. For two days and nights we ate our meals standing up. At night I slept on my back with my feet spread out and my arms extended over the sides to keep me from rolling out of my bunk. At about 1:00 A.M. on the third night, we backed off the typhoon and prepared the planes for the coming attack.

We were in a group of aircraft carriers and all the flattops launched their planes in the dark of the night, so they would arrive at their targets just before dawn. The attacks went well and when the bombers returned, the task force retreated at high speed to get out of range of the land-based Japanese bombers.

Each carrier had fighter planes assigned to combat air patrol. The fighter pilots flew high above the task force, waiting to be directed to intercept any of the enemy bombers coming out to attack our ships. Everyone was happy that the operation had gone well, but no one was ready to celebrate. We were not yet out of the range of the Japanese bombers. As each hour passed the prevalent feeling was, "So far so good." But the peace and quiet didn't last.

We had been at our battle stations since dawn. Every person aboard wore a metal helmet, a life jacket, and was outfitted in flash-proof clothing. I was on the LSO's platform landing our returning planes when I first noticed trouble. There was a half-hour of daylight left. Out on our perimeter a destroyer began to fire it's five-inch guns. I couldn't see their target, but I knew it had to be an attack. Immediately, I began waving off the returning fighter planes. Planes on a carrier deck during an attack create the added possibility of explosion and fire. Just then the ships squawk box opened up, "Prepare for attack!" One of the scout planes had reported that five hundred Japanese bombers were headed for the carriers.

What happened next is the nearest thing I have ever

261

experienced to a living dream. This was a dream in which I couldn't run or do anything right, no matter how hard I tried. It was a nightmare! Looking in the direction of the destroyer that was still firing, I saw a twin engine camouflaged bomber coming at us just above the waves. I knew it was a Japanese *Betty*. Quickly, I put on my Mae West life jacket and reached for my helmet on the bulkhead just below the LSO platform. Someone had taken my helmet. The only one left was a communications helmet that was extra wide at the bottom to accommodate a large set of earphones. It looked like an inverted Wok. I ran forward to the bow of the ship, because smoke and flames are swept back when a ship is hit. The *Betty* bomber had a nose gunner firing and the bullets were bouncing off the deck in front of me. A member of our deck crew was running forward about twenty feet in front of me and one of the bullets hit him in the ankle. This spun him around in the air. This stopped me.

Then the Japanese plane went low to the water. I thought for sure this was a Kamikaze pilot ready to crash into the side of the ship. It looked as if it would hit directly under me, so my first thought was to jump over the end of the ship. I started to run aft without too much thought of surviving such a leap. Just then the *Betty* dropped a torpedo. The torpedo appeared as large as a telephone pole. It seemed much larger than the one-ton torpedoes we dropped from our *Avenger* torpedo planes. I dropped to the deck, so the explosions from the torpedo would not break my legs. I could now see the gunner on the *Betty* and felt very exposed to his fire. I was a perfect target with my yellow shirt, life jacket and helmet. What made it worse, when I dove to the deck, the two release tabs that inflate the life jacket snagged. The jacket inflated lifting me higher and higher on the deck. At the last moment, the Japanese plane pulled up into an abrupt climb to clear the side of the ship. It wasn't a suicide plane after all. It was a torpedo bomber. However, the pilot was so low that when he pulled up to clear the ship the plane stalled and the left wing hit the deck in front of me. Four feet of the wing tip broke off and came to a stop just in front of me. The rest of the plane went into the water on the other side of the carrier. The torpedo never hit the ship. I think the pilot was too close when he dropped it. Torpedoes usually dive deep when dropped and then regain the desired setting as they level out for their run. The torpedo must have gone underneath the ship! It was a close call for us. In the overall action between October 12th and October 18th, 1944 we lost seventy-six planes in combat, thirteen in operations, and sixty-seven pilots and crew. Six of our ships were damaged, but none were sunk.

As darkness fell on that final day of this operation, emergency orders came that our Task Group 38.4 of the Third Fleet under Admiral William "Bull" Halsey was to rush south to protect the landing of U.S. forces in the Philippines. There were four carriers in our group: the Enterprise, the San Jacinto, the Belleau Wood and our carrier the Franklin. Little did I realize we were sailing to an engagement that would be recorded as the largest naval battle in the history of the world. This would forever be known as The Battle of Leyte Gulf. This sea engagement would be composed of four separate, yet closely interrelated actions, each of which involved forces comparable in size to any of those that had been engaged in the largest battles of the Pacific War. The four battles, two of them fought simultaneously, were joined in three different bodies of water separated by as much as 500 miles. Yet all four were fought between dawn of October 23rd, 1944 and dusk of October 24th. We were to repulse the huge Japanese operation that was aimed at destroying the U.S. landing operation underway at Leyte. It is only in retrospect that I have any comprehension of what we faced. At the time all I knew was that we were racing back to the Philippines to protect our troops that were storming the beaches to retake the islands from the Japanese.

We arrived off Cape Engano at the northwest end of the Philippines early on the morning of October 23rd. At 2:00 A.M. I reported to the pilots' Ready-Room in response to a general call to Flight Quarters. The Plexiglas board on the wall detailed the position of the enemy. The Japanese ships were coming directly at us from the north at speeds of twenty knots. As we turned to meet them, it gave us a closing speed of forty knots between the two opposing fleets. We would meet in about eight hours. It was imperative that our planes attacked first and at a distance. Time was of the essence. The order came; launch planes! Off our squadrons flew in the darkness. At dawn they were in position to attack the incoming Japanese fleet. They caught their planes at the moment they were preparing to take off from their carrier decks. Our pilots created havoc on the attacking force, setting fires and damaging a number of their ships. The few Japanese planes that the Japanese had been able to launch headed toward the Philippines. Their airmen showed no desire to fight and the carriers they had left fled north. Actually, this entire engagement had been a diversionary action planned by Admiral Ozawa to take Halsey's fleet north, leaving another Japanese naval force free to come undetected through the San Bernadino Strait.

Then we received a desperate cry from Admiral Kincaid who commanded the task force made up primarily of the light *jeep* carriers that were supporting the landing operation on Leyte. This central Japanese force had come undetected through the San Bernadino Strait, and was now attacking several of his little *jeep* carriers assigned to protect the northern flank of the landing troops at Leyte. These little carriers with their planes were holding off the Japanese attackers but they desperately needed help.

What even made it worse, we found out later, was that a third Japanese naval force had slipped in from the south through Surigao Strait and was threatening the Leyte operations from that direction. Here again, Admiral Kincaid had only a few little carriers between the Japanese and our landing troops on the southern perimeter. Not incidentally, one of these little carriers was the Manila Bay, the ship I had flown from on my first combat tour. Flyers from this heroic little carrier took on the Japanese capital ships and actually stopped their initial advance. Our job was to quickly give them support so that the United States landing operation at Leyte could be secured. There were hundreds of ships and landing craft that were severely threatened, not to mention the men of the Sixth Army who were storming the beaches on MacArthur's return to the Philippines.

The big question had been, "Where is the main body of the Japanese fleet?" We had engaged a decoy portion of their naval power on that initial attack. Now we knew where two other large Japanese fleets were operating against our landing forces. These ships had to be destroyed if the landing operation to retake the

Philippines was to be successful. This would be the key to eventually moving on for a direct attack and invasion of Japan, and hopefully the end of the war. The gauntlet was down and here was our chance.

The Japanese also knew this engagement was decisive. It would decide their future. In desperation they, for the first time in the war, sent out their suicide planes to attack us. Pilots intent on destroying U.S. forces at the cost of their own lives flew these planes. They were the Kamikaze. Hundreds of these suicide planes were sent against us during the Battle of Leyte Gulf. I saw many of them attempt to strike our ships. I remember one that made a run on the battleship, New Jersey. As the Kamikaze went into its dive, the battleship was outlined in fire. All of the guns on the battleship blazed away at the attacking plane. I could not understand how the pilot kept flying through that barrage—unbelievable! Then at the last moment the pilot veered the plane and turned toward the aircraft carrier San Jancinto, which was on our starboard. The Kamikaze pulled out of his death dive just at sea level, hitting the San Jacinto in the hangar deck just forward of the fantail. The plane crashed through the rear bulkhead, wrecking the planes on the hangar deck. Some fires started, but there was no explosion. They pulled the dead and mutilated pilot from the plane. He was dressed in a ceremonial shirt and shorts and wore no parachute. He had forgotten to arm the bomb. A rod inside the bomb needs to rotate before the detonator is activated. When this is not done, the bomb cannot explode. That was another close call.

Although the battle for our forces to secure Leyte became a prolonged and vicious battle for us, the Japanese naval forces took a disastrous beating and never did recover. In all phases of the Battle of Leyte Gulf the Japanese Imperial Navy lost four aircraft carriers, three battleships, six heavy cruisers, four light cruisers, nine destroyers and 387 aircraft. It marked the unquestionable demise of the enemy fleet as a world class fighting force. The U.S, lost the light carrier Princeton, two escort carriers and three destroyers. Much of the damage to our ships came as a result of the Kamikaze attacks, which continued to bring a lot of disaster and heartache.

Several months later, on March 19, 1945, a Kamikaze finally hit our carrier. Here is how it happened. Admiral Spruance daringly led Task Force 58 to Okinawa within sixty miles of Japan. This was a final step for the United States forces as they fought their way to Tokyo Bay. Before dawn on March 18th, we turned into the wind and launched a series of massive sweeps. The next day the Kamikazes struck our ships. Between midnight and 10:00 A.M. the Franklin repulsed twenty-six of these attacks. General Quarters had sounded so often that in a haze we just kept responding and responding to these attacks. "We have a Bogey. Raid number twenty-seven coming in from 280, angels ten, speed 250," the horns sounded. An unidentified plane was approaching at an altitude of ten thousand feet from the West at a speed of 250 miles an hour. I put on my life jacket, leather gloves and my battle helmet again. I tucked the bottoms of my trousers into my socks and wrapped a bath towel like a scarf around my head. This would protect me from burns in case I was caught in the flash of an explosion.

The next thing I heard were the ship's five-inch guns firing irregularly and shaking the ship with each blast. It was apparent that the attacking plane had successfully penetrated our Air Patrol. I knew this because our planes always stopped their pursuit when an enemy plane got within range of our own anti-aircraft fire. Then I heard the rhythmic firing of the twin forty-millimeter Bofors. The attacking Kamikaze had gotten by the five-inch guns and was still coming in. Then the ripping sound of the twenty-millimeters filled the air. I thought, this is one that will get me. I had escaped so many times, but how long could the Lord protect me?

I was in the Bomber Pilots' Ready Room when bombs exploded the ship. I was blown into the air. I came down on my back, crumbled, with chairs, debris and litter all around me. The Kamikaze had hit the Franklin just aft of the five-inch gun mount.

I struggled through the mess and gradually regained my bearings. There were two doors to the Ready Room. I forced one door open and braced it with my foot. Smoke came in but there were no flames. Out of the smoke came an enlisted man, bleeding from many small holes. Fragments had penetrated his face. His bloody shirt was torn and smudged from the explosion. His trousers were ripped and a piece of flesh hung from his thigh. I reached to assist him. "Grab on to my shoulders", I shouted in the melee. "I'll lead you through this mess and get you some help". He desperately needed a first-aid station and a medic. We struggled through the dark and smoke filled passageway to the Officers Wardroom, where corpsmen were set up for just such an emergency. By the time we arrived the medics were already treating some of the injured. The tables began to fill with broken bodies. The medic laid the seaman I had brought on a table alongside another one of the injured. On the table next to them were two others in critical condition. "You hold them while I get some more supplies," the corpsman requested. The hair on these two bodies was singed. Their eyes were open, showing only white eyeballs and they tossed in agony. Their bodies were already swollen and in restraining them from further injury my fingers just seemed to sink into their puffy flesh. In all the time that I had spent in this terrible war, this was the first time I had been faced with the direct human tragedy of it all. I was swept with nausea. I fought to control my psychological reaction as I worked and assisted in holding bottles that were feeding fluid into these shipmates who were fighting for life. Some died and were covered with sheets, but the survivors were moved on stretchers to beds and the wardroom was closed as a first aid station.

The explosions continued, the debris blowing up through the fire and smoke. I thought the Franklin was finished, but the men on deck never did quit their fight during the continued hours that fires burned and the heavy smoke enveloped the wrecked ship. As a result of the crew's historic valor, by nightfall the Franklin was still afloat and making fourteen knots. Miraculously, the Franklin limped into the safety of the Ulithi lagoon.

Navy tradition dictates that when a warship receives damages so great it has to return to the United States for repair, all hands will receive thirty days of survivors leave. Many of us checked the maps to see where Bremerton was in relation to our hometowns. We were trying to decide what transportation was available for a trip home. My hometown was Ashtabula, Ohio. I had been away a lifetime and longed to be there again with my family and friends.

It was not to be. While we were anchored at Ulithi, I received a message, "Report to the ship's communication office for new orders." They read, "Report immediately for Landing Signal Officer duty on the USS Enterprise." This was a dark moment. The Enterprise would be underway again to support the troops that were still fighting for their foothold at Leyte. I was dazed and sick at heart as I came aboard the Enterprise.

There is a tragic facet to this episode. I found out later that the Senior Landing Signal Officer had his request approved to join one of the ship's bomber squadrons. He wanted the experience of flying in combat. Thus, at the last minute I was ordered fill the vacated LSO position. That was why I had received the orders. Three weeks later the officer was killed on one of his first missions.

Compared to the Franklin, the USS Enterprise had a long, proud history in World War II. Tokyo Rose, the propaganda radio voice from Japan, had reported the "Big E" as sunk or damaged several times, only to have to later acknowledge that the carrier had again taken part in action against the Japanese. Some felt the Enterprise had a charmed life.

This is the account of what happened during the time I was on the Enterprise. One afternoon, while we were operating off the coast of the Philippines, a lone Japanese plane dove on us. At the time, I was on duty at my position on the Landing Signal's Officers platform. At first I thought the plane was a Kamikaze, as their attacks continued against our forces. But, at about two thousand feet, the pilot released two small bombs. The plane then flew off with our fighter cover in pursuit. From my position on the L.S.O. platform, I thought the bombs were going to hit us amidships. As the bombs descended, one of them had a steep trajectory and missed us off the starboard side. The other bomb had a shallow trajectory and exploded in the water on the far side of the ship. The concussion was so tremendous that, without hitting the ship, it still blew up the catwalk on the starboard side. This killed three of our pilots who were standing on that side of the flight deck. These

268

pilots were buried at sea in a ceremony scheduled between flight operations. The Enterprise, again, did not lose a moment in its routine flight operations.

Several more weeks went by. Then we were ordered back to Pearl Harbor for new squadrons and new Landing Signal Officers. I had spent more than a year performing on three different carriers. I had participated in the largest naval battle in history and experienced first hand the destruction, anxiety, fear and loneliness that faced many of our generation. Now it was time for me to go home.

The *USS Enterprise*

There is a tragic epilogue to my story. I relate the final chapter of what happened to the USS Franklin after I left the ship and my shipmates after that   initial Kamikaze attack. Following the repair of the aircraft carrier in the Bremerton, Washington shipyard, the ship returned to the Pacific War.   On March 19, 1945, Admiral Spruance daringly led Task Force 58 to Okinawa, taking the armada within sixty miles of Japan, a final step for the United States forces as they fought their way to Tokyo Bay. Before dawn the carrier turned into the wind and launched a series of massive sweeps. That day a Japanese Kamikaze, laden with two 500-pound bombs came out of the low clouds at about 6000 yards and crashed onto the flight deck of the Franklin. The bombs penetrated and exploded the ship's magazine, detonating the bombs and the ammunition. The carrier began to explode in a fiery panorama of chaos.   Under the tremendous explosions, the ship reeled and gasoline fires spread from one end of the ship to the other. All communication was lost and the ship took on a thirteen-degree list.   Casualties were disastrous; 724 men killed and 264 wounded. The aircraft carrier Franklin sustained more casualties and took more damage without sinking than any other ship in the history of naval warfare. Even though the USS Franklin valiantly made port under its own power, the proud ship was beyond repair and never again returned to the sea of battle.

It is with sorrow and pride that I will always remember these brave men and the ship on which they served. They endured much to help ensure the defeat of Japan!

Arnold Erickson remained in the U.S. Navy, and served as a dive-bomber pilot during the Korean War. During the Cold War, he flew Super Constellations as part of the Airborne Early Warning Wing in the Pacific. He also served on the staff of Admiral Leonard B. Southerland in Hawaii. Due to a combat related injury, he was forced to give up flying and retired in 1957 as a Lieutenant

Commander, USN.

His employment included business and education. He worked for the National Education Association for thirteen years.

Erick retired in his hometown of Ashtabula, Ohio where he is now actively involved in the writing of children's' stories and does volunteer work in the public schools. He writes:

> My life is now engrossed in writing stories, which I pretend are coming from the Creative Well. I hope they will help the many "someone's" who try to help our young people to rescue themselves from the many problems they face by using their Divine Gift, their brain. I believe that the words are true in the hymn that reads, "For everyone who goes astray, someone will come to show the way".

In December 2000 I called my old friend Arnold Erickson at his home in Ashtabula, Ohio and heard his voice for the first time in fifty-seven years. Memories flooded in from time long gone. Erick was still fighting the establishment in his own idealistic and committed way, forever true to the drumbeat of his own heart.

The USS Franklin
Hit by a Kamikaze in March 1945

A massive blast shook the entire ship. Sudden death was everywhere, for everyone, for the whole ship; death by fire, explosion and disintegration.

As in a great storm, disaster had struck with a wild wind, followed later by thunder and lightning. But this wind was flame and burning gasoline. It burst forward with hurricane speed and fury, leaving the hangar deck heaped with corpses.

Father Joseph Callahan, Chaplain, USS Franklin

18

FRED DUNGAN,
LIEUTENANT, USNR

There were about twenty-five applicants finally selected for navy flight training at the Long Beach Naval Air Station the week after the Japanese bombed Pearl Harbor. Most of us were from the University of Southern California, but there were a few from some of the other colleges in southern California. It was here that I met Fred Dungan, a native of Pasadena who was a mechanical engineering student at Pasadena Junior College. We signed up and began our training that eventually led to our commissioning as Naval Aviation Cadets. That was December 8, 1941.

Fred Dungan would later go on to be a night carrier fighter pilot and was credited with shooting down seven enemy planes. To my knowledge he was the only pilot in our beginning class who became a decorated ACE.

I lost track of Fred Dungan after we graduated as naval aviators from the Corpus Christi Naval Air Station in Texas in the fall of 1942. I did not see him again until the late summer of 1944 when we were both under medical care at the Long Beach Naval Hospital. He had been shot through the upper chest by a fifty-caliber bullet while engaging a Japanese *Zero* on a 1944 Fourth of July attack on Chichi Jima in the Bonin Islands. He showed me where the bullet had entered his chest, just missing his spinal cord, but shattering his clavicle. Here is the story that he told me about his engagement with the Japanese flyers and his miraculous survival, a story later recorded in part by Eric Hammel in *Aces Against Japan*, published by Presidio Press.

*   *   *

I am Lt. Fred Dungan, Naval Aviator, USNR. After Robbie Robinson and I completed our basic training at the main base at the Corpus Christi Naval Air Station, I was sent to the outlying base at Kingsville for advanced training in fighters. I returned to the main base at the Corpus Christi Naval Air Station on November 13, 1943, where those of us in the class of 5A-42-C (C) were commissioned as Ensigns and received our Wings of Gold.

It was then that I received orders to report for night fighter training at Quonset Point, Rhode Island. That was a special project where we worked at developing operational radar and night-fighter tactics. When I finished this training, I got my orders to VF(N)-76, the U.S. Navy's first *Hellcat* night-fighter squadron.

Then in January 1944, I was assigned with four other night fighter pilots to the aircraft carrier Hornet. There I flew both day and night missions. My first victory was a Japanese bomber that I shot down on April 24, 1944. It was daytime. I had just gone up to calibrate my radar and check to see that everything in the plane was ready for a night mission. Would you believe it, a Japanese bomber just flew by and I shot it down. That was off the coast of New Guinea.

*   *   *

The next two planes I shot down came during a flight I made a couple of months later. Our four-man night detachment was assigned as a division that joined a daylight strike by Fighter SquadonVF-2 against Guam. We were still flying off the carrier USS Hornet. The airplane I flew on this raid was a brand-new *Hellcat* that belonged to the commander of Air Group 2. It was painted navy blue, and had camera gear in the belly. All I had to do to operate the camera was to point the left wing at the target and press the trigger on the throttle. The flying conditions that afternoon were perfect. It was warm and clear, with puffy broken clouds at around 7,000 feet. It was a fine day for flying.

After the dive-bombers and torpedo planes made their attacks, the fighters swooped in to strafe. On my last low pass over the airfield, I noticed what I felt certain were planes in the revetments, concealed by the trees along the main runway. Too, there appeared to be stockpiles of fifty-gallon drums that I assumed were filled with aviation gasoline. I wasn't prepared to take pictures as I streaked by. When I joined up with the strike leader I told Russ Reiserer that I had cameras in my airplane and asked if I could make another run on the field to take some reconnaissance pictures. Russ said, "Okay," and Bill Levering said, "I'll stay with him."

Bill and I climbed up to about 10,000 feet and positioned ourselves over the northeast end of the runway. This placed the revetments I had seen on my port side, the side to which the cameras would be aimed. We dove straight down to build up as much speed as we could. I wanted to flash down the runway downwind, and take my pictures as quickly as possible. On the dive, I was hit in one of the starboard guns by what appeared to be 37mm anti-aircraft fire, but I kept going and pulled out low, right over the runway.

On my way down the runway, I strafed the AA battery that had hit my *Hellcat*. It was on the starboard side, toward the water. Then I pressed the camera trigger and hoped that I was taking pictures of the airplanes in the revetments.

At the end of the runway there was a cliff overlooking the water. Instead of pulling up, I led Bill down the cliff and recovered over the water a couple of miles out. As we began to climb again, I could see where my track had been during the dive. There was a trail of smoke left by the AA exploding shells that had been fired at me.

Flying back up to 6,500 feet to set up for another camera run, I looked back down at the field. There were no more AA shells coming up at us, but that wasn't because we had knocked out the gun batteries. It was because a Japanese carrier air group was breaking up in the landing pattern. The whole formation was circling counterclockwise into the wind, and several flights of bombers were peeling off and going in to land.

I got on the radio and yelled, "There's a whole Japanese air group landing on the field. They're right down there where we just attacked. We need help." While this went on I turned to Bill, who was on my wing. I pointed down so he would see the enemy planes. He had already seen them, so we just dove down into the landing pattern. I wanted to break up the formation by flying head-on into them. As we approached the bombers, I quickly looked back over my shoulder. Bill was beside me, but behind him there looked like there were a hundred *Zeros* coming right on us. Luckily, the *Zeros* broke off and did not come down through their own bomber formation. That saved Bill and me.

Only three of my port guns were working smoothly. The other one had been hit by anti-aircraft fire during the photo run and now was working only intermittently. Back over the field again, the first plane I saw was a *Kate* torpedo bomber. It was on the base leg, just ready for a final letdown. I led it very slightly from dead ahead and let my tracers trail back into his wing root. I had trouble holding the gun sight on the *Kate* because of the uneven recoil caused by the faulty gun. The *Hellcat* kept skewing to the left, but I could bring it back on target by applying a little more right rudder. The *Kate* blew

276

up in front of me and I flew through the explosion. I could feel the heat right through the canopy of my plane. It was awesome.

I was still worried about the *Zeros* that had been flying above the formation. It was time to get out of there, so I dove down to the water. As I came back up, I looked around and all the enemy fighters and bombers had just disappeared. I turned and made another run down the field to be sure that none of them had landed. Sure enough, there was a *Zero* taxing out to take off. I gave him a short burst and saw the plane start to smoke. Just as I flashed over the top of the airplane, I saw the pilot jump out and run into the palm trees bordering the runway.

I pulled up and around and headed back to the harbor. Three *Zeros* had a *Hellcat* pinned just above the water. I just knew it must be Bill Levering. He was in deep trouble. Everytime a *Zero* made a pass at him he jinked and turned, but to no avail. They had him in their sites and they kept bouncing him. I dove in and the *Zeros* broke off, but that was because other *Hellcats* came in right after me and we had them out numbered.

About then, tracers flashed past my cockpit. A *Zero* had come out of nowhere and had closed in on me. I made what I consider the finest evasion maneuver ever developed, a slow full power climbing turn to the left. As my speed dropped from an initial 200 miles an hour to about half that during that turning climb, the *Zero* tried to stay with me. Naturally with his greater speed he couldn't turn inside me and bring his guns to bear, although he was firing as he flew by me. I had felt some hits in the tail of my plane but he couldn't lead me enough to get hits into the cockpit or engine.

The *Zero* turned back again and we made two or three parrying circles on our way up to 5,000 feet. As I continued to climb and turn as efficiently as possible, I slowed to about 115 miles and hour and faked the Japanese pilot into making a tighter turn than his airplane could manage. He spun out. I executed a controlled spin to come down on him. I now had the advantage of position behind his plane and soon had him in my sites about 1,000 feet away. That was the perfect position for my bore-sighted pattern. I had time to give him one burst. It was perfect. In spite of my *Hellcat's* tendency to skid to the left because of the uneven recoil, the shots I fired appeared to be going right into the cockpit. I lost track of him for a second, but soon I had him spotted again. The plane was in normal straight and level flight and then it went into a gliding turn toward the field. I soon realized, however, that this was a plane without a pilot in control, as it never did pull out of that gliding turn. Two other *Hellcat* pilots came in for an easy kill, for the undoubtedly dead pilot never did take an evasive action. Although I saw the plane crash into the water, I could not take credit for that *Zero.*

I saw another *Zero* about a mile ahead. It was pulling up and away from me, so I applied full throttle and went after it. I chased at full power, but the *Zero* was still about a mile from me when it went into a cloudbank. I kept course and just before I got to the cloud, out came the *Zero* on his back directly at me. His 7.7-millimeter machine guns were firing and so was his 20-millimeter canon. His plane just blinked with fire as he came at me. I was so taken by surprise and fright that I didn't know whether to pull up or dive or what. It was a terrible time for indecision. It was important that I not turn and give him a broadside target. What should I do? If I dived away, the Japanese pilot could execute a split-S and come right out on my tail. Almost by instinct I kept my heading right at him, easing back on the throttle ever so slightly, gently dropping the nose of the plane. That seemed to surprise the attacker, as he wanted to avoid a head-on. We passed so close that I could see the features on the face of the Japanese pilot.

As soon as we passed, I pulled up into an extremely tight vertical turn and chopped my throttle to kill my speed. This enabled me to execute a very tight, quick turn. The *Zero* pilot never did slow and went into a high-speed turn. As he came around, he presented me with a forty-five degree deflection target. I was ready for him and fired. I could see my tracers passing close by his airplane. As I continued my turn inside of him, I came right out on his tail. He was now dead in my sights and a burst of fire went right into him. The *Zero* headed toward the water in a diving follow-through of the left-hand turn that had brought it open to my fire. I knew the plane had been seriously hit so I just followed the pilot down to confirm the kill. I got within fifty feet of the plane. The canopy was open and the pilot was throwing books and papers out of the cockpit. He might have been the air-group commander, getting rid of anything that might be helpful to us. It was apparent that he had been wounded by my last burst, as I could see the blood. He looked over at me and made a motion that I took for a valiant salute. Right then his wingtip caught the water and he plunged in, cartwheeling in a cascade of spray, as the plane disintegrated.

Alone, I went straight back to the Hornet and landed. I then learned how much damage Bill Levering's plane had sustained in his tangle with the three *Zeros* over the water. His *Hellcat* was so shot up that he had to land aboard the Hornet with the *Hellcat's* wheels and flaps up. Somehow he got the hook down and stopped the plane. As soon as he climbed out, they pushed his *Hellcat* over the side. He was fortunate to get back alive.

A little later, the pictures I took over the enemy field were developed. The film showed that there were indeed many airplanes and war supplies stored all around the runway. That night they sent the battleships and cruisers in to shell the area. I heard the whole place just erupted as a fuel or ammunition dump was hit.

At the end of that day's action, I was credited with the *Kate* and one of the two *Zeros* I shot down. That brought my score up to three downed enemy planes.

*   *   *

My last fight against the Japanese airmen was when I flew again from my carrier, the U.S.S. Hornet, on July 4, 1944. That is one Fourth of July that I will always remember. It was over Chicki Jima in the Bonin Islands about 500 miles south of Tokyo, Japan. Flying my F6F-3N *Hellcat* night fighter, I intercepted four Nakajima A6M2-N Zero-type Rufe float fighters in the predawn darkness and shot them down. Not one of the pilots in these planes knew what had hit them. That was the advantage we had with our night fighters, which had the ability with the new radar equipment to seek out enemy planes in the night. This was my final night flight and now I could fly peacefully back to the carrier Hornet as an Ace, with a total of seven kills to my credit. It didn't work out that way. I almost got killed just as dawn was breaking.

This is how it happened. In the dim light of that breaking day I saw that the harbor was alive with every type of Japanese ship, fleeing to the open sea. I decided to record the ships and transmit the information back to the fleet. My VHF radio wouldn't communicate to the carrier from this distance, so I wrote down everything that I was seeing on the notepad that I always kept strapped on my leg. I was on the east side of harbor, continuing to make wide counter clockwise circles and recording the information that would be helpful.

Suddenly, to my left, I saw a flash of light. Then I heard my wings being ripped by bullets. I thought I had been alone and made the mistake of concentrating on my report rather than covering my tail. Instinctively, I made a short evasive turn to the left. As a result, a *Zero's* 7.7-millimeter bullet penetrated the cockpit in front of the armor plate behind me and went through my left shoulder, shattering my clavicle. I'll never know how I got through that one, but somehow my sharp turn did enable me to elude the *Zero* and avoid further attack. It was like a terrible dream but I did manage to fly back to our task force, but my carrier, the Hornet, was not ready to take on planes. The carrier Yorktown was in position so I made my approach on her. Here I was faced with another crisis. It takes two good arms to land a plane, one to handle the control stick and the other to manipulate the throttle. This was next to impossible for me, because the bullet I had taken tore up and busted my left shoulder. With great difficulty, I eased my left arm over and was able to get my left hand on the throttle with just enough strength left to control my speed and take the final cut when I reached the flight deck. Somehow I hit the deck, caught the third arresting wire, and taxied ahead of the cable barrier. It was a miracle, but there I was on the Yorktown. I remember that a deck hand jumped up on my shot up plane and yelled, "This pilot is dying. Get some help up here so we can get him out."

"I can make it O.K.," I yelled back, and I got out of the cockpit. They got me to sick bay, and would you believe it, an old poker playing buddy I had not seen for some time, Dr. Metcalf, was on duty. We had always had banter between us, so I said, "High Doc. You play with fire-crackers long enough on the Fourth of July and you'll blow yourself up."

"Well, shut up and I'll work on you," Dr. Metcalf said, and then he sedated me and began to operate on my bloody body. My shoulder was badly busted up.

I found out later that John Drew, another member of our fighter squadron, had landed right behind me. His *Hellcat* fighter plane had been badly shot up and the engine had lost oil. Just as he hit the deck the plane's engine froze up. That was a close one. Had he been just in front of me, I would have gotten a wave off, and no way could I have gone on around again for another landing attempt.

*   *   *

I was in for a long recovery and my combat flying was over. I eventually made it back to the Long Beach Naval Hospital and it was there that I met Robbie Robinson again who was recovering from blast injuries suffered in the Marshall Island invasion. Despite the injuries and long recovery process, it was a wonderful time of sharing as we caught up on everything that had happened to each of us since graduating from the Corpus Christi Naval Air Station in Texas.

Later I returned to Quonset Point to train night-fighter pilots. This lasted well into the summer of 1945. I was one of the first navy pilots to be demobilized at the end of the war. Well, that's my story and I'm just glad that I am still here.

*   *   *

The last time I saw Fred Dungan was in 1999. He and his wife Lorayne now live in a beautiful home overlooking San Clemente. There they enjoy the sweeping vista of the magnificent California coast. They look over the last horizon where far beyond the blue Pacific, Fred, fought valiantly in those once war torn skies.

F6F *HELLCAT* Fighter

"The airplane I flew on the attack on Guam was a brand new *Hellcat* fighter. It was painted navy blue and had camera gear in the belly. The flying conditions were perfect. It was a fine day for flying."

Fred Dungan, Lt. USNR

19

JOAN L. ROBINSON

I first became aware of Joan Larrimer when she was in the Tenth Grade at Long Beach Polytechnic High School, and I was a Senior. Poly had an enrollment of 3,000 students, but even in such a large prestigious school this vivacious, attractive, and excellent student soon became a recognized leader and personality on the campus.

We first met when, as a senior debate team member, I was asked to moderate a Tenth Grade debate held before a civic organization meeting at the

Lakewood Country Club in Long Beach, California. Following the debate that evening, I asked Joan if I could drive her home. She was fifteen years old.

When Joan was twenty-one, we were married in Seattle, Washington. This was March 4, 1943. Our life together during those months of World War II, like so many others during that difficult, uncertain and challenging time was unique, to say the least. When I began to write the personal accounts of those who lived through World War II, I soon realized that I would be remiss if I did not include Joan's recollections. The young wives of this historic period were heroines of their time. Their stories need to be preserved to give those who follow an added and important perspective. Joan's courage, loyalty, and love gave me a steady mooring as I plied the rough seas of separation, anxiety, uncertainty, danger, and loneliness during World War II. Here is the story she tells.

*   *   *

I will begin my story with the stunning blow of the Japanese attack on Pearl Harbor, December 7, 1941. This traumatic event hit me with an emotional impact that, to this day, I can still feel. The anger and shock still cause me pain. My twentieth birthday was just three days away. I was completing my study at Long Beach Junior College, but my future looked bleak, vague and frightening. The Great Depression that started in 1929 was still lingering on in 1941. It had been a desperate twelve years for my parents as they fought to simply endure. We were like so many others struggling through the Depression's deprivations: lost jobs, lost homes, and lost hope. On top of this, we now would face a tragic global war.

I finished school and applied for work at the Cherry Avenue Branch of the First Security National Bank in Long Beach, California. I was elated to get the job and started working immediately. The bank was without experienced personnel. When war was declared, all of the men left to join the armed forces. Mr. Brown, the branch manager, was left to run the bank with untrained, very young women. My salary was eighteen dollars a week. I knew nothing about the banking business, but I spent over fifty hours a week working and learning. It is a wonder that the entire banking world didn't sink, never to recover, from this influx of inexperienced workers. But somehow we did prevail, and I found personal satisfaction in knowing that I was doing something necessary for the continued stability of our country in a time of great need. I worked at the bank for about twelve months, proud that I was able to reconcile the books at the close of each banking day.

At that point in time, Ensign F. Willard (Robbie) Robinson came back into my life. I hadn't seen or heard from Robbie for at least two years. When he came unexpectedly into the bank and asked me to have dinner with him, I was very surprised. However, we had known each other and had dated off and on in the earlier days of our acquaintance. We had always cared for one another, but dating was difficult. So, we went out to dinner that February night in 1943. We talked through the circumstances of our lives during the many months we had been apart. Then it was time to go. He drove me back to my parent's house and just as he was ready to leave he dumbfounded me. "I'm leaving for Seattle the first thing in the morning to join my new torpedo squadron that is being commissioned at the Sand Point Naval Air Station," he began. "I am asking you to come to Seattle and marry me. It is a big decision, so don't answer me now. I will call you in three days, and if you will come, I'll send you a train ticket and make all of the arrangements."

When he called three days later, I told him I would come. I knew, of course, that my friends would look upon this decision as impulsive, but I felt very sure and right about our marriage. Robbie and I would have whatever time together the risks of war would allow. We wanted this. We laugh now, fifty-five years later, and remark, "It was an impulsive war marriage that may still work out." Anyway, Robbie was fortunate enough to get a train ticket to Seattle for me. I say fortunate because during the war all travel was almost exclusively reserved for servicemen. When the day for my departure arrived, my folks drove me to the train station in Los Angeles. I said good-bye and began the lumbering 1200-mile journey to Seattle. It was the first time I had ever been away from home. By the second night I reached Portland, Oregon. The next train did not leave until the following morning, so I found a hotel room for a lonely stay. This was the greatest adventure I'd ever been on in my twenty-one years of life. I was nervous and even scared.

The next day Robbie was there to meet me when the train arrived in Seattle. He settled me in the Edmond Meany hotel near the University of Washington campus and then took me to an office where we could apply for our marriage license. After the three day required wait, we were married at the University Methodist Church. The men in the newly commissioned navy flight squadron attended our wedding. It was a sweet ceremony, all that a girl could ever hope for. Robbie had planned it all. The organist was the only other woman at the church, but it was just perfect as far as I was concerned.

We lived at the hotel in a room that looked out over the University campus. In the distance we could see snow-capped Mt. Rainier. It was a beautiful place and only cost us five dollars a day. We had dinner every evening at the Sand Point Navy Officers' Club, which was fun for me. It gave me the opportunity to become acquainted with the pilots in the torpedo squadron. They really were such boys! Robbie was one of the oldest and he was only twenty-four.

We had wonderful weather the month we were in Seattle and the pilots had a chance to fly almost every day. They needed to feel comfortable in that monster new torpedo bomber that would play such an important role in the war with Japan. I never grew to have any positive feeling about those powerful *Avengers* that they flew. To me the plane always seemed like a huge, ungainly, fire-spitting brute. The pilots loved the bomber, and naturally the wives, though afraid, were proud of their men.

We left Seattle the first week in April when Navy Flight Squadron VC-31 was transferred to El Centro, California for bombing and night flight training. Robbie did not have to make the flight because he got permission to drive us back to California. He owned the most impractical but impressive car one could imagine. It was a 1934 yellow Cadillac convertible, a custom made wonder that had originally belonged to the famous motion picture actress Norma Shearer. We drove to Portland and then over to the beautiful coast highway, almost abandoned during the war because of gas rationing. What a fantastic drive it was, all along the Oregon coast and then through the gigantic redwood forests of northern California. There was a rim on the wheel of the car that kept pinching one of the tire tubes. Robbie had to repair it thirteen times on that trip! He never lost his temper. That impressed me and I know that set a true direction for our marriage that has remained steady all of these years.

We stopped in Long Beach to see our families and drove on to El Centro. Robbie's squadron, VC-31, was stationed at the Marine Air Base there until July 1943. All of the married couples set up housekeeping at the Barbara Worth Hotel. Our salaries, even with flight pay, were so low that we did our laundry in the bathtub and ate a lot of grilled cheese sandwiches prepared on a little hot plate we kept in the hotel room. Our generation was one that would never have considered asking parents for financial help, and we found ways to make our money stretch. However things did get a little lean by the end of each month.

Despite the financial pinch, we did have a lot of good times while we were in El Centro. We became friends with the other newly married couples. All of the squadron wives had only what we could create for ourselves to fill the long days in that small town. Since I had our Cadillac convertible available, some of us would drive to Calexico once in a while, or out to the base to meet our husbands for dinner at the Officers' Club. That big yellow car was easy to spot on those empty roads and our squadron pilots, when they were out practicing, would love to make low-level torpedo runs on us. The way their motors roared as they dove by us in those massive bombers scared us half to death. Now, all these years later, I still can remember and feel that thundering vibration that shook us as they zoomed by. They would pull up at the last moment to clear the trees that lined the fields. These windbreaks protected the crops. I'm sure that was forbidden play, but no one was hurt and it did provide a diversion. It was also good practice in the life-and-death low flying they were destined to do.

I shall never forget Easter Sunday, 1943. We had a wonderful day together. All of the pilots were decked out in their white uniforms and the girls were in their pretty 1940 dresses. We decided to top off our perfect day by going for a spaghetti feed in one of El Centro's Main Street restaurants. Before we finished our dinner a couple of shore-patrol officers came in. "All pilots report immediately to the base!" they ordered. I drove some of the pilots and their wives out to the base. Our skipper, Commander Bill Bartlett, was waiting in the base ready-room for all of the pilots to arrive. He had received orders that a flight of unidentified planes was approaching the area and that the squadron was to intercept the enemy. We girls waved them good-bye as they took off and then we left the base wondering what in the world would happen to our husbands. That was my first brush with the reality of war and how fast the fun of a wonderful day could evaporate. Though this suspected attack later turned out to be just a false alarm, it was a forerunner of times to come.

By the summer of 1943 we were on the move again, this time to Coronado. The squadron was based at the North Island Naval Air Station across the bay from San Diego. Squadron VC-31 was decommissioned. The fighter pilots were reassigned to squadrons who were fighting in the Solomon Islands in the South Pacific. One of the fighter pilots who left was Pat Patterson who had been a very close friend. A few weeks later we were saddened to learn that he was missing. He never returned. The report came that the last time he was seen a Japanese *Zero* was firing at him. That was so hard. Robbie went to see his mother who was living in Hollywood. She always believed Pat would return.

The torpedo pilots who had been in VC-31 were now the nucleus of a newly commissioned squadron, VC-7. We didn't understand at the time, but the bomber pilots in this new squadron, including Robbie, were assigned to a very secret project. They would be the key in the development of air-to-ground rocket warfare. This new assignment would take further training and a new type of precision flying. They were also being trained for night attack work, so they were gone a lot at night. It was all pretty scary work. We lived in a room we rented from a marine colonel's wife.

It was less than a block from the entrance to the North Island Naval Air Station and this was convenient. Coronado was a delightful little military town, but it was rather hard to fill the days when we knew that it was just a matter of time until the squadron would be assigned to an aircraft carrier and leave to fight the Japanese somewhere in the far Pacific. Soon our husbands would be sent into the unknown of the war for which they had trained with such intensity. There was no way for us who were the wives of navy aviators to adequately prepare for this eventuality.

Several months before Robbie left on the aircraft carrier Manila Bay for the war, I had an ectopic pregnancy. This necessitated an emergency operation at the North Island Naval Hospital. What a physical and emotional blow that was. It took some time for me to recover and to readjust. I remember the sadness we felt because we had been hoping for a child and now this wasn't to be. It had been quite a year. We had lived in thirteen different places, our future together was out of our control and life had become very real and very earnest.

The year of 1944 began with our good-byes. The squadron had completed their intensive training, including carrier qualifications on the Manila Bay, and the pilots were ready to go. It is difficult to describe the mixture of emotions that I felt on the day that their carrier left the dock at North Island. There was a kind of hectic inner excitement that bordered on hysteria, even as it was necessary to maintain an appearance of calm assurance. As I think about it now, I wonder at the immense self-control that the wives displayed. We were all so young! Once the ship left the dock and turned into the open channel that led to the sea, several of us went to the home of the skipper's wife, Sis Bartlett, to spend a few more moments before saying good-bye. We had become very close during those months we had spent together. Now we would be going our separate ways, in most cases never to see one another again. The anxiety that I had experienced for so long only intensified as I returned to live with my parents in Long Beach. As loving as my parents were, there was no way they could relate to the loss of those close relationships I had developed in the squadron. There was no one I could talk to about all that I had been through during the year of 1943.

In the spring of 1944 I received a telegram that Robbie had been seriously hurt in a crash during combat somewhere in the Pacific. I had no idea where the squadron was fighting. Their movements were kept very secret. He has written about this tremendously difficult time in detail and the impact this tragedy had on the rest of our life together. I wished the war to be over for us, but that was not to be. There were months ahead of separation and anxiety before we could put it all behind and build our lives anew. From the time I received the telegram from the War Department telling of the crash at sea, until the end of the war in 1945, I could only live a day at a time, praying continually for the survival of my husband. I was simply waiting for real life to begin.

Finally, in 1945 VJ-Day (Victory over Japan) came. Our daughter, Gail, was born on November 2, 1945 when Robbie and I were both patients at the same time at the Long Beach Naval Hospital. Now fifty-five years later we look back on a rich and eventful life, full of blessings beyond our greatest dreams. The war years were formative for us. Looking back I think it is now possible to say that the tragic events thrust upon our life, and those around us, permanently molded our soul and our character in such a way that we could deeply appreciate the many blessings God had ahead for us. Although the beginnings were difficult, we were put on a path of faith and courage that has sustained us to this day. God can take the bad experiences in life and turn them to build the good things. This has happened for us. We have been blessed!

*   *   *

I have watched Robbie write these accounts. It has been a labor of love and tenacity, as with endurance he has pursued those who now recount their personal stories. In a sense they are my stories, too, for I have lived, loved and waited for these wonderful boys who left their youth in the skies and on the seas of war. Read their stories with awe, with wonder and with appreciation. They represent a generation set apart.

Robbie and Joan Robinson

Married March 4, 1943
Seattle, Washington

F. Willard and Joan L. Robinson
1998

This picture of Robbie and Joan Robinson was taken September 1998 in San Diego, California, on the occasion of the last official reunion of World War II Navy Flight Squadrons VC-31 and VC-7. Squadron VC-31 was commissioned fifty-five years before at the Sand Point Naval Air Station in Seattle, Washington, January of 1943.

TBM Grumman *Avenger* Launches Torpedo

Navy Flight Squadron VC-7

This picture of a TBM *Avenger* Torpedo Plane was painted by Joe Cavanaugh, a crewman who served with Navy Flight Squadron VC-7 during World War II. His drawings were used in all the communications that were sent to members of VC-7 as they planned for their reunions for the fifty years following World War II. Joe Cavanaugh died in 1997. This quiet, brave and talented brother is sorely missed.

Lt. F. W. Robinson, USNR

Epilogue

Long now have the remains of our comrades and loved ones rested in the depths of the sea. World War II was a devastating but perhaps necessary tragedy—fifty million dead, civilians and military alike. Nations in the farthest reaches of the earth were not untouched—none fully escaped. In the uncertain dawn of peace the survivors moved on, spawning new generations to face the joys and sorrows of the human experience. Let us live in the remembrance of those who gave so much that liberty would not die with their dreams, that out of that long long war, we now never give up on our search for peace.

Two brave and sterling air crewman who left too soon. . .

George Driesbach, Jr. Age 19, Rockford, Illinois

Harold Eckert, Age 22, Los Angeles, California

About the Author

Following his military service as a Naval Aviator in World War II, Lt. Robinson returned to the University of Southern California to earn his doctoral degree in Educational Administration and Philosophy.

For three decades Dr. Robinson worked in public education as a teacher and as a secondary school administrator, culminating in his seventeen-year tenure as Principal of Beverly Hills High School in Beverly Hills, California. There he directed and supervised the development of an educational program of excellence that received national recognition. He also contributed extensively to the improvement of education nationally, by serving as a Director on the College Entrance Examination Board and chairing numerous accreditation teams for the Western Association of Schools and Colleges.

Dr. Robinson is the author of the provocative book, *Beverly Hills Principal*, published by Writers Press, Boise, Idaho in 1999. It is a story of school leadership during the 1970's, a time that unraveled America.

Dr. and Mrs. Robinson now reside in Boise, Idaho where they celebrated their 58th wedding anniversary and remain active in church and civic affairs.